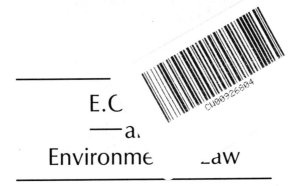

E.C

—a.

Environme   _aw

second edition

AUSTRALIA

The Law Book Company
Brisbane · Sydney · Melbourne · Perth

CANADA

Carswell
Ottawa · Toronto · Calgary · Montreal · Vancouver

AGENTS

Steimatzky's Agency Ltd., Tel Aviv
N.M. Tripathi (Private) Ltd., Bombay
Eastern Law House (Private) Ltd., Calcutta
M.P.P. House, Bangalore
Universal Book Traders, Delhi
Aditya Books, Delhi
MacMillan Shuppan KK, Tokyo
Pakistan Law House, Karachi, Lahore

E.C. Treaty
—and—
Environmental Law

second edition

DR LUDWIG KRÄMER
Judge at Landgericht in Kiel, LL.D.
Head of Legal Matters and Application of Community Law
in DG XI of the European Commission

LONDON
SWEET & MAXWELL
1995

Published in 1995 by
Sweet & Maxwell Limited of
South Quay Plaza, 183 Marsh Wall, London E14 9FT.
Computerset by York House Typographic Ltd, London W13 8NT.
Printed and bound in Great Britain by Butler and Tanner Ltd, Frome and London.

A CIP catalogue record for this book is available from the British Library

ISBN 0 421 50890 6

Contents

1. COMMUNITY ACTIVITY TO DATE IN THE FIELD OF ENVIRONMENTAL LAW

Origins of Community Environment Policy; Environment Programmes ... 1
Environmental measures adopted at Community level 5
    Water 5
    Air 11
    Noise 14
    Chemicals 15
    Nature conservation 18
    Waste 20
    General measures 23
Integrating environmental requirements in other policies 27
    Agricultural policy 27
    Regional policy 28
    Competition policy 30
    Transport policy 31
    Energy policy 33
    Development policy 34
    Industrial policy 36

2. OBJECTIVES, PRINCIPLES AND CONDITIONS OF EUROPEAN ENVIRONMENTAL LAW

The notion "Environment" 41
The objectives 45
The principles 53
Article 130r, paragraph 3, conditions to be taken into account 65

3. THE DECISION-MAKING PROCESS

Introduction 71

Majority decisions [Article 130 s(1)] 71
Unanimous decisions [Article 130 s(2)].. 74
   (1) Provisions primarily of a fiscal nature 75
   (2) Town and country planning, land use................................... 76
   (3) Management of water resources 78
   (4) Choice of energy sources; energy supply 79
Decisions on programmes [Article 130 s(3)]..................................... 80
Co-operation with other countries [Article 130 r(4)]......................... 84
Decisions based on other Treaty provisions 86
   Article 43.. 86
   Article 84.. 88
   Article 100a 89
   Article 113 97
   Article 130o... 98

4. COMMUNITY LAW AND NATIONAL LAW

Introduction: the effect of Community law.................................... 99
Article 130t 99
Article 100a(4) 106
The safeguard clause of Articles 130r(2)(2) and 100a(5) 110
Articles 30–36 111

5. FINANCING AND IMPLEMENTING COMMUNITY LEGISLATION

Financing legislation.. 129
Implementation: general questions 131
Monitoring implementation by the Commission 135

6. ASSESSMENT

The Treaty framework for law and policy 145
Programmes and secondary legislation 146
Water legislation 147
Air pollution... 148
Chemicals 150
Noise 150
Nature 151
Wastes 151

Horizontal measures 151
Implementation and enforcement 153
General evaluation 156

BIBLIOGRAPHY 161

INDEX 169

Table of Cases

ALPHABETICAL LIST

Assurpol 1.54

Celulosa Beira (C-266/91) 4.45
Commission v. Belgium (73/81) 1.13
Commission v. Belgium (C-42/89) 1.13, 5.01
Commission v. Belgium (C-290/89)................................ 1.13
Commission v. Belgium (C-2/90)............ 1.41, 1.42, 2.18, 2.22, 3.22, 3.33
Commission v. Council (22/70) 3.21
Commission v. Council (300/89)................... 1.18, 3.30, 3.34, 3.35, 4.18
Commission v. Council (C-155/91)........................ 1.41, 1.42, 3.30, 3.33
Commission v. Council (C-187/93)................................. 1.42
Commission v. Denmark (Danish bottles) (302/86).... 3.29, 4.31, 4.32, 4.35
Commission v. Denmark (C-47/88)............................4.45, 4.49
Commission v. Germany (C-131/88)...................... 5.05, 5.15
Commission v. Germany (C-361/88) 5.16
Commission v. Germany (C-58/89) 1.13
Commission v. Germany (C-237/90)............................... 1.14
Commission v. Greece (68/88) 5.12
Commission v. Italy (91/79) 3.18, 3.27
Commission v. Italy (92/79) 3.18, 3.27
Commission v. Italy (22/86) 1.13
Commission v. Netherlands (C-339/87)......................... 5.15
Commission v. Spain (C-355/90) 3.09
Commission v. United Kingdom (C-337/89).................1.13, 5.10
Compagnie Commerciale de l'Ouest and others v. Receveur principal
    des douanes de la Pallice Port (78-83/90) 4.45

Enichem Base SpA v. Cinisello-Balsamo (380/87) 4.33

France v. Commission (C-41/93) 4.36

Greece v. Council (62/88) 3.23, 3.38

Ianelli v. Volpi (64/76)... 4.45

I.L.O. (Op. 2/91) 3.21

Lornoy (C-17/91) 4.45

Mondiet v. Islais (C-405/92) 3.24, 3.30

Nijman (125/88) 4.35

Pretura di Torino v. X (228/87) 1.13
Procureur du Roi v. Dassonville (8/74) 4.58

Rewe-Zentral A.G. v. Bundesmonopolverwaltung (Cassis de Dijon)
    (120/78) 4.30, 4.58

United Kingdom v. Council (68/86) 3.24

Vessoso-Zanetti (206-207/88) 1.41
VOTOB 1.54

Zanetti and others (C-359/88) 1.41

NUMERICAL LIST

22/70, Commission v. Council: [1971] E.C.R. 263, [1971] C.M.L.R. 335 3.21

8/74, Procureur du Roi v. Dassonville: [1974] E.C.R. 837, [1974] 2
C.M.L.R. 436 .... 4.58

64/76, Ianelli et Volpi: [1977] E.C.R. 557, [1977] 2 C.M.L.R. 688 ...... 4.45

120/78, Rewe-Zentral A.G. v. Bundesmonopolverwaltung (Cassis de
Dijon): [1979] E.C.R. 649, [1979] 3 C.M.L.R. 494 .... 4.30, 4.58

91/79, Commission v. Italy: [1980] E.C.R. 1099, [1981] 1 C.M.L.R.
331 .... 3.18, 3.27

92/79, Commission v. Italy: [1980] E.C.R. 1115, [1981] 1 C.M.L.R.
331 .... 3.18, 3.27

73/81, Commission v. Belgium: [1982] E.C.R. 189 .... 1.13

68/86, United Kingdom v. Council: [1988] E.C.R. 855, [1988] 2
C.M.L.R. 534 .... 3.24

302/86, Commission v. Denmark (Danish bottles): [1988] E.C.R. 4607,
[1989] 1 C.M.L.R. 619 .... 3.29, 4.31, 4.32, 4.35

322/86, Commission v. Italy: [1988] E.C.R. 3995 .... 1.13

228/87, Pretura di Torino v. X: [1988] E.C.R. 5099 .... 1.13

C-339/87, Commission v. Netherlands: [1990] I E.C.R. 851 .... 5.15

380/87, Enichem Base SpA v. Cinisello-Balsamo: [1989] E.C.R. 2491,
[1991] 1 C.M.L.R. 313 .... 4.33

C-47/88, Commission v. Denmark: [1990] I E.C.R. 4509 .... 4.45, 4.49

62/88, Greece v. Council: [1990] I E.C.R. 1527, [1991] 2 C.M.L.R.
649 .... 3.23, 3.38

68/88, Commission v. Greece: [1989] E.C.R. 2965, [1991] 1 C.M.L.R.
31 .... 5.12

125/88, Nijman: [1989] E.C.R. 3533 .... 4.35

C-131/88, Commission v. Germany: [1991] I E.C.R. 825 .... 5.05, 5.15

206-207/88, Vessoso-Zanetti: [1990] I E.C.R. 1461 .... 1.41

C-359/88, Zanetti and others: [1990] I E.C.R. 1509 .... 1.41

C-361/88, Commission v. Germany: [1991] I E.C.R. 2567, [1993] 2
C.M.L.R. 821 .... 5.16

C-42/89, Commission v. Belgium: [1990] I E.C.R. 2821, [1990] 1
C.M.L.R. 716 .... 1.13, 5.01

C-58/89, Commission v. Germany: [1991] I E.C.R. 4893 .... 1.13

C-290/89, Commission v. Belgium: [1991] I E.C.R. 2851 .... 1.13

300/89, Commission v. Council: [1991] I E.C.R. 2867, [1993] 3
C.M.L.R. 359 .... 1.18, 3.30, 3.34, 3.35, 4.18

C-337/89, Commission v. United Kingdom: [1992] I E.C.R.
6103..1.13, 5.10

C-2/90, Commission v. Belgium: [1992] I E.C.R. 4431, [1993] 1
C.M.L.R. 365 .... 1.41, 1.42, 2.18, 2.22, 3.22, 3.33

78-83/90, Compagnie Commerciale de l'Ouest and others v. Receveur
principal des douanes de la Pallice Port: [1992] I E.C.R. 1847..... 4.45

C-237/90, Commission v. Germany: [1992] I E.C.R. 5973................. 1.14

C-355/90, Commission v. Spain: [1993] I E.C.R. 4221...................... 3.09

Op. 2/91, I.L.O.: [1993] 3 C.M.L.R. 800 .... 3.21

C-17/91, Lornoy, judgment of December 16, 1992 .... 4.45

C-155/91, Commission v. Council: [1993] I E.C.R. 939 1.41, 1.42, 3.30, 3.33

C-266/91, Celulosa Beira, judgment of August 2, 1993...................... 4.45

C-405/92, Mondiet v. Islais: [1993] I E.C.R. 6133 ....3.24, 3.30

C-41/93, France v. Commission, judgment of May 17, 1994............... 4.36

C-187/93, Commission v. Council, judgment of June 28, 1994............ 1.42

T-475/93 .... 1.42

Table of Legislation

EUROPEAN UNION TREATIES AND CONVENTIONS

1951   Paris. Treaty establishing a European Coal and Steel Community (ECSC) (April 18) 4.10

1957   Rome. Treaty establishing the European Community (E.C.) (March 25) [1992] 1 C.M.L.R. 573.

Arts. 1–7............... 2.18

Art. 2...........1.07, 1.08, 1.52, 2.01, 2.05, 2.06, 2.33, 2.35, 4.13, 6.01

Art. 3.............2.06, 2.35

Art. 3a 6.01

Art. 3b 2.18, 2.28

Art. 3k 2.01

Art. 3t.................. 1.56

Art. 5.... 1.30, 4.16, 5.01

Art. 7.................... 1.07

Art. 7a 3.31, 3.32, 4.23

Art. 8a 4.23

Arts. 30–36........... 1.58, 4.01, 4.10, 4.13, 4.27–4.58

Art. 30 ....1.30, 1.41, 1.42, 2.14, 3.33, 4.27–4.58

Art. 36 .... 4.04, 4.27–4.58

1957   Rome. Treaty establishing the European Community—*cont.*

Arts. 38–48.....1.52, 3.24

Art. 38(2).............. 3.24

Art. 39 ....1.52, 2.06, 3.02

Art. 43 ....1.36, 2.03, 3.01, 3.23–3.25, 4.08, 4.13, 4.25

(2).......3.24, 3.25

Arts. 74–84.....1.55, 3.26

Art. 75 .... 3.26

(3).............. 3.27

Art. 84 ....3.01, 3.23, 3.26, 4.13, 4.25

(2).......3.26, 3.36

Art. 85 .... 1.54

(3).............. 1.54

Art. 92 ....1.54, 1.58, 4.50

(1).............. 1.54

(3)(a) 1.54

(b) 1.54

(c) 1.54

Art. 95 ....1.20, 1.58, 4.45, 4.47, 4.50

Art 99 ....1.56, 3.01, 3.07, 3.23, 4.13, 4.47

Art. 100........1.42, 3.17, 3.18, 3.22, 3.24, 3.27, 3.34

1957   Rome. Treaty establishing
       the European
       Community—*cont.*
       Art. 100a 1.18, 1.42,
           1.58, 2.02, 2.03,
           2.10, 2.11, 3.01,
           3.06, 3.08, 3.14,
           3.17, 3.23, 3.27–3.36,
           3.38, 4.08, 4.12,
       4.13, 4.16–4.18, 4.47
           (3) 2.01,
           2.05, 2.11, 2.14,
           2.15, 2.17, 3.27,
           4.34, 6.01, 6.16
           (4) 2.01,
           2.05, 2.11, 2.15,
           2.35, 3.27, 3.32,
           3.34, 4.01, 4.08,
           4.17–4.23, 4.34,
           4.35, 4.57, 6.16
           (5) 4.01,
               4.24–4.26
       Art. 100b 3.32
           (2)........... 2.35
       Arts. 110–115 .... 3.37
       Art. 113 ....2.03, 3.01,
           3.23, 3.37, 3.38
       Art. 118a.......2.01, 2.02,
               3.23
           (3)....4.02, 4.21
       Art. 120a 1.07
       Art. 128................ 2.25
       Art. 129.........2.10, 2.25
       Art. 129a 2.10, 3.23
           (3) 4.02
       Art. 129b 2.05
       Art. 129d 3.08
           (2) 3.08
       Art. 130.........1.58, 2.02
       Arts. 130a–130e 1.53
       Art. 130d 1.53, 2.01,
               2.05, 5.12
       Art. 130e 3.23
       Arts. 130f–130o 3.39

1957   Rome. Treaty establishing
       the European
       Community—*cont.*
       Art. 130f.............. 3.39
           (3) 3.39
       Art. 130n 3.39
       Art. 130o 3.01, 3.23
       Art. 130q 3.39
       Title XVI...... 1.01, 2.01,
           3.01, 4.05, 5.02
       Arts. 130r–130t 1.01,
           1.06–1.08, 2.01, 2.33,
           3.16, 4.12, 4.23
       Art. 130r.......2.05, 2.06,
           2.10, 2.27, 3.02,
           3.15, 3.17, 3.21,
           4.02–4.04, 6.01
           (1) 2.01,
           2.03, 2.04, 2.06,
           2.07, 2.10, 2.26,
           2.30, 2.31, 2.34,
           3.02, 3.07, 3.14,
           3.25, 3.27, 3.31,
           4.04–4.06, 4.09,
           5.01, 5.03, 5.12,
               6.01
           (2) 2.14–
           2.19, 2.26, 2.38,
           3.02, 3.35, 4.12,
               4.34, 6.16
           (1)........ 1.08
           (2)....... 1.07,
           1.08, 2.07, 2.25,
           2.27, 2.35, 3.24,
           3.25, 3.31, 4.01,
           4.24–4.26, 6.01
           (3)....... 2.16,
           2.27, 2.37–2.41
           (4)....... 2.28,
       2.33, 3.20–3.22, 3.37
           (5)........ 3.20

1957 Rome. Treaty establishing
the European
Community—*cont.*
Art. 130s....... 1.07–1.09,
1.18, 1.24, 1.42,
1.56, 2.03, 2.10,
2.11, 2.18, 2.35,
2.41, 3.01, 3.02,
3.12, 3.13, 3.17,
3.21, 3.23–3.28,
3.31–3.33, 3.35–3.39,
4.02, 4.06–4.09,
4.11, 4.12, 4.18,
4.26
(1) 3.01–
3.05, 3.08, 3.12,
3.13, 4.24
(2) 1.16,
2.01, 2.12, 3.06–3.13,
4.24
(3) 3.14–3.19
(4) 5.01–5.04
(5) 1.09, 3.05
Art. 130t.......1.24, 1.58,
2.05, 2.08, 2.11,
2.15, 2.18, 2.35,
3.25–3.27, 3.31,
3.32, 3.35, 4.01,
4.02–4.16, 4.23,
4.26, 4.34, 6.01,
6.16
Art. 130u *et seq.* 1.57,
2.33
Art. 148................ 3.02
Art. 149................ 3.03
Art. 155.........5.07, 5.10
Art. 169........ 1.11, 3.01,
4.16, 4.23, 5.10–5.14,
5.18, 6.20, 6.21
Art. 170................ 4.16
Art. 171 .... 5.11
Art. 173................ 2.18
Art. 175.........2.17, 3.18
Art. 177................ 4.33

1957 Rome. Treaty establishing
the European
Community—*cont.*
Art. 186................ 5.13
Art. 189.........3.02, 5.03
Art. 189a 2.17, 3.03,
3.06
Art. 189b 2.17, 3.01,
3.13, 3.39
Art. 189c 2.17,
3.01–3.03, 3.13, 3.39
Art. 189d 2.17
Art. 190........2.37, 4.18,
4.36
Arts. 198a–198c 3.04
Art. 222................ 3.08
Art. 228................ 3.20
(4) 3.20
(7) 3.20
Art. 235........1.42, 1.56,
3.12, 3.22, 3.34, 3.37
1957 Rome. Treaty establishing
the European Atomic
Energy Community
(Euratom) (March
25) 1.56, 4.10
1986 Luxembourg (February 17)
and The Hague
(February 28) Single
European Act: [1987]
O.J. L169/1 ...... 1.01,
1.06, 2.01, 2.04,
2.06, 2.08, 2.12,
2.18, 2.21, 2.37,
3.07, 3.16, 3.23,
3.34, 3.39, 4.02
1989 Lomé. ACP-EEC
Convention (Lomé IV)
(December 15) [1991]
O.J.
L229/1 .... 1.57

1992 Maastricht. Treaty on
      European Union
      (February 7): [1992]
      O.J. C191/1, [1992] 1
      C.M.L.R. 719... 1.01,
          1.16, 1.43, 1.53,
          1.56, 2.01, 2.06–
          2.09, 2.12, 2.13,
          2.14, 2.18, 2.21,
          2.28, 2.35, 2.37,
          2.40, 3.04, 3.05,

1957 Maastricht. Treaty on
      European Union
      —cont.
          3.06, 3.07, 3.09,
          3.14, 3.16, 3.20,
          3.35, 3.37, 3.39,
          4.02, 4.24, 5.03,
                          6.16
      Preamble........2.01, 2.06
      Art. B ... 2.06, 2.31, 2.33

REGULATIONS

Reg. 17 [1959–62] O.J. Eng. Spec.
Ed. 87.......................... 5.07

Reg. 3481/81 on imports of
cetacean products: [1981] O.J.
L39/1 .... 1.37

Reg. 3626/82 on trade in
endangered species: [1982]
O.J. L348/1... 1.37, 4.54, 6.11

Reg. 1872/84: [1984] O.J.
L176 ....5.02, 5.03

Reg. 3529/86 on the protection of
forests against air pollution:
[1986] O.J. L326/5 .. 1.52, 3.24

Reg. 2247/87: [1987] O.J.
L207/8 .... 5.03

Reg. 3955/87 on trade in
radioactively contaminated
agricultural products: [1987]
O.J. L371/14 .... 3.39

Reg. 1734/88 on the import
and export of certain
dangerous chemicals: [1988]
O.J. L155/2.................. 3.13
Art. 9............................. 3.13

Reg. 2052/88 on the reform of the
Structural Fund: [1988] O.J.
L185/13................1.53, 5.12
Art. 7......................1.53, 5.12

Reg. 3322/88 on the protection of
the ozone layer: [1988] O.J.
L297/1 .... 1.24

Reg. 2496/89 on import of ivory
from African elephants: [1989]
O.J. L240/5... 1.37, 2.08, 4.28

Reg. 1210/90 setting-up a European
Environment Agency: [1990]
O.J. L120/1 (see, also, [1993]
O.J. L294/29 and [1993] O.J.
C323/1) 1.46,
2.28, 2.38, 3.10,
5.07, 6.05
Art. 2............................. 1.46

Reg. 563.91: [1991] O.J. L63/1. 5.03

Reg. 594/91 on the import,
export, production and
consumption of CFCs: [1991]
O.J. L67/1 ....1.24, 3.33,
4.26, 5.19, 6.08,
6.09

Reg. 2092/91 on labelling of
agricultural products: [1991]
O.J. L198/1...........1.47, 1.52

Reg. 3254/91 on import of skins of
animals caught in leg traps:
[1991] O.J. L308/1 ..1.37, 4.28

Reg. 3907/91: [1991] O.J.
L370/1 .... 5.03

Reg. 3908/91: [1991] O.J.
L370/28 .... 5.03

Reg. 345/92 on drifting nets: [1992]
O.J. L42/15...........3.24, 4.28

Reg. 880/92 setting up a
Community-wide system for
an eco-label: [1992] O.J.
L99/1...................1.47, 2.28,
4.11, 4.13, 5.19,
6.05

Reg. 1973/92 setting up an
environmental fund (LIFE):
[1992] O.J. L206/1..1.48, 5.02

Reg. 2078/92 on agricultural
production methods: [1992]
O.J. L215/85 .... 1.52

Reg. 2080/92 on financial aid to
afforestation: [1992] O.J.
L215/96 .... 1.52

Reg. 2455/92 on export and import
of certain dangerous
chemicals: [1992] O.J.
L251/13.1.31, 1.57, 2.10, 4.26

Reg. 3280/92: [1992] O.J.
L327/3 .... 4.42

Reg. 259/93 on the transport of
hazardous waste: [1993] O.J.
L30/1.......... 1.39, 1.41, 1.42,
1.57, 2.20, 3.22,
4.12, 4.26, 6.15

Art. 4............................. 1.41
Art. 7............................. 1.41
Art. 18 .... 1.57

Reg. 792/93 on a Provisional
Cohesion Fund: [1993] O.J.
L79/74 .... 1.54, 2.05, 5.12

Reg. 793/93 on use of chemicals:
[1993] O.J. L84/1 ...1.29, 6.10

Reg. 1738/93 on transport
infrastructure: [1993] O.J.
L161/4 .... 1.55

Reg. 1836/93 on eco-auditing:
[1993] O.J. L168/1.1.33, 1.47,
2.28, 5.19, 6.05,
6.10, 6.15

Reg. 2081/93 on Structural Fund:
[1993] O.J. L193/5 .... 1.53

Reg. 2807/93: [1993] O.J.
L261/1 .... 5.07

DIRECTIVES

Dir. 67/548 on the classification, packaging and labelling of dangerous substances: [1967] O.J. Spec. Ed. 234 .... 1.02, 1.27, 3.02

Dir. 70/157 on noise level: [1970] O.J. Spec. Ed. 111 ..1.02, 1.25

Dir. 70/220 on pollutant emissions from motor vehicles: [1970] O.J. L76/1 ... 1.02, 1.20, 3.02, 3.07, 3.28, 6.08, 6.09, 6.15

Dir. 72/306 on diesel car emissions: [1972] O.J. Spec. Ed. 889 .... 6.08, 6.09, 6.25

Dir. 73/173 on solvents: [1973] O.J. L189/7 .... 1.28

Dir. 75/439 on the disposal of waste oils: [1975] O.J. L194/23 1.40, 6.08

Dir. 75/440 on the quality of surface waters: [1975] O.J. L194/26........ 1.11, 1.13, 6.05

Dir. 75/442 (Framework Directive on waste): [1975] O.J. L194/23................1.38, 5.18
Art. 5............................. 1.41

Dir. 75/716 on the sulphur content of liquid fuels: [1975] O.J. L307/22................1.21, 6.09

Dir. 76/160 on bathing water: [1976] O.J. L31/1 .... 1.11, 1.12, 6.05
Art. 6............................. 5.18

Annex V 5.18

Dir. 76/403 on the disposal of PCBs and PCTs: [1976] O.J. L108/41 .... 1.40

Dir. 76/464 (Framework Directive on discharges into the water): [1976] O.J. L129/23 ...... 1.14, 1.16, 1.33, 2.39, 6.05
Art. 7............................. 6.05

Dir. 76/769 on the use and prohibition of chemicals: [1976] O.J. L262/201 ..... 1.29, 6.08

Dir. 77/312 on the screening of the population for lead: [1977] O.J. L105/10 .... 2.10

Dir. 77/728 on paints and varnishes: [1977] O.J. L303/23 .... 1.28

Dir. 78/159 on water supporting fish life: [1978] O.J. L222/1 .... 1.11, 1.13

Dir. 78/176 on waste from the titanium dioxide industry: [1978] O.J. L54/19........ 1.18, 1.40, 1.58
Art. 9............................. 3.34

Dir. 78/319 on toxic and dangerous waste: [1978] O.J. L84/43 .... 1.38, 5.08, 5.18

Dir. 78/659 on fishwater: [1978] O.J. L222/1................... 6.05

Dir. 78/611: [1978] O.J. L197/19 .... 6.09

Dir. 78/631 on classification, packaging and labelling of pesticides: [1978] O.J. L206/13 .... 1.28

Dir. 78/1015 on motorcycles: [1978] O.J. L349/21 .... 1.25

Dir. 79/113 (Framework Directive on construction machinery and equipment(: [1970] O.J. L33/15 .... 1.25

Dir. 79/117 on plant protection products: [1977] O.J. L33/36 .... 1.29

Dir. 79/409 on the conservation of wild birds: [1979] O.J. L103/1 .... 1.34, 3.09, 6.11, 6.15
Art. 4.............................. 3.09

Dir. 79/869 on methods and sampling for the abstraction of drinking water: [1979] O.J. L271/44 .... 1.11

Dir. 79/923 on shellfish water: [1979] O.J. L281/47 1.11, 1.13

Dir. 80/51 on subsonic aircraft: [1980] O.J. L18/26......... 1.25

Dir. 80/68 on groundwater: [1980] O.J. L20/43... 1.11, 1.13, 6.15

Dir. 80/372 on CFCs in aerosol cans: [1980] O.J. L90/45 . 1.24

Dir. 80/609 on the limitation of emissions from large combustion plants: [1988] O.J. L336/1 .... 2.39

Dir. 80/778 on water for human consumption: [1980] O.J. L229/11 .... 1.11, 1.13, 2.32, 6.05, 6.15

Dir. 80/779 on limit-values for sulphur dioxide and suspended particulates: [1980] O.J. L229/30 ....1.23, 4.14, 4.48, 6.08, 6.15

Dir. 82/176 on mercury: [1982] O.J. L81/29 .... 1.15

Dir. 82/501 on major accident hazards: [1982] O.J. L230/1 .... 1.33, 2.20, 5.19, 6.10, 6.15

Dir. 82/795 on CFCs in aerosol cans: [1982] O.J. L329/29 1.24

Dir. 82/883 on titanium: [1982] O.J. L378/1 .... 1.18

Dir. 82/884 on limit-values for lead: [1982] O.J. L378/15 ...... 1.23, 4.14, 6.08, 6.15

Dir. 83/129 on import of certain seal skins: [1983] O.J. L91/20 ....1.37, 4.28

Dir. 83/189 on restrictions on chemicals: [1983] O.J. L109/8 .... 1.30, 1.44, 1.58, 2.20, 4.36

Dir. 83/206 on subsonic aircraft: [1983] O.J. L117/15........ 1.25

Dir. 83/513 on cadmium: [1983] O.J. L291/1 .... 1.15

Dir. 84/156 on mercury: [1984] O.J. L74/49 .... 1.15

Dir. 84/360 on pollution from industrial plants: [1984] O.J. L188/20...............1.22, 1.33, 5.18, 6.09
Art. 13 ....5.18, 6.09

Dir. 84/491 on lindane: [1984] O.J. L274/11....................... 1.15

Dir. 84/533 on compressors: [1984] O.J. L300/123............... 1.25

Dir. 84/534 on tower cranes: [1984] O.J. L300/130............... 1.25

Dir. 84/535 on welding generators: [1984] O.J. L300/142...... 1.25

Dir. 84/536 on power generators: [1984] O.J. L300/149...... 1.25

Dir. 84/537 on powered hand-held concrete breakers picks: [1984] O.J. L300/156...... 1.25

Dir. 84/538 on lawn-mowers: [1984] O.J. L300/171 .... 1.25

Dir. 84/631 on transfrontier shipment of hazardous waste: [1984] O.J. L326/31 1.39, 3.22

Dir. 85/203 on limit-values for nitrogen dioxide: [1985] O.J. L87/1 .... 1.23, 6.08, 6.15

Dir. 85/210 on lead content of petrol: [1985] O.J. L96/25 .... 1.21, 5.18, 6.08, 6.09

Art. 3 .... 5.18

Dir. 85/337 on environmental impact assessment: [1985] O.J. L175/40 1.33, 1.43, 1.55, 2.02, 2.20, 3.08, 4.14, 5.12, 6.10, 6.15

Dir. 85/339 on containers of liquids for human consumption: [1985] O.J. L176/18 1.40, 1.42

Dir. 85/467: [1985] O.J. L269/56 .... 6.08

Dir. 85/501 on the prevention of major accident hazards: [1985] O.J. L230/1 .... 2.02, 5.19

Dir. 86/278 on use of sewage sludge in agriculture: [1986] O.J. L181/6 .... 1.40

Dir. 86/280 on DDT and pentachlorophenol: [1986] O.J. L181/16 .... 1.15

Dir. 86/594 on household appliances: [1986] O.J. L344/24 .... 1.25

Dir. 86/609 on the protection of animals used in research and scientific experience: [1986] O.J. L358/1 .... 1.36

Dir. 86/662 on hydraulic excavators dozers, etc.: [1986] O.J. L384/1 .... 1.25

Dir. 87/178 on tests on chemical substances: [1987] O.J. L15/29 .... 1.27

Dir. 87/217 on asbestos: [1987] O.J. L85/40 .... 1.32, 6.08

Art. 8 .... 4.14

Dir. 87/219 on the reduction of liquid fuels: [1987] O.J. L91/19 .... 1.21, 6.09

Dir. 87/416 on the prohibition of regular leaded petrol: [1987] O.J. L225/33 .... 1.21, 4.12

Dir. 88/76 on catalytic converters: [1988] O.J. L36/1 ... 1.20, 3.30

Dir. 88/77 on standards for diesel-engined vehicles: [1988] O.J. L36/33 .... 1.20

Dir. 88/320 on test on chemical substances: [1988] O.J. L145/35 .... 1.27

Dir. 88/347 on limit-values and quality objectives for discharges of certain dangerous substances: [1988] O.J. L158/35 .... 1.15

Dir. 88/379 on chemical preparation: [1988] O.J. L187/14 .... 1.28, 4.11

Dir. 88/436 on catalytic converters: [1988] O.J. L214/1 .. 1.20, 3.30

Dir. 88/609 on emissions from large combustion installations: [1988] O.J. L336/1 . 1.22, 2.41, 6.08, 6.09, 6.15

Art. 3(5) 3.13

Dir. 88/610 on major accident hazards: [1988] O.J. L336/14 .... 1.33

Dir. 89/106 on construction material: [1986] O.J. L40/12 .... 1.59, 4.50

Dir. 89/235 on motorcycles: [1989] O.J. L98/1 .... 1.25

Dir. 89/369 on pollution from new municipal waste incinerators: [1989] O.J. L163/32 ...... 1.22, 4.13, 6.08, 6.15

Dir. 89/392 on machinery: [1989] O.J. L183/9 .... 1.58

Dir. 89/428 on the harmonisation of national programmes for the reduction of pollution: [1989] O.J. L201/56 .... 1.18, 3.30, 3.34, 4.18

Dir. 89/429 on pollution from existing municipal waste incinerators: [1989] O.J. L203/50 .... 1.22, 4.18, 6.08, 6.09, 6.15

Dir. 89/458 on catalytic converters: [1989] O.J. L226/1 .. 1.20, 3.30

Dir. 89/491 on catalytic converters: [1989] O.J. L238/43 1.20, 1.25

Dir. 90/219 on contained use of genetically modified organisms: [1990] O.J. L117/1 .... 1.32

Dir. 90/220 on deliberate release of modified organisms: [1990] O.J. L117/15 . 1.32, 2.20, 6.10

Dir. 90/313 on freedom of access to environmental information: [1990] O.J. L158/56 ...... 1.45, 6.10, 6.15

Dir. 90/396 on appliances burning gaseous fuels: [1990] O.J. L196/15 .... 1.59

Dir. 90/415 on TRI, PER and TCB: [1990] O.J. L219/49 .... 1.15

Dir. 90/667 on agricultural waste: [1990] O.J. L363/51 .... 1.40

Dir. 91/156 (Framework Directive on waste): [1991] O.J. L78/32.. 1.38, 1.42, 1.44, 3.30, 3.33, 4.26
Art. 6 .... 5.12, 6.13

Dir. 91/157 on waste from batteries and accumulators: [1991] O.J. L78/38 .... 1.40, 3.30, 3.33

Dir. 91/173: [1991] O.J. L85/34 .... 3.30, 4.18, 4.36

Dir. 91/271 on urban waste water treatment: [1991] O.J. L135/40 .... 1.17, 6.05, 6.15

Dir. 91/338: [1991] O.J. L186/59 .... 1.32

Dir. 91/414 on licensing of pesticides: [1991] O.J. L230/1 .... 1.28, 1.29, 3.25, 4.26
Art. 11 .... 4.26

Dir. 91/441 on catalytic converters: [1991] O.J. L242/1 . 1.20, 1.58, 3.07, 3.30
Art. 3 .... 1.58, 3.07

Dir. 91/542 on standards for diesel-engined vehicles: [1991] O.J. L29/1 .... 1.20

Dir. 91/628 on the protection of animals during transport: [1991] O.J. L340/17 .... 1.36

Dir. 91/676 on the protection of waters from pollution by nitrates from agricultural sources: [1991] O.J. L375/1 ... 1.17, 1.52, 6.15

Dir. 91/689 on hazardous waste: [1991] O.J. L377/20 ...... 1.38, 4.14, 4.26, 6.15

Dir. 91/692 on the standardisation and rationalisation of environmental reports: [1991] O.J. L377/48 .... 1.13, 1.22, 1.46, 5.08

Dir. 92/3 on the transport of nuclear waste: [1992] O.J. L35/24 1.39

Dir. 92/12 on products subject to excise duty: [1992] O.J. L76/1 .... 4.45

Dir. 92/14 on subsonic aircraft:
[1992] O.J. L76/21 .... 1.25
Dir. 92/32 on classification,
packaging and labelling of
chemical substances
(amending for the seventh
time Dir. 67/548): [1992] O.J.
L154/1 .. 1.27, 2.20, 4.25, 6.10
Dir. 92/43 on the conservation
of natural habitat and of flora
and fauna: [1992] O.J.
L206/7 .... 1.35, 3.03, 3.09,
6.11, 6.15
Art. 1.............................3.05
Art. 5.............................3.09
Dir. 92/72 on ozone concentrations:
[1992] O.J. L297/1 .... 1.23

Dir. 92/112 on reduction of wastes:
[1992] O.J. L409/11.......1.18,
3.34, 4.18, 6.08
Dir. 93/12 on fuel for diesel-
engined vehicles: [1993] O.J.
L74/81 .... 1.21, 6.08
Dir. 93/59 on car emissions: [1993]
O.J. L186/21 .... 3.30
Dir. 93/76 on energy efficiency
(SAVE): [1993] O.J.
L237/28 .... 1.56
Dir. 93/389 on control of energy:
[1993] O.J. L167/31 .... 1.56
Dir. 94/10 [1994] O.J.
L100/30 .... 1.44
Dir. 94/12: [1991] O.J. L100/42......
1.59

DECISIONS

Dec. 76/431: [1976] O.J.
L115/73 .... 5.09
Com. Dec. 78/618 setting up a
Scientific Committee on the
Toxicity and Ecotoxicity of
chemicals: [1978] O.J. L198/
17 .... 2.38
Dec. 85/338 on the CORINE
project: [1985] O.J.
L176/14 .... 3.10
Counc. Dec. 86/234 adopting an
environmental research
programme (1986–1990):
[1986] O.J. L159/31 .... 3.18
Counc. Dec. 91/354 adopting an
environmental research
programme (1990–1994):
[1991] O.J. L192/29 .... 3.18
Com. Dec. 93/464: [1993] O.J.
L219/1 .... 2.38
Dec. 93/500: [1993] O.J.
L235/1 .... 1.56
Com. Dec. 93/701: [1993] O.J.
L328/53 .... 1.48

ENVIRONMENTAL PROGRAMMES

1973 First Environmental Action
Programme: [1973] O.J.
C112/1 .... 1.04, 1.50,
2.02, 2.12, 2.18
1977 Second Environmental Action
Programme: [1977] O.J. C139/
1 .... 1.04, 2.12
1983 Third Environmental Action
Programme: [1983] O.J.
C46/1 .... 1.04, 2.12
1987 Fourth Environmental Action
Programme: [1987] O.J.
C328/1 .... 1.04, 1.18, 2.12,
2.18, 2.28, 3.16,
6.05
1990 Environmental Programme for
the Regions (ENVIREG):
[1990] O.J. C115/3 .... 1.53
1993 Fifth Environmental Action
Programme: [1993] O.J.
C138/1 .... 1.04, 1.18,
1.53, 1.54, 1.55,
1.56, 1.59, 2.24,
3.10, 3.16, 3.18,
5.07

INTERNATIONAL TREATIES AND CONVENTIONS

1963   Berne. Agreements and
        Protocols on the
        protection of the
        Rhine. See Dec. 77/
        586: [1977] O.J.
        L240/35, Dec. 82/460:
        [1982] O.J. L210/8,
        Dec. 88/381: [1988]
        O.J. L183/27 ..... 1.19
1973   CITES Convention to
        improve protection of
        endangered species of
        flora and fauna ... 1.37
1974   Paris. Convention for the
        prevention of marine
        pollution from land-
        based sources (June
        4). See Dec. 75/437:
        [1975] O.J.
        L194/5 .... 1.50
1976   Barcelona. Convention for
        the protection of the
        Mediterranean Sea
        against pollution
        (February 16). See
        Dec. 77/85: [1977]
        O.J. L240/1 .... 1.50
1976   Bonn. Convention for the
        protection of the
        Rhine against
        chemical pollution
        (December 3). See
        Dec. 77/586: [1977]
        O.J. L240/51...... 1.50

1979   Bonn. Convention on the
        conservation of
        migratory species
        of wild animals
        (June 23). See Dec.
        82/461: [1982] O.J.
        L210/10 .... 1.50
1979   Berne. Convention on the
        conservation of
        European wildlife and
        natural habitats
        (September 19). See
        Dec. 82/72: [1982]
        O.J. L38/1
1979   Geneva. Convention on
        long-range
        transboundary air
        pollution (November
        13). See Dec. 81/462:
        [1981] O.J.
        L171/11 .....1.00, 1.50
1985   Vienna. Convention for the
        protection of
        the ozone layer
        (March 22). See Dec.
        88/540: [1994] O.J.
        L297/8 ......1.24, 1.50
1987   Montreal. Protocol on
        substances that
        deplete the ozone
        layer (September 16).
        See Dec. 88/540:
        [1988] O.J. L297/8;

Dec. 91/690: [1991] O.J. L377/82 and Dec. 94/68: [1994] O.J. L33/1 .1.24, 1.50

1987 Regensburg. Convention on the Danube. See Dec. 90/160: [1990] O.J. L90/18 .... 1.19

1989 Basle. Convention on the transport of hazardous waste (March 22). See Dec. 93/98: [1993] O.J. L39/1 .... 1.39, 1.50, 3.22

1990 Magdeburg. Convention on the Elbe. See Dec. 91/598: [1991] O.J. L321/25 .... 1.19

1992 New York. Convention on climate change (May 9). See Dec. 94/69: [1994] O.J. L33/11 .... 1.50, 2.19, 3.12, 4.51

1992 Rio de Janeiro. Convention on biological diversity (June 5). See Dec. 93/626: [1993] O.J. L309/1 .... 1.50

ONE

Community Activity to date in the Field of Environmental Law

Origins of Community Environment Policy; Environment Programmes

A new title "Environment" consisting of the three Articles 130r to 130t was **1.01** incorporated, as Title VII, into the EEC Treaty by the 1987 Single European Act. The Maastricht Treaty on European Union brought a number of amendments to these provisions and transferred them to Title XVI.

Concepts such as "environment", "environmental protection" or "environment policy" were absent in the original Treaty. However, even before 1987, the Community had adopted numerous measures to protect the environment which can be grouped under the overall heading of "Community environment policy".

It was realised soon after the entry into force of the Rome Treaties that the **1.02** creation of a European Economic Community with a common market, in which national borders no longer constituted economic frontiers, gave rise to a corresponding need for mechanisms at Community level to safeguard man and the environment. Since the end of the transition period for constructing the common market, the Community has, therefore, increasingly engaged in activities to protect the environment. In 1967 Directive 67/548 on the classification, packaging and labelling of dangerous substances was adopted.[1] In 1970, the Council adopted a Directive on noise levels[2] and pollutant emissions[3] of motor vehicles. Also in 1970, the Commission declared in a

---

[1] [1967] O.J. Spec. Ed. 234.
[2] Dir. 70/157: [1970] O.J. Spec. Ed. 111.
[3] Dir. 70/220: [1970] O.J. L76/1.

1

memorandum to the Council that it was necessary to draw up a Community action programme on the environment; this was followed by a formal communication in July 1971.[4]

1.03　This communication gave rise to vigorous debate, both at Community level and in the Member States. It concerned, among other things, the question of whether environment matters were best dealt with at Community level or in the form of intergovernmental agreements and co-ordination of national environment policies. The Commission, backed by Parliament, was emphatically in favour of Community provisions. This view was eventually accepted by the Heads of State and Government of the then nine Member States, who in October 1972 declared:[5]

> "Economic expansion is not an end in itself. Its first aim should be to enable disparities in living conditions to be reduced. It must take place with the participation of all the social partners. It should result in an improvement in the quality of life as well as in standards of living. As befits the genius of Europe, particular attention will be given to intangible values and to protecting the environment, so that progress may really be put at the service of mankind."

1.04　The Community's institutions were requested to draw up a programme of action on the environment. This programme was adopted at the end of 1973.[6] However, the programme was agreed not only by the Community, but also by the representatives of the Governments of the Member States meeting in Council, because France in particular maintained its stance in favour of intergovernmental co-operation rather than a Community policy on environmental matters. Also the Second to Fifth Community Programmes on the environment were approved by the Community and the representatives of the Member States.[7]

1.05　In 1984, Parliament presented a draft Treaty establishing the European Union. Articles 55 and 59 of the draft gave the European Union concurrent competence for environment policy. In part as a reaction to Parliament's initiative, the European Council of Heads of State and Government appointed an all ad hoc Committee on Institutional Affairs, known as the Dooge Committee. The "Dooge Report" made only general reference to the environment as a sector in which increased co-operation would be necessary in future. The European Council discussed the Dooge Report in June 1985. It

---

[4] Commission SEC(71) 2616 final, July 7, 1971.
[5] Commission, Sixth General Report (1972), p. 8.
[6] [1973] O.J. C112/1.
[7] [1977] O.J. C139/1; [1983] O.J. C46/1; [1987] O.J. C328/1; [1993] O.J. C138/1.

decided to call an Intergovernmental Conference to consider amending the Treaty.

In July 1985, the Luxembourg Presidency presented a draft containing the **1.06** objectives of an amended Treaty, which provided in general for the inclusion of new areas of activity in the EEC Treaty, without explicitly mentioning the environment. The Commission submitted to the Conference proposals for a section on the environment containing four articles on the objectives and principles; a non-exhaustive list of the areas of Community activity in environmental protection; on the possibility for Member States to take more stringent measures; and the rule that the Council take decisions on environmental matters by majority vote.

Following discussions of the Intergovernmental Conference, the Commission presented a revised version of its proposals, which contained for the first time, a clause on the distribution of tasks between the Community and the Member States, but retained the principle of decisions by majority vote. After further discussions at the Conference, the Presidency submitted a text for the Single European Act to the Heads of State and Government at their meeting on December 2 and 3, 1985, which largely followed the structure of the Commission proposal. With regard to Articles 130r to 130t, this proposal was adopted as the definitive text.

In 1990, the discussion on the creation of European Political Union started **1.07** again. The European Council of Heads of State and Government in June 1990, adopted a basic statement on Community environmental policy and law.[8] The Commission, in its opinion of October 21, 1990, commented that "the question is one of improving decision-making, in other words the use made of qualified majority voting, rather than re-defining powers".[9] This statement was taken up by the European Council at its meeting in Rome in December 1990, which stated that environmental protection was one of the areas where there was a need to extend or re-define the Community's powers. It also noted that environmental protection needed to be improved in order to ensure sustainable growth.[10] Following this framework, the Commission's first proposal to the Intergovernmental Conference on Political Union[11] suggested, on the one hand, the qualified-majority voting in Article 130s and, on the

---

[8] [1990] 6 E.C. Bull. point 1.13 and Annex II.
[9] Opinion of the Commission of October 21, 1990, on the proposal for amendment of the Treaty establishing the European Economic Community with a view to political union: [1991] 2 E.C. Bull. Supp. 80.
[10] [1990] 12 E.C. Bull. point 1.8.
[11] First contributions by the Commission to the Intergovernmental Conference "Political Union": SEC(91) 500 of March 30, 1991. See: [1991] 2 E.C. Bull. Supp. 83 *et seq.*

other hand, a new formula of the integration principle in Article 130r(2)(2).[12] The Commission in addition, suggested environmental provisions in the chapter on Union Citizenship,[13] energy[14] and transeuropean networks,[15] and general provisions on external economic policy.[16] Member States also presented minor changes to the Intergovernmental Conference, only, presumably because the introduction of the environmental chapter into the Treaty was of such a recent nature.

1.08   In April 1991, the Luxembourg Presidency submitted a draft Treaty which introduced some linguistic and minor substantive changes into the environmental chapter. It suggested a new wording of Article 130r(2)(2) and provided for majority voting under Article 130s. Furthermore, the draft introduced the environment into Articles 2 and 3 and suggested that a general subsidiarity clause be put into the Treaty; the reference to the environment in the chapter on citizenship was deleted.

Following further discussions at the Intergovernmental Conference, the Dutch Presidency submitted, on September 25, 1991, a new draft text. The suggestions from the Luxembourg draft were maintained in this text in Articles 130r to 130t, but added in particular: (a) the precautionary principle in Article 130r(2)(1), and (b) the express mention of the adoption of environmental action programmes by majority co-decision. Article 2 was slightly changed.

1.09   Further discussions led to a new draft text from the Dutch Presidency on November 11, 1991, which was discussed in a conclave of November 12 and 13, 1991. Since, in particular, Spain and the United Kingdom were in favour of maintaining unanimous decisions in Article 130s, this draft, while maintaining the principle of majority voting, suggested that decisions on fiscal matters, town and country planning and soil use should be adopted unanimously. The proposal also introduced for the first time the derogation clause, which later became Article 130s(5) and which was largely initiated by

---

[12] Article 130s: "The measures required under Article 130r shall be adopted as laws . . . under the co-decision procedure . . . "
    Article 130r(2)(2): "Environmental protection requirements must be integrated into the definition and implementation of the Community's other policies".
[13] Article 7: "Every Union citizen shall have the right to enjoy a healthy environment and the obligation to contribute to protecting it. To this end, he shall have the right to information and the right to consultation where appropriate".
[14] Article 2: "The common energy policy shall have the following objectives: . . . (e) to promote energy savings and the use of new and renewable energy sources. It shall ensure a high level of protection in relation both to the environment, and to health and safety".
[15] Article 120a: (Action by the Union or trans-European networks) "shall take account of the demands of economic and social cohesion, environmental protection and cooperation with Third World countries".
[16] Articles Y 0 to Y 32 of the Commission; contributions (note 11 above).

Spain. The subsequent discussions, in particular during the Maastricht conference itself, only led to minor changes in the environmental provisions.

Environmental measures adopted at Community level

The salient environmental protection measures adopted at Community level **1.10** described below have been divided into different sections to ease presentation. The division is not always clear-cut; thus the measures to protect the ozone layer could come under either chemicals, air pollution or nature conservation. While many measures in the sphere of other policies, such as transport, agriculture or regional policy, may have substantial effects, favourable or otherwise, on the environment, they are not all considered below for obvious reasons.

WATER

The Community has adopted a wide range of provisions for the protection and **1.11** improvement of the aquatic environment.

A first set of Directives lays down quality objectives for water for specific uses. These include the provisions on surface waters for the abstraction of drinking water[17]—supplemented by a specific Directive on measurement methods and sampling[18]—the quality of bathing water,[19] water supporting fish life,[20] shellfish waters,[21] groundwater[22] and water for human consumption (drinking water).[23] The Directives specify the minimum quality required of the water for the use in question, sampling frequency and measurement methods. Member States were required to take measures and prepare programmes to ensure that the water quality specified was achieved within the lengthy lead times for the Directives, namely five years for water supporting fish life and drinking water, six years for shellfish water and 10 years for surface water and bathing water, respectively.

Implementation of the legislation proved extraordinarily difficult, particularly since the Commission did not systematically monitor application of the

---

[17] Dir. 75/440: [1975] O.J. L194/26.
[18] Dir. 79/869: [1979] O.J. L271/44.
[19] Dir. 76/160: [1976] O.J. L31/1.
[20] Dir. 78/659: [1978] O.J. L222/1.
[21] Dir. 79/923: [1979] O.J. L281/47.
[22] Dir. 80/68: [1980] O.J. L20/43.
[23] Dir. 80/778: [1980] O.J. L229/11.

Directives in the first few years after their entry into force.[24] The stipulated programmes were seldom drafted and rehabilitation work was only occasionally initiated. There were also considerable differences from one country to another. It has taken the increased application of the Treaty infringement procedure pursuant to Article 169 since the middle of the 1980s,[25] to make Member States face up to their responsibilities and gradually step up their efforts to meet the Community quality standards, though the situation is, at present, far from satisfactory.

1.12   The Directive on bathing waters covers some 16,000 bathing areas in the Community, 10,977 coastal waters and 5,266 inland waters. Portugal and the United Kingdom have not identified any inland bathing water.[26] During the bathing season, bathing waters must be regularly monitored; if necessary, measures must be taken to improve the quality of the water, or for instance, prohibit the bathing. The basic philosophy of the Directive is that in places, where a great number of persons bathe, water has to have a certain minimum quality.

Member States report annually to the Commission on their monitoring. The Commission publishes regular reports on the quality of bathing waters.[27] It follows from the 1992 report that measurements often concern total and faecal coliforms only, though the Directive is broader. In 1992, some 19 per cent. of the bathing waters did not conform to the Directive as regards total and faecal coliforms; in fact, only 63 per cent. of the inland waters complied. In the report to the Commission, only Denmark, the Netherlands and Germany indicated places where they had prohibited bathing due to the poor quality of the water.

For a number of years a private initiative, mainly from local authorities, has set up a "Blue Flag Scheme", which attributes a blue flag to bathing waters that comply with the criteria set up by the initiators.[28] The scheme is actively and financially supported by the Commission.

---

[24] See Haigh, *Manual of Environmental Policy: The E.C. and Britain* (Looseleaf) (London); Kromarek, "Vergleichende Untersuchung über die Umsetzung der E.G.-Richtlinien Abfall und Wasser", Environmental Research Plan of the Federal Minister of the Interior, Research Report 83–103 03 306 (December 1986), *passim*; Bennett, *Netherlands: Water and waste, a study of the implementation of the EEC Directives* (London, 1986); Lavoux, *France: Water and waste, a study of implementation of the EEC directives* (London, 1986); Capria, *Directive Ambientali CEE; Stato di attuazione in Italia* (Milan, 1988); Cabot, *EEC Environmental Legislation, a Handbook for Irish local authorities* (Dublin, 1987). With regard to practical application see also Parliament's Resolution of March 10, 1988: [1988] O.J. C94/154 (aquatic environment).

[25] By the end of 1993, the Court of Justice had given some 25 judgments on the application of Community water directives by Member States.

[26] Figures from the Commission, the Quality of bathing water 1992 (Bruxelles-Luxembourg) 1993.

[27] The 1992 report is already the 10th report which is published.

[28] See, for instance, Written Questions 1578/91 and 1579/91 (Amendola): [1992] O.J. C102/13.

6

Only some Member States apply the Directive on the quality of surface waters[29] in full. In particular, the clean-up plans which are required under the Directive have not been drawn up, or not been communicated to the Commission.[30] In 1992, the Commission stated that 25 per cent. of the waters did not comply with the Directive's requirements,[31] though reliable data is rare. A replacement general directive on the ecological quality of water has been proposed.[32]

1.13

The Directive on protecting groundwater against pollution by certain substances[33] prohibits completely the direct discharge of certain particularly dangerous substances contained in list I, and makes indirect discharges subject to prior consent, for which it lays down formal and material preconditions. The direct and indirect discharge of substances contained in list II is to be made subject to an authorisation procedure.

It would appear that groundwater pollution by agricultural activities: nitrates; pesticides, is a growing problem in most countries. Since Member States have no reporting obligations towards the Commission[34] and hardly any of them publish national data, there is a lack of precise information. Groundwater contamination by waste tips is in principle covered by the Directive, but has not led to systematic monitoring and where necessary, to remedial actions. A general revision of the Directive is announced.[35] Directive 80/778 fixed maximum concentrations of undesirable substances in drinking water.[36] Member States were disposed until 1985 to clean up their waters; they could ask for longer delays, which no Member State did. By the end of 1993, the standards for drinking water quality were not yet fully complied with by any Member State. The greatest problems were raised by nitrates, pesticides, coliforms and heavy metals in the water. The failure to prevent or combat pollution of surface or groundwater led almost everywhere to the difficulty of respecting the requirements of the Directive.[37]

The Directive's rules on methods and frequency of sampling are not very strict. No obligation was laid down to report on its implementation to the

---

[29] Dir. 75/440: [1975] O.J. L194/26.
[30] See, Cases 73/81, *Commission* v. *Belgium*: [1982] E.C.R. 189; C-290/89, *Commission* v. *Belgium*: [1991] I E.C.R. 2851; C-58/89, *Commission* v. *Germany* [1991] I E.C.R. 4983.
[31] The State of the Environment in the European Community: COM(92) 23 final, vol. III of March 27, 1992, point 2.1.
[32] Legislative Programme 1993: [1993] O.J. C125/1, point 241.
[33] Dir. 80/68: [1980] O.J. L20/43.
[34] Dir. 91/692 introduced such an obligation from 1996 onwards: [1991] O.J. L377/48.
[35] Council Resolution of December 12, 1991: [1992] O.J. C59/6.
[36] Dir. 80/778: [1980] O.J. L229/11; the Commission has announced for 1993, a proposal for a revision: [1993] O.J. C125/1, point 241.
[37] See, for instance Cases 228/87, *Pretura di Torino* v. *X*: [1988] E.C.R. 5099; C-42/89, *Commission* v. *Belgium*: [1990] I E.C.R. 2821, [1990] 1 C.M.L.R. 716; C-237/90, *Commission* v. *Germany*: judgment of November 24, 1992, not yet reported; C-337/89, *Commission* v. *United Kingdom*: [1992] I E.C.R. 6103.

Commission.[38] Considerable pressure exists to lower the standards, in particular as regard pesticides.[39]

The Directives on the quality of fresh waters supporting fish life and of shellfish waters[40] are not systematically monitored. Member States often designated waters which already complied with their requirements, or did not designate waters to which the Directives would be applicable. Only three Member States notified any waters at all supporting fish life, covered by Directive 78/659, and only four designated shellfish waters. It took a Court judgment in 1988 to establish that such conduct was not permissable.[41]

1.14   Another set of Directives concerns protection of the aquatic environment from pollution by certain dangerous substances. The basic rules for the Community were laid down in a framework Directive in 1976.[42] The groups of dangerous substances were assigned to two lists. List I contained substances which are particularly dangerous owing to their toxicity, persistence and bioaccumulation, while seven different groups of dangerous substances were included in List II. For List I substances, the Directive stipulated the establishment of Community limit values, which were not to be exceeded by the emission of standards set for the individual dischargers. In place of limit values, Member States could also opt for emission standards based on observance of Community quality objectives.

Until such time as limit values and quality objectives had been set for List I substances, they were to be treated according to the procedures for List II substances. Member States had to establish programmes for all List II substances based on national or Community quality objectives, which were to lead to a reduction in water pollution. Authorisation for individual discharges were to be in line with the quality objective for the receiving water.

The Commission presented the Council with a list of 1,500 substances eligible for inclusion in List I of the Directive. Of these, 129 were to be investigated as a priority and appropriate provision made. The Council agreed to this procedure.[43]

---

[38] See, however, Dir. 91/692: [1991] O.J. L377/48, which introduces such a reporting requirement. The first Community report is to be published in 1997.

[39] The maximum concentration is 0.1 μg per pesticide and 0.5 μg for all pesticides together. There are some 20,000 pesticides and 700 effective substances in use in the E.C. The request is to fix different concentrations for the different pesticides; however, enforcing and controlling would then be impossible.

[40] Dir. 78/659 (fishwater): [1978] O.J. L222/1; Dir. 79/923: [1979] O.J. L281/47 (shellfish water).

[41] Case 322/86, Commission v. Italy: [1988] E.C.R. 3995.

[42] Dir. 76/464: [1976] O.J. L129/23.

[43] Council Resolution of February 7, 1983: [1983] O.J. C46/17.

To date, Community limit values and quality objectives have been set for the 1.15
following substances in List I: mercury,[44] cadmium,[45] HCH (lindane),[46]
carbon tetrachloride, DDT, pentachlorophenol,[47] aldrin, dieldrin, endrin,
isodrin, hexachlorobenzene, hexachlorobutadiene dieldrin, endrin, isodrin,
hexachlorobenzene, hexachlorobutadiene chloroform,[48] 1,2-dichloroethane,
TRI, PER and TCB (trichlorobenzene).[49] Quality objectives for any List II
substances have not yet been established.[50]

The Directives in question have not yet been complied with in form and
substance in all Member States. Only some Member States have drawn up
pollution reductions programmes for some substances in List II. A comparison of the individual programmes by the Commission, as provided for by
Directive 76/464, has not taken place. Likewise, the Commission has so far
failed to produce the comparative assessments of implementation of the
Directives on mercury, cadmium and HCH.

The Community's work was considerably slowed down by a difference of 1.16
opinion between the United Kingdom and the other Member States.[51] The
view of the United Kingdom is that the decisive criterion for all substances is
the extent to which they damage the environment. Consequently, all that is
necessary is to set and monitor quality objectives. This contrasted with the
view that the particularly dangerous substances in List I should be regulated
by limit-values for discharges. The compromise written into Directive 76/464,
allowing Member States a choice of the two methods, did not end the
discussion. More importantly, the Commission has not yet notified the
Council of the instances in which it has accepted application of the quality
objectives approach, although the framework Directive made specific provision for this; in addition, comparative assessments of the actual effects of the
Directives have not so far been undertaken.

In 1988, Member States and the Commission agreed that the limit-value
approach and the quality-objective approach should be used jointly.[52]
However, this consensus which was also expressed at different North Sea
Conferences, had not yet materialised by the end of 1993. A Commission
proposal to adopt Community standards for dangerous discharges into water

---

[44] Dir. 82/176: [1982] O.J. L81/29 and Dir. 84/156: [1984] O.J. L74/49.
[45] Dir. 83/513: [1983] O.J. L291/1.
[46] Dir. 84/491: [1984] O.J. L274/11.
[47] Dir. 86/280: [1986] O.J. L181/16.
[48] Dir. 88/347: [1988] O.J. L158/35.
[49] Dir. 90/415: [1990] O.J. L219/49.
[50] A proposal for a Directive on chromium discharges was submitted to the Council in 1985:
[1985] O.J. C351/33, but never adopted.
[51] See on this subject in depth comments by Rehbinder-Stewart, *Environmental Protection Policy*
(Berlin-New York, 1985), pp. 216 *et seq.*; Haigh, *Manual of Environmental Policy: The E.C.
and Britain* (looseleaf) (London).
[52] [1988] 6 E.C. Bull. point 2.1.175.

by majority decisions under Article 130s(2)[53] has since 1991, been blocked by the Council and was withdrawn in 1993. Whether the Maastricht Treaty will now allow majority decisions on water issues, will be discussed in points 3.10 below.

1.17   Directive 91/271 on urban waste water treatment,[54] requires all agglomerations with more than 2000 persons to be equipped with collecting systems for urban waste water by the year 2005. The water shall be subject to secondary treatment before discharge. This Directive will require considerable investment from several Member States.

Directive 91/676 on the protection of waters from pollution by nitrates from agricultural sources,[55] obliges Member States to designate areas at risk, *i.e.* where the nitrate level risks are too high. For these areas Member States have to set up action programmes for the limitation of fertilisers or manure per hectare.

1.18   Efforts to reduce water pollution by individual industries had only resulted in legislation on titanium dioxide production.[56] A directive of mid-1989 on the harmonisation of national programmes for the reduction of pollution,[57] (which fixed binding dates for the reduction of wastes, in particular, as regards discharges into waters), was annulled by the Court of Justice because it had been based on Article 130s rather than 100a.[58] It was replaced by Directive 92/112[59] which fixed binding dates as of 1994: however, these obligations may be set aside temporarily, where "major technical and economic difficulties" so require and reduction programmes are submitted to the Commission.

The Commission had, generally, suspended its work on water pollution by certain industries owing to "obvious differences of opinion within the Council".[60] The particular case in point concerned the failure to adopt the proposal for a directive on water pollution by pulp mills. The announcement in the Fourth Action Programme to the effect that work on pollution by individual industries was to be resumed,[61] had not produced concrete results by the end of 1993 and was not repeated in the Fifth Action Programme.

1.19   There are no specific directives as yet on the prevention and reduction of marine pollution, although some of those mentioned—*e.g.* on bathing waters,

---

53 [1990] O.J. C55/7.
54 Dir. 91/271: [1991] O.J. L135/40.
55 Dir. 91/676: [1991] O.J. L375/1.
56 Dir. 78/176: [1978] O.J. L54/19; Dir. 82/883; [1982] O.J. L378/1.
57 Dir. 89/428: [1989] O.J. L201/56.
58 Case C-300/89, *Commission* v. *Council*: [1991] I E.C.R. 2867, [1993] 3 C.M.L.R. 359.
59 Dir. 92/112: [1992] O.J. L409/11.
60 Commission, "Progress made in connection with the environment action programme and assessment of the work to implement it" COM(80) 222 final of May 7, 1980, p. 5.
61 Fourth Environment Action Programme: [1987] O.J. C328/1, point 3.4.2.

waste from the titanium dioxide industry—also cover the marine environment. A proposal for a directive on the dumping of waste at sea was first put to the Council in 1976, and again in amended form in 1985,[62] but failed to be adopted and was finally withdrawn in 1993.

The Community is party to several international Conventions on the protection of the marine environment. However, in this capacity it shares powers with the Member States.[63] The Community as an entity does not conduct its own, intensive monitoring of observance of the Conventions.

There is a similar situation regarding the Rhine, the rehabilitation of which is governed by international and not Community regulations, despite the fact that the Community has ratified various agreements and protocols on protection of the Rhine.[64] The Community also adhered to Conventions on the Danube[65] and the Elbe[66] water management and clean-up, though again the Conventions are not monitored at Community level.

AIR

The Community bases its air pollution legislation on a variety of approaches.   **1.20**

One group of provisions regulating specific products was designed to reduce pollutant emissions from motor vehicles and motorcycles. The measures taken in 1970 to reduce pollutant emissions from motor vehicles have been tightened up since the beginning of the 1980s.[67]

Owing to the fact that the extent of environmental damage due to air pollution is not equally apparent in all Member States, and to differences in the importance attached to environmental protection by the individual Member States, it took the Community several years to reach a decision on emission standards for cars which were strict enough to require the use of catalytic converters. The standards, which were finally agreed by majority decisions in 1987 and 1988—with a decisive participation of the European Parliament—require all new cars, marketed in 1993 or later, to be equipped with catalytic converters.[68] No rules for existing cars were laid down. Economic incentives by Member States to promote the use of catalytic converters were only authorised for transitional periods, and under the strict condition that a car with a converter remained more expensive than a car

---

[62] [1976] O.J. C40/3; [1985] O.J. C245/23; amended [1988] O.J. C72/8.
[63] See paras. 3.20 *et seq* below.
[64] See, Dec. 77/586: [1977] O.J. L240/35; Dec. 82/460: [1982] O.J. L210/8; Dec. 88/381: [1988] O.J. L183/27.
[65] Dec. 90/160: [1990] O.J. L90/18.
[66] Dec. 91/598: [1991] O.J. L321/25.
[67] Dir. 70/220: [1970] O.J. L76/1; this Directive was amended five times between 1988 and 1991.
[68] Dir. 88/76: [1988] O.J. L36/1; Dir. 88/436: [1988] O.J. L214/1; Dir. 89/458: [1989] O.J. L226/1; Dir. 89/491: [1989] O.J. L238/43; Dir. 91/441: [1991] O.J. L242/1.

without that technology.[69] It is at present, highly controversial as to whether or not Member States are free to decide on non-discriminatory economic incentives under Article 95 of the Treaty. Community standards were also fixed for diesel-engined vehicles,[70] though not yet for trucks.

1.21   Product-related provisions were also adopted on the lead content of petrol.[71] Unleaded petrol was to be available throughout the territory of Member States from October 1989. The real situation of consumption of unleaded petrol is, at present, still rather unsatisfactory.[72] In order to allow the speeding up of the introduction of lead-free petrol, Member States were allowed to prohibit regular leaded petrol,[73] a measure which abolished its free circulation. The sulphur content of liquid fuels was progressively reduced by different Directives.[74] Since 1987, these Directives have allowed Member States to further reduce, for environmental reasons, the use of liquid fuels with too high sulphur content on their territory.[75] In 1993, this possibility was abolished; however, at the same time the scope of application of the Directive was reduced; it now only covers fuel for diesel-engined vehicles.[76] Other gasoils are to be regulated by Member States.

1.22   A Directive adopted in 1984 provides for a system of special authorisation for emissions to the atmosphere from pollutant industrial plants.[77] New plants must use the best available technology without entailing excessive costs. In the case of existing plants, Member States must draw up strategies and programmes for the gradual reduction of emissions. To what extent these requirements are observed, is unclear. No reporting requirements exist for Member States.[78] The Commission, together with Member States, regularly elaborates and publishes technical notes on best available technologies for specific sectors of industry. However, information on these notes is limited; they have no binding legal nature and their observation is neither monitored

---

[69] This approach is based on the assumption, that a complete recovery of the cost for the catalytic converter would lead to the introduction of a second technical standard.

[70] Dir. 88/77: [1988] O.J. L36/33; Dir. 91/542: [1991] O.J. L29/1.

[71] Dir. 85/210: [1985] O.J. L96/25.

[72] See, Written Question 2276/92 (Pollack): [1993] O.J. C32/42: at the end of 1991, lead-free petrol had the following market-share: Germany 79 per cent., Denmark 67 per cent., Netherlands 59 per cent., Luxembourg 45 per cent., United Kingdom 42 per cent., Belgium 42 per cent., France 28 per cent., Ireland 27 per cent., Greece 9 per cent., Italy 7 per cent., Spain 4 per cent., Portugal 3 per cent.

[73] Dir. 87/416: [1987] O.J. L225/33.

[74] Dir. 75/716: [1975] O.J. L307/22.

[75] Dir. 87/219: [1987] O.J. L91/19.

[76] Dir. 93/12: [1993] O.J. L74/81.

[77] Dir. 84/360: [1988] O.J. L188/20.

[78] See, however, Dir. 91/692: [1991] O.J. L377/48, which introduces a reporting requirement. The first report by the Commission will be published in 1998.

nor known. It does not seem that these notes have reached Community-wide consensus on what constitutes the "best available technology".

Following five years of discussion, the Community reached a compromise in 1988 on emissions from large combustion installations which are to be reduced by certain percentages with 1980 as the reference year.[79] In 1989, two Directives on the prevention and reduction of air pollution from new and existing municipal waste incinerators were adopted.[80] These Directives fix emission limit values for certain pollutants, and control requirements for Member States. A directive on the incineration of dangerous waste is currently being discussed in the Council.[81]

Media-specific Directives establish limit-values for sulphur dioxide and suspended particulates (black smoke),[82] lead[83] and nitrogen dioxide,[84] that may not be exceeded throughout the territory of the Member States. For a transitional period, Member States were allowed to designate vulnerable zones in which the limit values were to be observed only at the end of the transition period. These periods have since elapsed for sulphur dioxide; suspended particulates and lead, and will elapse in 1994 for nitrogen dioxide. Clean-up programmes which were required for these zones during the transitional periods, have only very rarely been set up. As Member States decide on the emplacement and number of measuring stations, and since measuring instruments are not very precise and the measuring results are based on average figures, the Directives have, overall, had only limited success in improving air quality. **1.23**

A Directive on ozone concentrations adopted in 1992,[85] obliges Member States to regularly measure ozone concentrations and to warn the population where ozone concentrations exceeded certain limits.

The Community joined in the international efforts to protect the ozone layer from chlorofluorocarbons. In 1980 it decided to freeze CFC production at 1976 levels and to reduce their use in aerosol cans.[86] It became a party to the Vienna Convention and the Montreal Protocol in 1988 and adopted a Regulation controlling imports, exports, production and consumption of these substances,[87] which was gradually tightened. Some ozone-destroying substances were prohibited; proposals to reduce the use also of substances with a less **1.24**

---

[79] Dir. 88/609: [1988] O.J. L336/1.
[80] Dir. 89/369: [1989] O.J. L163/32 (new plants); Dir. 89/429: [1989] O.J. L203/50 (existing plants).
[81] [1992] O.J. C130/1.
[82] Dir. 80/779: [1980] O.J. L229/30.
[83] Dir. 82/884: [1982] O.J. L378/15.
[84] Dir. 85/203: [1985] O.J. L87/1.
[85] Dir. 92/72: [1992] O.J. L297/1.
[86] Dec. 80/372: [1980] O.J. L90/45; Dec. 82/795: [1982] O.J. L329/29.
[87] Reg. 91/594: [1991] O.J. L67/1 which replaced Reg. 3322/88: [1988] O.J. L297/1.

destroying effect, (the so-called HCFCs), are being discussed.[88] It is to be noted that these measures are based on Article 130s and make explicit reference to the Member States' possibility to take more stringent measures to protect the environment pursuant to Article 130t.

The Community also became party to the Geneva Convention on long-range transboundary air pollution, which establishes several principles regarding the reduction of air pollution and promotes international co-operation and the exchange of information.[89] The Community does not monitor implementation on its own account.

NOISE

1.25 Community noise protection measures taken so far exclusively concern standards for certain products, in particular transport media—motor vehicles,[90] motorcycles,[91] construction machinery and equipment,[92] and household appliances.[93] The Directives concerning these product sectors are optional; they therefore set maximum noise emission levels only for those products implicated in intra-Community trade. By contrast, Member States set independent noise protection standards for products intended exclusively for the domestic market.

The maximum permissible noise emission level from subsonic aircraft is regulated by three Directives that adopt the arrangements of the International Civil Aviation Organisation for the Community.[94]

A framework Directive was adopted in 1986 which permits the establishment of maximum noise levels for household appliances; implementing regulations have not so far been adopted at Community level.[95] A separate Directive lays down maximum noise levels for lawnmowers and provides for them to be labelled accordingly.[96]

---

[88] [1992] O.J. C90/16.
[89] Dec. 81/462: [1981] O.J. L171/11.
[90] Dir. 70/157: [1970] O.J. L42/6; latest amendment Dir. 89/491: [1989] O.J. L238/43.
[91] Dir. 78/1015: [1978] O.J. L349/21; latest amendment Dir. 89/235: [1989] O.J. L98/1.
[92] Framework Directive 79/113: [1979] O.J. L33/15.
  Dir. 84/533 (compressors): [1984] O.J. L300/123.
  Dir. 84/534 (tower cranes): [1984] O.J. L300/130.
  Dir. 84/535 (welding generators): [1984] O.J. L300/142.
  Dir. 84/536 (power generators): [1984] O.J. L300/149.
  Dir. 84/537 (powered hand-held concrete breakers and picks): [1984] O.J. L300/156.
  Dir. 86/662 (hydraulic excavators, dozers, etc.): [1986] O.J. L384/1.
[93] Dir. 86/594, [1986] O.J. L344/24.
[94] Dir. 80/51. [1980] O.J. L18/26.
  Dir. 83/206, [1983] O.J. L117/15; Dir. 92/14: [1992] O.J. L76/21.
[95] Dir. 86/594: [1986] O.J. L344/24.
[96] Dir. 84/538: [1984] O.J. L300/171.

All the specific Directives, which are largely based on the work of inter-   **1.26**
national standardisation organisations, specify maximum levels for products
new on the market, but contain no provisions on noise emissions throughout
the lifetime of a product. In addition, they tend to enshrine the current state of
the art rather than oblige product manufacturers to reduce noise emissions.
This is understandable bearing in mind that the primary objective of the
regulations adopted to date has been the establishment of free intra-
Community trade and the elimination of technical barriers.

The Community has not so far fixed quality objectives for noise emissions,
for instance in urban agglomerations, in the vicinity of airfields, hospitals or
residential areas.

CHEMICALS

Community measures in the field of chemicals are targeted at specific products   **1.27**
or production processes.

A Directive from 1967 regulates the classification, packaging and labelling
of chemical products at Community level.[97] Since the sixth amendment of this
Directive, new chemicals, *i.e.* substances not in circulation in the Community
on September 18, 1981, have to be notified to the Commission before they are
placed on the market. The notification must be supplemented by the results of
tests conducted to evaluate the potential risk posed by the substance to man
and the environment. In this respect a Directive from 1986 lays down the
principles of good laboratory practice for tests on chemical substances.[98] The
notification is forwarded to all Member States to give them the opportunity to
express reservations or demand further tests.

New substances may not be placed on the market until 45 days after
notification; if the subsequent examination by the 12 Member States takes
longer, the bringing into circulation would probably, as a precautionary
measure, only be permissible on completion of examination, notwithstanding
any claims for compensation by the notifying party.

Dangerous substances are included in Annex I to the Directive and may be
placed on the market in all Member States on the common conditions applying
throughout the Community. By mid-1993, approximately 2,500 substances
were notified in the Community, including 1,800 substances under a
simplified procedure.

Old substances (those which were on the Community market before
September 18, 1981—an inventory first drawn up in 1987 lists all old
substances,[99] totalling just over 100,000) are classified, packaged and labelled

---

[97] Dir. 67/548: [1967] O.J. 196/1; seventh amendment by Dir. 92/32: [1992] O.J. L154/1.
[98] Dir. 87/18: [1987] O.J. L15/29; see, also, Dir. 88/320: [1988] O.J. L145/35.
[99] The list is published in [1990] O.J. L196/4.

according to their hazard potential by the manufacturer or Community importer; they may then be circulated freely in the Community.

1.28   Chemical preparations are subject to the provisions of Directive 88/379.[1] The Directive covers the classification, packaging and labelling of dangerous preparations for which it lays down uniform rules; no pre-marketing notification of new preparations is required. Rather, marketing is free. Marketing in one Member State permits the entry to the whole Community market. The Directive replaced earlier Directives on solvents,[2] paints and varnishes,[3] but not the Directive on the classification, packaging and labelling of pesticides,[4] introduced in 1978. There are specific Directives on the Community-wide licensing of pesticides[5] and also on medicinal products and cosmetics.

If a Member State considers that a substance or a preparation, while complying with the requirements of Directives 67/547 or 88/379 poses a risk to man or the environment it may impose restrictions on its circulation or prohibit it. Such measures may only be temporary and must be notified to the Commission. Then, a Community procedure is opened which leads to a Community-wide decision, taken by a qualified majority.

1.29   Community-wide restrictions on use and prohibitions of chemicals are issued pursuant to Directive 76/769,[6] which is regularly updated. Restrictions and bans are imposed, among others, on asbestos, PCBs, benzen, cadmium and pentachlorophenols. At present, any amendment of the Directive must be in the form a special Council Directive, which is a slow and laborious procedure considering the risk which many chemicals pose.[7] A new Regulation adopted in 1993, tries to systematically assess the risk of existing chemicals and accelerate the Community decisions on restrictions of use, where necessary.[8] Bans of some plant protection products are the subject of a specific Directive,[9] which allows for other pesticides to be banned at national level. This system will, however, be replaced once Directive 91/414 on the Community-wide authorisation of plant protection products[10] is fully operational.

---

[1] Dir. 88/379: [1988] O.J. L187/14.
[2] Dir. 73/173: [1973] O.J. L189/7.
[3] Dir. 77/728: [1997] O.J. L303/23.
[4] Dir. 78/631: [1978] O.J. L206/13.
[5] Dir. 91/414: [1991] O.J. L230/1.
[6] Dir. 76/769: [1976] O.J. L262/201.
[7] Attempts by the Commission to introduce a simplified procedure have failed, see, [1974] O.J. C126/33 and COM(83) 556 final of September 9, 1983.
[8] Reg. 793/93: [1993] O.J. L84/1.
[9] Dir. 79/117: [1979] O.J. L33/36.
[10] Dir. 91/414: [1991] O.J. L230/1.

National restrictions or bans of chemicals must be notified to the Commission **1.30** in their draft stage, under Directive 83/189.[11] Notification gives rise to a standstill period of at least three months, during which the compatibility of the planned measure with Community law is examined in particular the provisions of Article 30. This period is extended to 12 months if the Commission decides to adopt the national measure in full, or in part, in the form of a Community legal measure. After that period there are—more or less legally substantiated—standstill obligations resulting from the principle of Community-spirited conduct (Article 5 of the Treaty), particularly if the Commission has already proposed a Community solution. The content of the planned national measure is examined to ascertain in particular whether it has a discriminatory effect or whether it is unreasonably severe in relation to the desired objective.[12]

Exports and imports of chemicals which are banned or severely restricted by **1.31** virtue of Community measures—but not where only national measures exist— are regulated by a specific Regulation.[13] Exports may only take place where the importing country has given its consent to such an import. This consent must be given after the importing country has been informed of the intended import and the risks which the chemicals present.

Imports into the Community of dangerous chemicals must be expressly authorised.

Two Directives on the contained use of genetically modified micro-organisms **1.32** and the deliberate release of genetically modified organisms were adopted in 1990.[14] The Commission must be notified of the intention of a deliberate release, it then, in turn, informs the other Member States. The release may take place only where all Member States have given clearance; in case of divergence a Community decision is taken by majority. There are deliberations to adopt more specific directives in the food, pharmaceutical and pesticide sector.

Horizontal Community-wide measures on existing chemical products have also been announced, but so far only one such measure has been adopted, for asbestos.[15] A programme on reducing the use of cadmium adopted in 1988, has, until now, only been implemented by one Directive, which restricts the use of cadmium in certain products.[16]

---

[11] Dir. 83/189: [1983] O.J. L109/8.
[12] See below paras. 4.26 *et seq.*
[13] Reg. 2455/92: [1992] O.J. L251/13.
[14] Dir. 90/219: [1990] O.J. L117/1 (contained use); Dir. 90/220: [1990] O.J. L117/15 (deliberate release).
[15] Dir. 87/217: [1987] O.J. L85/40.
[16] Council Resolution of January 25, 1988: [1988] O.J. C30/1; Dir. 91/338: [1991] O.J. L186/59.

1.33   Legislation on chemical installations has, in the past, not been very systematic. Discharges into water,[17] or emissions into the air were subjects of authorisation requirements.[18] A general directive covering all authorisations has been proposed.[19]

Following a number of serious accidents in the Community, a Directive was adopted in 1982 on the major accident hazards of certain industrial activities, which covers approximately 2,000 industrial plants in the Community.[20] The plant operators have to take whatever measures are necessary to prevent serious accidents. Thus, they have to make and forward to the competent authorities, safety audits for the plant, draw up risk prevention and emergency plans and notify in detail any accident with serious consequences for man or the environment. The Directive was extended following the Sandoz accident in Basle in 1986.[21] It now covers not only in-plant storage, but storage in general of dangerous chemicals. Furthermore, the Directive on environmental impact assessment[22] and the Regulation on eco-auditing[23] also apply to chemical installations.

NATURE CONSERVATION

1.34   The Council adopted a Directive on the conservation of wild birds[24] in the context of measures to protect flora and fauna. The Directive is an attempt to provide comprehensive, union-wide protection to birds and their habitats. It protects the habitats of 175 particularly endangered bird species, restricts the number of species that can be hunted and traded commercially and prohibits certain hunting and trapping methods. Full application of the Directive is encountering considerable difficulties in all Member States. The main problems concern the impairment of bird habitats as a result of anthropogenic activity, in particular agriculture and tourism, and the failure to adopt suitable measures for their protection; also in 1993, fewer than half the approximately 1,600 habitats falling within the Directive's field of application had been designated[25] and therefore hunting continued of bird species protected by the Directive, including the hunting and trapping practices. One further problem is the more than generous interpretation of the strict derogations allowed by the Directive at local, regional or national level.

---

[17] Dir. 76/464: [1976] O.J. L129/23.
[18] Dir. 84/360: [1984] O.J. L188/20.
[19] [1993] O.J. C31/6.
[20] Dir. 82/501: [1982] O.J. L230/1.
[21] Dir. 88/610: [1988] O.J. L336/14.
[22] Dir. 85/337: [1985] O.J. L175/40.
[23] Reg. 1836/93: [1993] O.J. L168/1.
[24] Dir. 79/409: [1979] O.J. L103/1.
[25] Answer to Written Question 1648/90: [1991] O.J. C248/1.

A general Directive on the conservation of natural habitats and of fauna and   **1.35**
flora was adopted in 1992.[26] It attempts to provide for a comprehensive
protection of species and their habitats, *inter alia*, because international
conventions, to which the European Community is a party, did not achieve too
satisfactory results and in particular, did not stop the slow but progressive
degradation and even disappearance of natural habitats in Western Europe.
The protection system, including the designation and protection measures for
habitats, is to be set up progressively within six years. In exceptional cases,
Community funding is foreseen in order to assist Member States.

Directive 86/809 concerns the protection of animals used in research and   **1.36**
scientific experiments, but not animals used in the production process.[27] The
Directive contains a number of fundamental rules regarding the use and keep
of animals, and the inspection of plants and installations that use animals in
their experiments and research. A Directive concerning the protection of
animals during transport, which is based on Article 43 was adopted in 1991,
and a Directive on the protection of animals in zoos was suggested.[28]

The Community intends to become party to the 1973 CITES Convention to   **1.37**
improve protection of endangered species of flora and fauna which is at
present open to ratification by Nation States only.[29] Regulation 3626/82 has
laid down uniform rules for intra-Community trade in endangered species of
animals and plants.[30] The Community territory is regarded as an entity, with
mutual recognition of import and export licences granted by Member States.
In practice, differences in monitoring, interpretation and routine application
by Member States, due in some cases to diverging commercial interests and
differing levels of environmental awareness, frequently lead to differences of
approach concerning trade in endangered species of flora and fauna.[31] A
fundamental revision by Regulation 3626/82 was suggested in 1992.[32]
    Imports of certain cetacean products have been prohibited since 1982[33];
imports of certain seal skins since 1983,[34]; of ivory from African elephants
since 1989[35] and skins of animals caught in leg traps since 1991.[36] Where such

---

[26] Dir. 92/43: [1992] O.J. L206/7.
[27] Dir. 86/609: [1986] O.J. L358/1.
[28] Dir. 91/628: [1991] O.J. L340/17 (transport of animals); [1991] O.J. C241/14 (animals in zoos).
[29] A 1983 amendment to the Convention has not yet been ratified by a sufficient number of
    contracting States.
[30] Reg. 3626/82: [1982] O.J. L384/1.
[31] European Parliament: [1988] O.J. C290/142. These differences caused the Commission to
    suggest a revision in 1992.
[32] [1992] O.J. C26/1.
[33] Reg. 3481/81: [1981] O.J. L39/1.
[34] Dir. 83/129: [1983] O.J. L91/20.
[35] Reg. 2496/89: [1989] O.J. L240/5.
[36] Reg. 3254/91: [1991] O.J. L308/1; the ban becomes effective in 1995.

Directives deal with hunting or capture practices, they come in conflict with rules of commercial policy.

WASTE

1.38 The Community has been legislating on waste since 1975. Its declared aim of bringing about integrated waste mangement in the Community[37] has, however, not been achieved.

The framework Directive 75/442 defines the concept of "waste" and lays down general obligations of waste management, including the obligation to prevent and reduce the production of waste, to promote its recovery and safe disposal.[38] Recovery and safe disposal must take place without endangering human health or harming the environment. Member States must draw up waste management plans. All disposal and recovery activities must be authorised, waste installations shall be periodically inspected and are subject to a number of obligations such as on record keeping and on the transport of waste. Directive 78/319 on toxic and dangerous waste[39] was replaced by Directive 91/689 on hazardous waste.[40] This new Directive undertakes to define hazardous waste. A provision requesting the drawing up of a positive list of hazardous wastes proved to be impossible to implement and was thus replaced by a provision to establish an indicative list.[41] Directive 91/689 again obliges Member States to dispose of hazardous wastes without risk to man or the environment. It introduces an authorisation system for installations which treat or dispose of hazardous wastes and requires management plans for hazardous wastes to be drawn up.

1.39 Directive 84/631 on transfrontier shipment of hazardous waste, adopted in 1984 and supplemented in 1986 to also cover the export of hazardous waste to third countries,[42] had proved inadequate to stop illegal waste transports. In 1993, it was replaced by Regulation 259/93[43] which at the same time, incorporated the provisions of the Basel Convention on the transport of hazardous waste of 1989[44] into Community law. The Regulation deals with export, import and intra-Community transport of all kinds of wastes. It introduces a complicated system of controls, differentiated according to types of waste—for which it establishes green, orange, and red lists—and countries of destination, giving Member States practically complete freedom to export

---

[37] Council Resolution of May 7, 1990: [1990] O.J. C122/2.
[38] Dir. 75/442: [1975] O.J. L194/23; amended by Dir. 91/156: [1991] O.J. L78/32.
[39] Dir. 78/319: [1978] O.J. L84/43.
[40] Dir. 91/689: [1991] O.J. L377/20.
[41] [1993] O.J. C271/16: [1994] O.J. C51/4.
[42] Dir. 84/631: [1984] O.J. L326/31.
[43] Reg. 259/93: [1993] O.J. L30/1.
[44] Dec. 93/98: [1993] O.J. L39/1.

wastes and to prohibit imports. The more than sophisticated surveillance system, which implies the existence of national-oriented mechanisms, will have to prove itself in an internal market without frontiers or frontier controls.

There is a general Directive on the transport of nuclear waste,[45] modelled according to Directive 84/631, and requesting essentially an authorisation for each transport of nuclear waste.

These general Directives are supplemented by Directives on specific types of wastes: Directive 75/439 concerns the disposal of waste oils;[46] Directive 76/403 the disposal of PCBs/PCTs;[47] Directive 78/176 waste from the titanium dioxide industry;[48] Directive 85/339 deals with containers of liquids for human consumption;[49] Directive 86/278 concerns the use of sewage sludge in agriculture;[50] Directive 91/157 the waste from batteries and accumulators.[51] Finally, a Directive on agricultural wastes covers specific aspects of such wastes.[52] **1.40**

Directives on the landfill of waste[53] and on packaging as well as wastes from packaging[54] have been proposed, along with Directives on the incineration of hazardous wastes[55] and on the liability for damage caused by waste.[56] A proposal for a directive on the dumping of wastes at sea was withdrawn in 1993.[57]

The reasons for the relative lack of success to achieve the declared aim of reaching an integrated waste management inside the Community are in particular: **1.41**

(1) A uniform definition of "waste" and "hazardous waste" has not been achieved.[58] Thus, for instance, until mid-1994, Germany considered recoverable waste not as waste, but as secondary raw material, which is

---

[45] Dir. 92/3: [1992] O.J. L35/24.
[46] Dir. 75/439: [1975] O.J. L194/23.
[47] Dir. 76/403: [1976] O.J. L108/41.
[48] Dir. 78/176: [1978] O.J. L54/19.
[49] Dir. 85/339: [1985] O.J. L176/18.
[50] Dir. 86/278: [1986] O.J. L181/6.
[51] Dir. 91/157: [1991] O.J. L78/38.
[52] Dir. 90/667: [1990] O.J. L363/51.
[53] [1991] O.J. C190/1; amended by [1993] O.J. L212/33.
[54] [1992] O.J. C263/1.
[55] [1992] O.J. C130/1.
[56] [1989] O.J. C251/3.
[57] [1976] O.J. C40/3 and [1985] O.J. C245/23; withdrawal [1993] O.J. C228/13.
[58] See, Statistical Office of the European Community (EUROSTAT), Environment Statistics 1991 (Bruxelles-Luxembourg, 1992) No. 9, p. 167: "Waste classified as 'hazardous' corresponds to anything from 1 per cent. (Ireland) to 57 per cent. (Netherlands)."

not submitted to the waste rules, despite contradicting court judgments.[59] Generally, the distinction between waste and non-waste was not
precise enough.

(2) The repartition of responsibilities between the Union and Member
States is not clear, despite a number of court decisions in that area.[60]
Thus, Article 5 of Directive 75/442 on waste states that Member States
shall

"in co-operation with other Member States where this is necessary or advisable
establish an integrated and adequate network of disposal installations which must
make the Community as a whole to become self-sufficient in waste disposal and
the Member States to move towards that aim individually".

In prolongation and deviation of these principles, under Regulation
259/93 Member States may pronounce general prohibitions of waste
shipments,[61] thus moving to national self-sufficiency and prohibiting
waste transports from other Member States. At the same time, wastes
have been declared "goods" under Article 30 of the Treaty.[62]

(3) Waste management plans were seldom drawn up and/or forwarded to
the Commission.

(4) There is a shortage of waste recovery and disposal facilities in Member
States. Local opposition to the siting of such installations favour
uncontrolled disposal, transport to other regions and uncontrolled or
controlled burning.

(5) The Community tools for monitoring the directives were insufficient.
Member States were reluctant to act in an integrated way and sometimes
considered the requirements of the directives as recommendations rather
than as binding obligations. The Commission did not insist on strict
compliance and failed to monitor the directives in a transparent
Community-wide manner.

1.42   Prior to the adoption of the Single European Act in 1987, the waste
Directives were based simultaneously on Articles 100 and 235 of the Treaty.[63]
Since 1987, the Commission has based its proposals on Article 100a of the
Treaty, except those on the incineration of domestic wastes. The Council

---

[59] Cases C-206-207/88, *Vessoso-Zanetti*: [1990] I E.C.R. 1461; C-359/88, *Zanetti and others*: [1990]
I E.C.R. 1509.
[60] Cases C-2/90, *Commission* v. *Belgium*: [1992] I E.C.R. 4431, [1993] 1 C.M.L.R. 365; C-155/91,
Commission v. *Council*: [1993] I E.C.R. 939.
[61] Reg. 259/93: [1993] O.J. L30/1, in particular Arts. 4 and 7.
[62] Case C-2/90 (note 60 above).
[63] An exception is Dir. 85/339 (note 49 above) which was based only on Article 235.

adopted the Directives on waste, hazardous waste and the Regulation on the transport of waste on the basis of Article 130s; the Directive on batteries on the basis of Article 100a. The Court of Justice declared waste to come under Article 30 of the Treaty.[64] It considered Article 130s to be the appropriate legal basis for Directive 91/156 on waste[65] and took a similar line on the legal basis as regards Regulation 259/93 on the transport of waste.[66] It is thus, more than doubtful whether an internal market for waste will develop over the next few years or whether waste management will not in fact, primarily take place at national level. In the author's view it is almost impossible to conceive an internal market without internal borders for goods and then, once these goods have ended their useful lifetime, to re-nationalise their future.

GENERAL MEASURES

Gradually, the Community tried to develop general legal instruments which are applicable to all environmental media and sectors. The first important measure was Directive 85/337 on the environment impact assessment of certain public and private projects.[67] The Directive requires a number of projects, such as motorways, ports, airports or incineration installations for hazardous wastes, to be assessed prior to administrative authorisation, as to their direct and indirect effects on the environment. A second group of projects must undergo such an assessment, if in particular, in view of the nature, size or location of the project's significant effects on the environment can be expected. The final decision whether a project is authorised or not, lies with the Member States. The Directive lays down principles for the impact assessment, the consultation of the general public and the participation of environmental administrations. It has undoubtedly had some influence on administrative planning at local and regional level in Member States,[68] though administrations quite often try to circumvent its provisions, in particular by deciding on (the siting of) a project before the impact assessment is made. The internal rules of the Commission, providing the procedures in the case of national projects that were co-financed by Community money,[69] have not

1.43

---

[64] Case C-2/90 (note 60 above).
[65] Case C-155/91 (note 60 above).
[66] The Commission withdrew its application to the Court on the legal basis of Directive 91/689, when the judgment on Directive 91/156 was issued. The legal basis of Regulation 259/93 was attacked by the European Parliament, which argued in favour of Article 100a. The Court of Justice rejected the application, Case C-187/93, judgment of June 28, 1994, not yet reported. Furthermore, individual firms have attacked that Regulation because of the different restrictions and bans on the transport of waste which it contains. The Court of First Instance rejected the application, Case T-475/93, *Buralux and others v. Council*, judgment of May 17, 1994, not yet reported.
[67] Dir. 85/337: [1985] O.J. L175/40.
[68] Commission (93) 28 final of April 2, 1993.
[69] [1988] 12 Bull. 100.

been published and were not really applied. A revision of Directive 85/337 has been announced,[70] although plans to extend its application to national policies, plans and programmes are politically contested.

As regards Community measures, no legal obligations for an environmental impact assessment exist. In a declaration annexed to the Maastricht Treaty it is stated: "The Conference notes that the Commission undertakes in its proposals and that the Member States undertake in implementing those proposals, to take full account of their environmental impact and of the principle of sustainable growth".[71] Legally, this declaration does not have importance.

1.44   The procedure which was set up to inform the Commission and other Member States of planned environmental measures,[72] agreed in 1973 by the representatives of the Governments of the Member States, was not on the whole successful, as it was purely a gentleman's agreement and the deadlines provided for were much too short. It has not been *de facto* replaced by Directive 83/189.[73]

This Directive requires Member States to notify the Commission draft legislation containing product specifications. In 1994, its application was extended to environmental requirements and to voluntary agreements as regards production and use of products.[74] Since the framework Directive 91/156[75] on waste, also contains a notification provision, most of product-related environmental legislation by Member States must already by now be notified to the Commission in the draft stage, with some uncertainties existing as regards production-related measures.

1.45   Directive 90/313 on the freedom of access to environmental information[76] came into effect in 1993. It gives everybody a right to have access to information on the environment which is held by public administration. Refusals to grant access may be made only in specific, expressly enumerated cases and must be motivated. Access to information may be enforced and is not dependent on the individual proving a specific interest in the information. Access to information on the environment held by Community institutions is not covered by the Directive.[77] Since the end of 1993 the Council and the Commission have granted access to documents which they hold.[77a]

---

[70] Legislative Programme 1993: [1993] O.J. C-125/1 point 241.
[71] [1992] O.J. C191/102, Declaration No. 20.
[72] Agreement of March 5, 1973, [1973] O.J. C9/1 and July 15, 1974, [1974] O.J. C86/2.
[73] Dir. 83/189: [1983] O.J. L109/8.
[74] Dir. 94/10: [1994] O.J. L100/30.
[75] Dir. 91/156: [1991] O.J. L78/32.
[76] Dir. 90/313: [1990] O.J. L158/56.
[77] The Commission has announced its intention to submit such a proposal, [1994] O.J. C60/4 no. 241.
[77a] [1993] O.J. L340/43 and [1994] O.J. L46/58.

Since the numerous obligations to report on the implementation of the **1.46** different environmental Directives have not really been complied with,[78] the Community adopted Directive 91/692 on the standardisation and rationalisation of environmental reports.[79] Member States will have to report on the implementation of Community Directives on the basis of questionnaires. The Commission then elaborates a sectorial report, which will be made public and which will, for the first time, be published in 1987 (water), 1998 (air, chemicals) and 1999 (wastes). As regards Community reports on the state of the environment, the European Environment Agency will publish such a report every three years.[80]

This Agency was set up in 1990 with the task of collecting, processing and distributing data on the environment. Since Member States were only able to agree on the seat of the Agency in 1993, the Regulation entered into effect in November 1993.

Regulation 880/92 sets up a Community-wide system for an eco-label[81] to be **1.47** given to products which have better environmental characteristics than others. A European quality label was created. The system leaves national eco-labelling schemes unaffected.[82] Agricultural products, produced under certain ecological conditions, may bear a specific label informing on these production methods.[83]

In 1993 Regulation 1836/93 set up a voluntary system of eco-auditing for industrial undertakings.[84] Companies which agree to subject their different sites to an ecological auditing, may use a logo to inform on their participation in the system.

As yet, the Community has practically no financial resources of its own to **1.48** combat environmental pollution. Attempts at the beginning of the 1980s to set up an environmental fund, failed.[85] In the 1980s and early 1990s several mini-funds were established to co-finance demonstration and pilot projects, in particular clean technologies and natural habitats. These efforts led, in 1992, to the creation of the environmental fund, LIFE, which is equipped with 400 million ECUs for four years and aims at assisting in the financing of pilot and

---

[78] Commission, Monitoring Application of Community Legislation, 8th Report, [1991] O.J. C338/1, pp. 204 *et seq.*
[79] Dir. 91/692: [1991] O.J. L377/48.
[80] Reg. 1210/90: [1990] O.J. L120/1, Art. 2.
[81] Reg. 880/92: [1992] O.J. L99/1.
[82] At present there are environment labelling schemes principally in Germany, France and the Scandinavian States.
[83] Reg. 2092/91: [1991] O.J. L198/1.
[84] Reg. 1836/93: [1993] O.J. L168/1.
[85] See, Johnson-Corcelle, *L'autre Europe "verte": la politique communautaire de l'environnement* (Bruxelles, 1987), pp. 299 *et seq.*

demonstration projects, clean technologies, technical assistance and habitat and species conservation.[86]

1.49 In 1993, a General Consultative Forum was established which groups trade and industry, environmental organisations, consumers and trade unions, and which has the function to increase public participation in environmental decision-making at Community level.[87]

Proposals on integrated administrative authorisation, which provide for an authorisation that covers all emissions, discharges, waste generation, etc., were made at the end of 1993.[88] A Greenbook on liability for environmental damage caused to the environment, published in 1993, might lead to the drafting of legislation at a later stage.[89]

1.50 The Community is party to a number of international environment Conventions and related Protocols, the most important being:

— Paris Convention of June 4, 1974, for the prevention of marine pollution from land-based sources;[90]
— Barcelona Convention of February 16, 1976, for the protection of the Mediterranean Sea against pollution;[91]
— Bonn Convention of December 3, 1976, for the protection of the Rhine against chemical pollution;[92]
— Bonn Convention of June 23, 1979, on the conservation of migratory species of wild animals;[93]
— Berne Convention of September 19, 1979, on the conservation of European wildlife and natural habitats;[94]
— Geneva Convention of November 13, 1979, on long range transboundary air pollution;[95]
— Vienna Convention of March 22, 1985, for the protection of the ozone layer;[96]
— Montreal Protocol of September 16, 1987 on substances that deplete the ozone layer;[97]

---

[86] Reg. 1973/92: [1992] O.J. L206/1.
[87] Commission decision 93/701: [1993] O.J. L328/53.
[88] [1993] O.J. C311/6 [Integrated Pollution Prevention and Control].
[89] COM(93) 97 of March 17, 1993.
[90] Dec. 75/437: [1975] O.J. L194/5.
[91] Dec. 77/585: [1977] O.J. L240/1.
[92] Dec. 77/586: [1977] O.J. L240/51.
[93] Dec. 82/461: [1982] O.J. L210/10.
[94] Dec. 82/72: [1982] O.J. L38/1.
[95] Dec. 81/462: [1981] O.J. L171/11.
[96] Dec. 88/540: [1988] O.J. L297/8.
[97] Dec. 88/540: [1988] O.J. L297/8; amended by Dec. 91/690: [1991] O.J. L377/28 and Dec. 94/68: [1994] O.J. L33/1.

— Basle Convention of March 22, 1989, on the control of transport of hazardous wastes;[98]

— Rio de Janeiro Convention of June 5, 1992, on biological diversity.[99]

— Rio de Janeiro Convention of July 1992 on climate change.[1]

The Community attends meetings relating to other Conventions in an observer capacity. The Conventions, all of which are joint agreements, do not in practice have a substantial impact in the Community because virtually no monitoring takes place of those parts of the agreements that fall within Community responsibility; consequently, each Member State applies the Conventions' rules in accordance with its own national practice. Thus the Conventions do more for Community participation in international discussions on environmental protection and its status as a legal personality than for protection of the environment as such. The position differs only where the Community adopts its internal legal instruments in performance of international Conventions.

Integrating environmental requirements in other policies

The very first Community Environment Action Programme stressed the importance of integrating the environmental dimension in other Community policies.[2] In 1987, the Single European Act stated that "environmental requirements shall be a component of the Community's other policies". This phrase was amended by the Maastricht Treaty and will be commented on below.[3]   **1.51**

The results of taking environmental considerations into account in the conception and implementation of other Community policies have, overall, not been very tangible.

AGRICULTURAL POLICY

Agricultural Policy is based on Articles 38 to 48 of the Treaty, which do not   **1.52**
mention the environment. Agricultural policy pursues the objectives of Article 39 and, more generally, of Article 2 of the Treaty. Agricultural statistics show increasing production from an ever smaller area of land, thus illustrating the phenomenon of intensification in agriculture. The use of

---

[98] Dec. 93/98: [1993] O.J. L39/1.
[99] Dec. 93/626: [1993] O.J. L309/1.
[1] Dec. 94/69: [1994] O.J. L33/11.
[2] First Environmental Action Programme: [1973] O.J. C112/1.
[3] See para. 2.25 below.

fertilisers increased between 1970 and 1989, of nitrogen fertilisers from 5 million tonnes to 8.3 million tonnes; of phosphate fertilisers it decreased from 4.6 million tonnes to 4.2 million tonnes and of commercial fertilisers it increased from 13.8 million to 17.2 million tonnes. The pesticide input as a proportion of the final output in agriculture developed from 1.5 per cent. in 1973 to 2.7 per cent. in 1990.[4]

A 1985 Green Paper for the first time, devoted a special section to the environmental effects of agriculture.[5] In 1988 followed a communication on "Agriculture and the environment" which discussed the environmental aspects with great tact and essentially announced studies and plans to improve the situation.[6] The general problems of agricultural policy led to increased efforts to finance farmers as conservationists of nature, such as for the setting aside of land or afforestation. A Regulation to protect forests against air pollution and fire was adopted in 1986 and several times amended and complemented[7] in order to allow reliable data collection and financial support to be granted to forest conservation measures. Regulation 2080/92 introduced a system of financial aid to afforestation.[8]

Regulation 2092/91 fixed and defined rules on ecological agriculture and the labelling of products thereof.[9] Regulation 2078/92, on agricultural production methods compatible with the requirements of the protection of the environment and the maintenance of the countryside,[10] aimed at a reduction of pollution caused by agriculture and took into account the function of farmers in nature conservation and the protection of landscapes. The Council also adopted rules on fiscal advantages for biocarburants from agricultural production.[11] Finally, Directive 91/676 should also be mentioned; its aim is the protection of waters against nitrates from agricultural production.[12]

REGIONAL POLICY

1.53 The relatively young regional policy of the Community is designed to promote harmonious economic development of the regions (Article 130a to 130e). In 1988, the Council adopted Regulation 2052/88 on the reform of the Structural Funds, which was based on (old) Article 130d of the Treaty.[13] Article 7 of this Regulation stated:

---

[4] Figures from Statistical Office (note 58 above), Chap. 11.
[5] Commission, Perspectives for the common agricultural policy, COM(85) 333 of July 23, 1985.
[6] Commission, COM(88) 338 of June 8, 1988.
[7] Reg. 3529/86: [1986] O.J. L326/5.
[8] Reg. 2080/92: [1992] O.J. L215/96.
[9] Reg. 2092/91: [1991] O.J. L198/1.
[10] Reg. 2078/92: [1992] O.J. L215/85.
[11] [1992] O.J. C73/6.
[12] Dir. 91/676: [1991] O.J. L375/1.
[13] Reg. 2052/88: [1988] O.J. L185/13.

"Measures financed by the Structural Funds or receiving assistance from the EIB of from another existing financial instrument shall be in keeping with the provisions of the Treaties, with the instruments adopted pursuant thereto and with Community policies, including those concerning . . . environment protection".

The expectations linked to this provision have not been fulfilled. The main reason for this is probably that the Community Regional Policy, since its reform in 1988, deals with regional programmes whereas the actual impairment of the environment stems from the individual project which is co-financed by virtue of the regional development programme. Such projects are decided by Member States with the support of steering committees set up by the Member States and in which environmental interests are clearly under represented. Another reason, linked to the first, is that in a number of Member States which benefit from regional aid, the environmental administration and general environmental infrastructure is weak, compared with the structures of agriculture, trade, transport, industrial development, etc. A third reason is that the notion of "provisions" and "policies" in Article 7 is too vague. Even the Commission is not of the opinion that "policy" has any independent substantive significance.[14] Instead of asking for each project that is co-financed by the Community for an environment impact assessment, credit is all too often given to the assurance that a specific project will have no significant impact on the environment.

In 1993, Regulation 2052/88 was amended by Regulation 2081/93.[15] It remains to be seen to what extent the new Regulation, which has not changed the substance of Article 7, will contribute to better ensure the integration of environmental requirements into regional development measures.

In 1990, the Commission approved a separate environmental programme for the regions, ENVIREG, which aimed at promoting regional socio-economic development and environment.[16] Between 1990 and 1993, 580 million ECUs were made available to finance measures, particularly in coastline areas, such as waste water treatment plants, waste disposal installations, marine oil pollution equipment in ports and habitat protection.

Numerous economical or infrastructure projects which affect landscapes, fauna and flora, persons or the environment would have never been realised without Community financial intervention. Beyond the purely legal question of whether a creditor is not responsible for the use of his money, there is the more ethical problem that the sharing of responsibilities claimed by the Fifth Environmental Action Programme also implies that Community institutions

---

[14] See the controversy between the Commission and the European Parliament, which is reflected in the Parliament's resolutions of April 22, 1993: [1993] O.J. C150/287 *et seq.*
[15] Reg. 2081/93: [1993] O.J. L193/5; see, also, Reg. 2081/93—2085/93: [1993] O.J. L193/20 *et seq.*
[16] [1990] O.J. C115/3.

must protect the general interest "environment", even where it is threatened by decisions which are only taken because the Community provides for the capital.

Already before the Maastricht Treaty (which provided for the creation of a Cohesion Fund with the task to (co)finance transport and environmental projects) entered into effect, the Council adopted Regulation 792/93, which provided for a provisional Cohesion Fund.[17] The Fund co-financed environmental projects in Ireland, Spain, Portugal and Greece, up to 85 per cent. of the total costs.

COMPETITION POLICY

1.54   Co-operation between undertakings on environmental matters may fall within the sphere of Article 85, but may be eligible for a derogation pursuant to Article 85(3). The Commission has only recently had to address the question of whether the objective of environmental protection could justify the application of Article 85(3), which it confirmed in the specific case.[18] National voluntary agreements or convenants between undertakings or between undertakings and public authorities[19] are to be assessed, as far as the agreements between undertakings are concerned, against Article 85; the Commission's approach to this form of measures in environmental policy, which is widely spread in Denmark, the Netherlands and Germany, is still not very detailed, though the Fifth Environmental Action Programme announces the elaboration of voluntary agreements at European level.[20]

As regards State aids, the Community has been allowing, since 1974, contrary to the prohibition in principle in Article 92 and contrary to the polluter-pays principle, national aid with environmental goals.[21] The aid was not to exceed a certain percentage of the overall investment. In addition to a basis in Article 92(3) (b), all other conditions being fulfilled, Article 92(3) (a) or (c) were also to be applied to aid for environmental purposes. The derogation from Article 92, originally limited to a transition period of 6 years, was extended by a further transition period of 6 years in 1980.[22] The maximum amount of aid permissible was not to exceed 15 per cent. of the total investment. Aid was to be granted only to companies whose production plant

[17] [1993] O.J. L79/74.
[18] XXIInd Report on Competition Policy 1992 (Bruxelles-Luxembourg, 1993) points 177 et seq. (VOTOB); see, also, Commission: [1991] O.J. C188/7 and XXIInd Report, point 140 (Assurpol).
[19] See, Commission XXIInd Report (note 18 above) VOTOB; see, also, J. van Dunne (Ed.) Contracts and Covenants (Rotterdam, 1993).
[20] [1993] O.J. C138/5, point 41.
[21] Commission Fourth Report on Competition Policy 1974 (Bruxelles-Luxembourg, 1975) point 175.
[22] Tenth Report on Competition Policy 1980 (Bruxelles-Luxembourg, 1981) points 222 et seq.

was more than two years old. In 1986 the Commission decided to extend the transition period during which national aid for environmental purposes could be granted by a further 6 years.[23]

At the end of 1993, new Community guidelines on State aids for environmental protection were adopted and published. These will apply until 1999.[24] The guidelines cover all sectors governed by the E.C. Treaty and intend to reflect the role which economic instruments can play in environmental policy. The basis of the exemption is Article 92(3)(c); however, Article 92 (3)(a) or 92 (3)(b) might be applicable in specific cases:

(a) Aid for investment—in land, buildings, plant and equipment—can be authorised up to 15 per cent. gross of the eligible costs, where aid is given in order to help firms adapt to new mandatory standards; for small and medium-sized enterprises, an extra 10 per cent. may be allowed. In keeping with the polluter-pays principle, no aid should normally be given towards the cost of complying with mandatory standards in new plants. Aid to encourage firms to attain significantly higher than the mandatory standards may be authorised up to 30 per cent. of the eligible costs (plus, for small and medium-sized enterprises, an extra 10 per cent.); these figures also apply, where no mandatory standards or other legal obligations to protect the environment exist.

(b) Aid for information activities, training and advisory services, where they fall at all within Article 92(1) "will normally exemptible" from that provision;

(c) Operating aids which relieve firms of costs resulting from the pollution or nuisance they cause will only in exceptional cases be approved by the Commission; such cases could be in the field of waste management or temporary relief from new environmental taxes;

(d) Measures to encourage final consumers to purchase environmental friendly products are not normally prohibited, because they do not give financial benefits to particular firms; where this is the case, they may be authorised if they are granted without discrimination and do not exceed 100 per cent. of the extra environmental costs.

TRANSPORT POLICY

As regards transport, the number of cars within the Community doubled   **1.55** between 1970 and 1988, rising from one car per 4.8 inhabitants in 1970 to one car per 2.5 inhabitants in 1988. The length of the motorway network went

---

[23] Sixteenth Report on Competition Policy 1986 (Bruxelles-Luxembourg, 1986) points 259 *et seq.*
[24] [1994] O.J. C72/3.

from 12,795 km in 1970 (10 Member States) to 30,408 in 1987. Both passenger and goods vehicle-kilometres have doubled since 1970. The railway network has been slightly reduced in size; goods traffic in railways was reduced from one billion tons in 1970 (10 Member States) to 765 million tonnes in 1989.[25]

Within the framework of the common transport policy (Articles 74 to 84 of the Treaty) in 1992, the Commission issued a Greenbook,[26] and in the same year a Whitebook on the inter-dependency between transport and the environment.[27] The Whitebook denounced the increase of environmental constraints[28] over the last 20 years and proclaimed the consideration of environmental aspects as an integrated part of a common transport policy. In order to reduce the environmental impact of transport, the Whitebook pleaded for the adoption of strict standards for exhaust emissions, energy consumption and noise emissions as well as standards on technical controls for cars; the fixing of noise levels in the neighbourhood of airports, and environment impact assessments for infrastructure plans and projects, including cost-benefits analyses.

At the same time the Whitebook stated that a stabilisation of CO_2 emissions by the year 2000 and a later reduction would not be achieved in transport, in view of the expected increase of road traffic.[29] Thus, it pleaded for the promotion of public transport, bicycles and electro cars, the reduction of private car use and of land use as well as a better assessment of transport infrastructure on the environment.

The Fifth Environment Action Programme stated that "because of the projected increases in the volume of cars used, the mileages driven and increases of road freight traffic, the transport . . . will offset any potential reduction attributable to the introduction of the new emission standards" and suggested to "reduce operational pollution, limit the infrastructural development of land use, reduce traffic and congestion and prevent or reduce risks inherent in the transport of dangerous goods and wastes". It suggested in particular road taxes, road pricing, regulation and fiscal incentives for fuels and vehicles and a change in the user behaviour.[30]

The Community Action Programme on Traffic Infrastructure, adopted in 1993, aimed at the improvement of the Community transport infrastructure, for which it provided 325 million ECUs within two years.[31] The criteria for supporting a measure were essentially the contribution to the establishment of

---

[25] Figures from the Statistical Office (note 58 above), Chap. 10.

[26] *Greenbook on the impact of transport on the environment*, COM(92) 46 final of April 6, 1992.

[27] Commission, *Whitebook on a Community strategy on sustainable mobility*, COM(92) 494 final of December 2, 1992.

[28] Increase of noise, water and soil pollution, land use, impairment of landscapes, traffic congestions, increase of accidents.

[29] Whitebook (note 27) paras. 172 and 173.

[30] Fifth Environmental Action Programme: [1993] O.J. C138/1, point 4.3.

[31] Reg. 1738/93: [1993] O.J. L161/4.

an efficient transport infrastructure. The environment was mentioned to the extent that individual projects had to comply with Directive 85/337 in order to receive financial support from the Community.

In general, it might not be exaggerated to state that only a small minority of Member States pursues a national transport policy which is respective of the environment. The attempts to increase car, road and railway production seem everywhere to be at the centre of transport policies, and the necessity to create the corresponding infrastructure for the ever increasing car park reduces the efficiency of environmental measures. This situation cannot remain without affecting the Community transport policy.

ENERGY POLICY

The Community energy policy—if one can talk of policy—operates in the **1.56** Treaty without an express legal basis.[32] Its objectives and priorities are thus rather general. As regards the environment, the Commission issued a communication in 1988, where it fixed its objectives until 1995, which included the research for a balanced pursuit of environmental and energetical objectives.[33] In 1990, a communication followed on "Energy and Environment"[34] which was marked by the discussion of the greenhouse effect. The Commission suggested a series of measures, concerning the promotion of energy technologies, of energy saving measures, codes of conduct to be adopted by the energy industry and the establishment of a consultative committee on energy. The communication indicated that nuclear energy could reduce air pollution and might thus be supported.[35] In October 1990, the Joint Council of Ministers of energy and of the environment agreed to have CO_2 emissions stabilised by the year 2000 with regard to 1990, in order to combat the greenhouse effect.[36] In pursuit of this decision—which was taken in the form of an unpublished resolution—the Commission proposed a number of actions:

(a) a directive to improve energy efficiency in housing, public investment measures, cars and industrial companies;[37]

(b) a decision to promote renewable sources of energy (ALTENER);[38]

---

[32] See, also, Article 3(t) of the Treaty and the declaration annexed to the Maastricht Treaty according to which it will be re-examined in 1996 to what extent there should be a specific provision on energy in the Treaty: [1992] O.J. C191/97 Declaration No. 1.

[33] Commission, COM(88) 174 final of April 6, 1988.

[34] Commission, COM(89) 369 final of February 8, 1990.

[35] Renewable energy sources counted for 1.6 per cent. of energy supply of the Community in 1973 and for 1.5 per cent. in 1989; Nuclear energy counted for 1.9 per cent. in 1973 and 14.2 per cent. in 1989, see, Commission COM(90) 1248 final of September 14, 1990, p. 2, No. 4.

[36] [1990] E.C. Bull. point 1.3.77.

[37] Commission, COM(92) 182 final of June 26, 1992.

[38] [1992] O.J. C179/4.

(c) a directive to introduce a combined tax on CO_2 emissions and on energy, of up to 10 dollars per barrel of oil;[39]

(d) a decision to control CO_2 emissions and other greenhouse gases.[40]

Measures (a) and (b) which essentially aim at setting up programmes and giving incentives, including financial incentives, were adopted in 1993; so was the decision to set up a control mechanism for CO_2 emissions.[41] As regards the CO_2 energy tax, it had been suggested by the Commission under the condition that other industrialised countries—this was aimed at the United States and Japan—took equivalent measures in order to fight the greenhouse effect. Since this was by the end of 1993, more than unlikely, the proposal which needs unanimity under Article 99 of the Treaty will probably not be adopted.

The Community's energy policy is in a triple difficulty: first, it lacks a clear legal basis, which leads to the result that most of the measures or proposed measures mentioned above were based on Article 130s; others will have to be based on Article 235 of the Treaty. This legal situation makes it difficult to develop a coherent energy policy. Second, the Euratom Treaty is conceived as a treaty to promote the peaceful use of nuclear energy, while six Member States—Greece, Italy, Portugal, Ireland, Denmark and Luxembourg—do not have nuclear energy production on their territory;[42] this is likely to influence Community decisions in the area of energy and internal market questions. Third, Member States rely heavily on national sources of energy—oil in the United Kingdom, gas in the Netherlands, nuclear energy in France and Belgium, coal in Germany, etc.,—which leads to preponderance being given to safety of supply questions rather than to environmental issues. These circumstances might make it extremely difficult to reach a Community energy policy whose aim is to seriously take into account environmental requirements. Stabilising CO_2 emissions by the year 2000 is an objective which, as it seems at present (late 1993), cannot be reached. As regards renewable energy resources—wood, solar energy, wind energy—they counted for 1.6 per cent. of energy supply in 1973 and 1.5 per cent. in 1989; nuclear energy counted for 1.9 per cent. in 1973 and 14.2 per cent. in 1989.[43]

DEVELOPMENT POLICY

1.57 The Community development policy, now based on Articles 130u *et seq.* of the Treaty, largely took place, apart from co-operation in the framework of the

---

[39] [1992] O.J. C196/1.

[40] COM(92) 181 final of June 1, 1992: [1992] O.J. C196/1.

[41] Directive 93/76: [1993] O.J. L237/28 (energy efficiency—SAVE); Decision 93/500: [1993] O.J. L235/14 (Altener); Decision 93/389: [1993] O.J. L167/31 (control).

[42] Italy stopped production after the Chernobyl accident in 1986.

[43] Commission, Safety of Supply, internal market for energy and energy policy, Communication. COM(90) 1428 final of September 14, 1990, p. 2, point 4.

United Nations and its daughter organisations, within the context of the so-called Lomé conventions, which were agreed between the Community and (now) some 70 African, Caribbean and Asiatic countries. The Lomé IV Convention, which came into effect in 1991,[44] contains for the first time, a chapter on environmental aspects. It suggests the strengthening of environmental considerations in the planning and financing of development projects and fixes a number of principles; the realisation of which depending largely on the will and determination of the ACP countries. Community help often consists of financial assistance; the Commission estimates that under the Lomé IV Convention some 400 million ECUs per year will be allocated to environmental programmes and projects, mainly on projects combating desertification, protecting marine sources and promoting renewable energies.[45]

Export of products that are banned or severely restricted by Community measures, shall only take place under the principle of prior informed consent.[46] Exports of dangerous waste to ACP countries is completely prohibited;[47] to other developing or Third World countries such exports are subject of serious restrictions. Imports of products and wastes into the Community follow the general rules. Imports of species of fauna and flora have very considerably been reduced during the last years.[48] This is not without problems, since on the one hand the E.C. also feels the need to protect fauna and flora in Third World countries, and on the other hand import restrictions can easily be regarded by Third World countries as a sort of ecological imperialism. This tension is particularly obvious in the question of tropical timber, where the Community has not yet developed a consistent approach.

In the context of its commercial policy the Community pleads for import restriction measures to be allowed only where such measures are agreed upon by international agreements. However, the prohibition of imports of certain seal skins, of ivory from the African elephant and the proposal to prohibit the import of furs obtained by use of leg-traps does not follow this general principle. In view of the considerable political influence to which global agreements and their adaptations are exposed, it is doubtful whether a responsible environmental policy can really wait for the existence of an international agreement before measures to protect the environment are taken; the Community itself is in an even more delicate position, since its failure to act might all too easily lead to action from one or the other Member States, thus affecting the internal coherence of the Community.

---

[44] [1991] O.J. L229/1.
[45] Commission, Fifth Environmental Action Programme (note 30), point 12.1.
[46] Reg. 2455/92: [1992] O.J. L251/13.
[47] Reg. 259/93: [1993] O.J. L30/1 Art. 18.
[48] Statistical Office (note 58 above), Chap. 12.

INDUSTRIAL POLICY

1.58 Community industrial policy, which has now a specific title (Article 130) in the E.C. Treaty, existed long beforehand. Its main aim in the past was, as regards environmental aspects, not to see the free circulation of products and services inside the European Union impeded by national measures to protect the environment, to ensure that European environmental rules are acceptable to industry and that production-related environmental measures do not lead to distortions of competition or too seriously burden the European industry.

In 1992, the Community adopted a general communication on "Industrial competitiveness and protection of the environment"[49] which lists a number of policy sectors that are of relevance to industry, where environmental issues could play a role. The communication concludes that there should be better integration of the environment into other policies; that the dialogue with industry should improve and that uniformity of the Internal Market should be maintained, while a high level of protection of the environment should be promoted.

As regards production-related measures, almost all relevant Community measures, e.g. environment impact assessment, eco-audit, emission standards, accident-prevention schemes for chemical installations and licensing requirements, were adopted in the form of horizontal environmental measures. With the one exception of the Directive on waste from the titanium dioxide industry, all these measures were adopted under Article 130s, thus allowing Member States to maintain or introduce more stringent protective measures at national level. Overall, limited use was made of the possibility to introduce new, more stringent measures in Member States. Environmental liability issues might, to some extent, be considered to be production-related. After the Seveso-barrel incident 1983, where large disregard of existing rules on the handling of dangerous waste was found to exist within the Community, the Commission suggested the introduction of strict liability rules for damage caused by waste.[50] The Council could not agree on that proposal and asked for a new proposal to be submitted by 1987. This proposal was made in 1988.[51] To date, the Council have not been able to agree on this proposal.

Following the industrial accident of Sandoz/Basle in 1986, the Council invited the Commission to examine legislation on environmental liability. The Commission submitted a Greenbook in 1993, without giving clear indications as to its intention of proposing legislation. The discussion on this Greenbook

---

[49] Commission, SEC(92) 1986 final of November 4, 1992.
[50] [1983] O.J. C186/3.
[51] [1989] O.J. C251/3.

continues.[52] As regards products, the conflict lines between national environmental measures and the free circulation of goods will be described below.[53] In that context, Directive 83/189 which requests Member States to notify the Commission of product-related legislation already at the draft stage, gains more and more importance.[54] The dispute on whether fiscal or other financial incentives may be taken at national level or whether they constitute a barrier to trade, was particularly violent during the discussion on the Community-wide introduction of catalytic converters for cars. The compromise, which was achieved, allowed national financial incentives under certain conditions.[55] Whether Member States are ready to follow this compromise beyond the individual car Directives, is doubtful. In my opinion a financial or fiscal measure is not a measure of equivalent effect which would have to be assessed under Articles 30–36, but instead under Article 92 and/or 95 of the E.C. Treaty. Rather, the European Union should more try to ensure that its measures indeed reach a high level of environmental protection: if this were the case, financial incentives to go even further would be less necessary.

The Commission announced, in 1991, a new approach for legislative measures under Article 100a and national financial incentive measures.[56] This approach provided legislation in two steps. In a first step, standards were to be adopted which were technically feasible; the second step was to provide for measures which were not yet technically achievable, but attainable within a specific time-span. This second step was to be decided immediately, but enter into effect only several years later. Financial incentives should only be allowed in order to speed up compliance with step two.

The proposal has not yet been realised in any legislation at European level, though it was again announced as a basic approach at the end of 1992;[57] thus it is doubtful, whether it will play any significant role in future. The main reason for this seems to be the reluctance to suggest or to adopt measures which industry cannot yet generally achieve.

In the mid-1980s, in its efforts to accelerate the achievement of the Internal Market, the Community adopted a new approach to technical harmonisation. Community legislation should, in future, only fix the essential criteria for health and safety of the product in question. Producers could obtain, for their **1.59**

---

[52] Commission, Green paper on remedying environmental damage, COM(93) 47 final of May 14, 1993.
[53] See, para. 4.27.
[54] Directive 83/189: [1983] O.J. L109/8.
[55] See, text of Dir. 91/441: Art. 3, [1991] O.J. L242/1.
[56] Commission, J.P. (91) 271 of March 26, 1991.
[57] Commission (note 49 above), p. 13 for an example of how this approach led to political declarations on future directives rather than to legally binding provisions see Directive 94/12 on car omissions: [1994] O.J. L100/42.

products, a Community certification mark, CE, which certified compliance with the essential health and safety requirements as well as with the relevant European standards. In the absence of European (CEN) standards, national or international standards had to be complied with. A number of technical directives were adopted under this new concept, which also have some impact on the environment.[58] Though these Directives did, generally, not refer to the environment, to environmental impairment or similar notions, technical standards could considerably affect the environment, such as air emissions from water heating installations, asbestos pipes or copper pipes for drinking water use, or construction material containing PVC. CEN-standards or international standards, which do not give the same protection as some national industrial standards, therefore may lead to a lowering of the degree of environmental protection, since and where the corresponding products are marked with the CE Mark.

CEN-CENELEC organisations are of a confederal structure: only national standardisation bodies are members. This is potentially detrimental to the input of environmental concerns into the work of CEN-CENELEC. CEN has set up a technical committee on standardisation and environment, and the Commission stated in its communication on standardisation and the environment[59] that high environmental standards were necessary. However, in the absence of any concrete structural measure, it is difficult to see the basic problem overcome.

One further aspect is added. In national standardisation, the administration—central Government, public agencies or others—regularly participate in the drafting of standards, or have other possibilities to infuse questions of national general interest in these national standards. At Community level, there is nobody to raise questions of Community general interest such as the environment. In particular, Commission officials do normally not participate in the standardisation work. Indeed, within the given framework of legislation and/or specific mandates, industry writes itself its European standards.

Agreements between industry and the Commission on environmental issues have, so far, only three times been concluded, in the area of ozone-depleting substances.[60] The problem of such agreements largely lies in the doubts on the capacity of industry to see such an agreement observed, not only by members

---

[58] Dir. 89/106 (construction materials): [1989] O.J. L40/12; 89/392 (machinery): [1989] O.J. L183/9; 90/396 (appliances burning gaseous fuels): [1990] O.J. L196/15.
[59] Commission: [1990] 456 final of October 3, 1990.
[60] Recommendations of April 13, 1989, L144/56; of June 27, 1990: [1990] O.J. L227/26; of June 27, 1990, L227/30.

of the industrial association in question, but by all companies concerned, furthermore in the problem of monitoring of such agreements and in sanctions.[61] The Fifth Environmental Action Programme announces new initiatives in this area.

---

[61] See, J. van Dunné (ed.), *Environmental Contracts and Covenants: New Instruments for a Realistic Environmental Policy?* (Rotterdam, 1993); H. Bocken and J. Traest (ed.), *Milieubeleidsovereen-komsten* (Bruxelles, 1991); M. Aalders and R. van Acht (ed.), *Afspraken in het milieurecht,* (Zwolle, 1991).

TWO

Objectives, Principles and Conditions of European Environmental Law

The notion "Environment"

Environment: the heading of Title XVI and the term used in Articles 130r to   **2.01**
130t, are not defined. The term also appears in: (a) in Article 2—"sustainable
and non-inflationary growth respecting the environment", (b) Article 3(k)
where the activities of the Community include "a policy in the sphere of the
environment"—(c) Article 130d in which it is laid down that the Cohesion
fund may provide a financial contribution to projects in the "fields of
environment". Article 100a(3) talks of "environment protection", Article
100a(4) of "protection of the environment". Finally, the Preamble to the
Maastricht Treaty mentions that economic and social progress shall be
promoted within the context of "environmental protection".
   Furthermore, Article 100a(4) and 118a talk of the "working environment";
Article 130 which deals with "industry" requests an "environment favourable
to initiative and development of undertakings" and an "environment
favourable to co-operation between undertakings".
   When the Single European Act first introduced the notion "environment"
into the Treaty, some considerations were made as to whether Article 130r(1)
should refer to "natural environment" or "natural and man-made environment", but any such attempts were abandoned. There was no attempt to
define "environment" during the Maastricht Treaty negotiations.
   It follows from Articles 130r(1) and 130s(2) that the environment includes
humans, town and country planning, land use, waste and water management
and use of natural resources, in particular of energy. This list, which was not
meant to be exhaustive, includes practically all facets of the environment, in
particular fauna and flora which are part of the natural resources, as well as
climate. The inclusion of town and country planning makes it clear that
"environment" is not limited to the natural environment.

41

2.02 In June 1990 shortly before the beginning of the negotiations of the Maastricht Treaty, the Heads of State and Government adopted a "Declaration of the Environment",[1] where they stated that the rights to a healthy and clean environment included, specifically, "the quality of air, rivers, lakes, coastal and marine waters, the quality of food and drinking water, protection against noise, protection against contamination of soil, soil erosion and desertification, preservation of habitats, flora and fauna, landscape and other elements of the natural heritage, the amenity and quality of residential areas".

Furthermore, it must be remembered that when "environment" was included in the Treaty in 1987, there was already extensive secondary Community legislation, adopted in the form of three or four Environmental Action Programmes and generally perceived as legislation on the environment which covered water and air, noise and chemicals, nature conservation, waste and some measures of general nature. It must be assumed that by using the notion "environment" in all these circumstances, the authors of the Treaty have given to the notion the shape, according to which it is generally understood. The term "environment" is thus all embracing and includes the economic, social and aesthetic aspects, its value, the preservation of natural and archaeological heritage, and the man-made and natural environment.

Secondary Community legislation provides no real assistance, since definitions in different regulations or directives are given for that specific context. With that restriction, the definition of Directive 85/337 may serve as a useful guidance for what "environment" means.[2]

The notion is different from the notion of "working environment" used in Articles 100a and 118a, which obviously have to do with the conditions at the working place, such as air pollution, noise, risk of accidents, etc. The specific conditions of the working place justify a different treatment of "environment" and "working environment", although in the beginning of EEC environmental policy this distinction was not made[3] and some directives do not really allow us to precisely differentiate between these two areas.[4] Working environment matters thus have to be adopted under Article 118a or, as the case may be, under Article 100a.

2.03 The notion "environment" in Article 130 has nothing to do with the notion of the environment used elsewhere in the Treaty. Indeed, the word "environment" is used only in some languages. Others use the word "Umfeld" or a

---

[1] European Council, Resolution June 25-26, 1990: [1990] 6 E.C. Bull. 18, point 1.36.

[2] Dir. 85/337: [1985] O.J. L175/40: "human beings, fauna and flora; soil, water, air, climate and the landscape; the interaction between the factors mentioned in the first and second indents; material assets and the natural heritage".

[3] See, for instance First Environmental Action Programme: [1973] O.J. C112/1 (p. 43: "improvement of the working environment").

[4] See, for instance Directive 85/501 on the prevention of major-accident hazards: [1982] O.J. L230/1.

corresponding translation, which is better translated by "circumstances", or "conditions". Therefore, "environment" in Article 130 must be understood to mean "general conditions", since the purpose of that provision is to create a climate which encourages co-operation, initiative and development of undertakings throughout the Community.

In the past doubts were raised as to whether "environment" also includes animal welfare.[5] However, animals are part of the natural environment; thus protection measures for animals are environmental measures. The question, whether such measures to protect animals are to be based on Article 43, 100a, 113 or 130s, is to be distinguished from the general question of whether animal welfare is part of the environment area, and will be discussed below.

Geographically, the environment knows no frontiers. During the drafting of the Single European Act attempts were made to limit the scope of the term to the Community environment,[6] but without success. The fourth indent of Article 130r(1) now clarifies that environmental problems outside the Community are equally enshrined in "environment". Consequently, the Community can take measures to protect the environment outside the territory covered by the Treaty, for example, measures to protect the ozone layer, combat climate change or desertification, or even to protect the environment in a third world country, such as measures in favour of the African elephant, or capturing methods for whales, seal pups or fur animals. Similarly, there is no Community environment distinguishable from any individual, national, regional, or local environment. As such, the measures taken by the Community need not be restricted to transfrontier environmental problems. The question, whether the Community should deal with purely local environmental issues, is a question to be solved under the general principle of subsidiarity. Even before the Maastricht Treaty had entered into effect, the Commission had rejected requests to take initiatives, arguing that such matters could be better solved at local or regional level.[7] In contrast to that the disposal of domestic waste, which might be considered to be a local problem has been the subject of Community measures; ambient levels of noise in the neighbourhood of airports might one day, for competitive reasons, be the subject of Community action.[8]

2.04

The Community measures with regard to the environment shall form a "policy". This notion was introduced by the Maastricht Treaty, whereas the

---

[5] E. Grabitz, "EWG-Kommentar" (looseleaf) (Munchen-Berlin) Art. 130r, note 10; J. Pernice, "Kompetenzordnung und Handlungsbefugnisse der Europaischen Gemeinschaft auf dem Gebiet des Umwelt-und Technikrechts". [1989] *Die Verwaltung* 1.

[6] See, de Ruyt, *L'Acte Unique Europeen*;. 2nd ed. (Bruxelles, 1987), p. 214.

[7] For details see below, para. 2.33.

[8] In this sense Commission Whitebook on sustainable mobility, COM(92) 494 final of December 2, 1992.

Single European Act only talked of "actions relating to the environment".[9] "Policy" means a coherent and consistent number of actions, grouped under a general orientation and with the aim of reaching certain objectives.

2.05   The notion of "environment" cannot be looked at separately from the objective of environmental action. Article 130r talks of preserving, promoting and improving the quality of the environment, or protecting human health, of making prudent use of the natural resources and of promoting measures at international level to solve environmental problems. Article 130t takes this idea up by allowing Member States to maintain or introduce more stringent protective measures. Also Articles 100a(3) and (4) talk of measures to protect the environment. Article 2 mentions that an economy must be sustainable and respect the environment. From this it can be concluded that it must be the objective of the policy to protect the environment, *i.e.* the different parts which compose it.

Only Article 130d talks in a neutral way of "projects in the fields of environment". However, the wording is not clear as to whether the only projects which can be co-financed by the Cohesion Fund, are those which aim at the protection of the environment and are to be financed by the Community.

The first decisions which were taken[10] concerning the financing of an urban sewer system, a system to install warning stations for water quality in different Spanish regions, a study to assess the sensitivity of Portuguese coastal waters, a study on a continuous clean-up policy in Portugal and clean-up measures for polluted water in the Alvida basin (Portugal). Also, some Member States have asked for financial support to finance a coastal walkway, a footpath, aqueducts to bring drinking water to an urban agglomeration or a road to bypass a city. However, it follows from the context of Article 130d that only environment protection measures may be financed by the Cohesion Fund. Indeed, that provision also mentions "trans-European networks in the area of transport infrastructure" as being capable of co-financing. Trans-European networks also exist under Article 129b in the area of telecommunications and energy. Such networks affect the natural environment within the Community. The limitation to transport networks would thus have no sense if, for instance, energy infrastructure measures could be subsumed under the "environment". The only possible interpretation of Article 130d is, therefore, that environmental projects are projects which aim at preserving, protecting or improving the quality of the environment. Thus, while the measures approved by the

---

[9] The German version of the Single Act was the only one which used the word "policy" instead of "action".

[10] Commission: [1993] O.J. L308/1 *et seq*. The decisions were based on Regulation 792/93: [1993] O.J. L79/74 which provided for a financial cohesion instrument; that instrument was called "interim financial instrument".

Commission seem to come under this provision, this is not the case with the other examples mentioned above. Their direct effect is not to improve the environment, but to improve transport and water distribution.

The objectives

Article 130r mentions the objectives of Community environmental policy. **2.06** These objectives were set by the Single European Act and slightly changed by the Treaty on European Union. Article 2 of the E.C. Treaty refers to the "tasks" of the Community, which are "to promote throughout the Community a harmonious and balanced development of economic activities, sustainable and non-inflationary growth respecting the environment". The Maastricht Treaty fixes a number of objectives for this Union, amongst others "to promote economic and social progress which is balanced and sustainable".

Article B of that Treaty indicates that its authors were "determined to promote economic and social progress for their people within the context of the accomplishment of the internal market and of reinforced cohesion and environmental protection.

It is a common understanding that the tasks of Article 2 E.C. Treaty are no longer an exhaustive enumeration.[11] As regards the environment, the new wording of Article 2 also clarifies that the respect of the environment is one of the objectives—indeed the words "tasks" and "objectives" are synonymous of the Community. This interpretation is confirmed by the Preamble and Article B of the Maastricht Treaty.[12]

Article B (Maastricht Treaty) and 2 (E.C. Treaty) fix the general objectives of the Community, which are completed by specific articles, such as Article 39 for agricultural policy or 130r(1) for the environment. The relationship between Article 130r(1) and the more general provisions is the same as, for instance, that between Articles 3 and 2 on the one hand, and agricultural policy objectives (Article 39) on the other.

No hierarchy between the objectives can be established. According to the **2.07** Treaty the Community's task is to attain all its objectives. Should individual objectives conflict, the Community institutions must give priority to the objective required in the concrete circumstances. It is, in particular, not

---

[11] See M. Zuleeg, in *Groeben-Thiessing-Ehlermann, Kommentar zum EWG-Vertrag*, 4th ed. (Baden-Baden 1991), para. 2.

[12] See, Preamble to the Treaty on European Union: " . . . Determined to promote economic and social progress for their peoples, within the context of the accomplishment of the internal market and of reinforced cohesion and environmental protection . . . "; Article B: "The Union shall set itself the following objectives: to promote economic and social progress which is balanced and sustainable . . . ".

possible to deduct from Article 130r(2)(2) a rule that environmental objectives prevail in case of conflict over other objectives.[13] Any such hierarchy of objectives would have needed a clearer expression in the Treaty.

The wording of the first three objectives of Article 130r(1) was slightly changed by the Maastricht Treaty and the fourth objective was added.

No hard and fast distinction can be drawn between the different objectives in paragraph 1. For instance, the maximum values set for pollutant concentrations in drinking water by the Directive on drinking water, contribute towards protecting human health. At the same time they entail measures to prevent or reduce inputs of pollutants into the soil, ground water or surface water so that the maximum concentrations can be observed. They also avoid wastage of a natural resource (water). Similar examples can be found in the Directives on waste, air pollution, etc.

1. "To preserve, protect and improve the quality of the environment" (2)

2.08   The wording is not exactly the same in every official language. Every version except the German reads "to preserve, protect and improve the quality of the environment", but the German reads "to preserve and protect the environment and improve its quality".

The formula of this objective is very broad and leaves almost unlimited possibility for Community action. "Environment" is again the natural and man-made environment. Sevenster and Jans are of the opinion that measures to protect the environment in third world countries could not be under this objective;[14] however, the text does not contain any limitation and Community practice is different. These arguments, taken from public international law and its limits on the territories of States or State organisations, were developed prior to the adoption of the Maastricht Treaty. They are not convincing; thus Community measures to protect the African elephant by prohibiting the import of ivory[15] aim at the protection of a specific species. It is not possible to argue that Zimbabwe, Zambia or another nation's environment is exclusively affected; since the environment knows no frontiers, it cannot be subdivided into national segments, not even under public international law. The import ban for ivory protects the elephant irrespective of national frontiers.[16]

Sevenster's statement that "protecting" is sufficiently wide a term to also include "preserving" and "improving"[17] is probably correct, all the more since the borderline between the notions is not precise and, for instance,

---

[13] See for more details below, paras. 2.35 et seq.

[14] J. Sevenster, *Europees Milieubeleid*. (Deventer, 1992), 96; J. Jans, *Europees Milieurecht in Nederland*. (Groningen, 1991), 28.

[15] Commission Regulation 2496/89: [1989] O.J. 240/5.

[16] This is the reason why international lawyers talk of "global commons" when they refer to aspects such as the ozone layer, the high sea, nature, tropical forests, etc.

[17] Sevenster (note 14 above), p. 97.

Article 130t uses only the word "protecting" without repeating the other two words.

Measures to preserve, protect and improve the quality of the environment includes schemes to combat or clean up pollution after it has occurred, action to prevent pollution and general plans or other measures to improve the state of the environment. For example, these could take the form of information campaigns, research, education or the promotion of clean technologies. Conservation measures in turn help protect the environment, *e.g.* schemes to restore buildings or to protect endangered species. Measures to protect the sea, such as bans on the dumping of waste at sea, help to preserve marine fauna and flora and the coasts. With the help of the regenerative capacity of the sea, they contribute towards improving the environment. **2.09**

The objectives do not lead to concrete requirements for legislative action; it is not possible to deduct from the requirement to protect the environment a limitation of to limit the use of land in a specific case. However the objectives require action by the Community institutions in order to reach fruition, which in turn entails a dynamic policy.

2. Protecting human health

This objective was introduced in the Treaty by the Single Act 1987 and only slightly changed by the Maastricht Treaty.

Measures to preserve, protect and improve the quality of the environment (Objective 1) often contribute towards protecting human health. To a certain extent this objective is, therefore, tautological. Nevertheless, it removes all doubts as to whether rules not designed to complete the internal Community market, or on the borderline between environmental and consumer protection or the protection of public health, could be based on Articles 130r and 130s. Drinking water regulations or rules to prevent pollution of swimming pools are such examples. **2.10**

For example, legislation to protect human health could take the form of a Directive on biological screening of the population for lead[18] or any other pollutant. This illustrates that this objective can include measures concerned with public health in general, as opposed to simply protecting human health. Another example is Council Regulation (EEC) No. 2955/92 concerning export from and import into the Community of certain dangerous chemicals.[19] These Community rules ban or restrict the sale and use of the chemicals covered by the Regulation. Since the Regulation stipulates that the country of destination must be notified whenever these chemicals are exported from the Community,

---

[18] Dir. 77/312: [1977] O.J. L105/10.
[19] Reg. 2455/92: [1992] O.J. L251/13.

it by no means promotes the free movement of goods and could not therefore be based on Article 100a. The Council rightly chooses to base the Regulation on Article 130r instead.

Community measures under Article 129 (public health), 129a (consumer protection) and 100a (internal market measures to protect health and safety of consumers), may also contribute to the protection of human health. It remains to be determined in the concrete circumstances which provision is applicable. For instance, a Directive to protect the population against electromagnetic waves from electric lines or limiting the noise level around airports might well be drafted in a way that it contributes to the protection of human health and thus constitutes an environmental measure under Article 130r(1).

2.11 Normally product related rules will not be able to be based on Article 130s, even when they (partly) include rules which affect consumers' health and safety. Indeed, it clearly follows from Article 100a(3) and (4) that they can also be based on Article 100a; therefore the choice of the legal basis is determined by the consideration of which rule allows the two objectives of the Treaty to be reached, *i.e.* environmental protection and free circulation of goods. Without doubt this is Article 100a because a legislation which is based on Article 100a is able to deal with consumer protection and free circulation, whereas a legislation that is based on Article 130s is not capable of ensuring the free circulation of goods because of the existence of Article 130t.

3. Prudent and rational utilisation of natural resources

2.12 The provision was introduced into the Treaty by the Single Act 1987 but the drafting was slightly changed by the Maastricht Treaty. "Natural resources" is a very vague term. It probably covers the management of all resources which are already to be found in the environment: fauna and flora, timber, minerals, water, oil and natural gas and chemicals. The use of the notion prior to the Single European Act (in particular in the four Environmental Action Programmes) does not lead any further either, since the terminology and the content of the notion varied.[20] A prudent utilisation will try to reach a sustainable, careful use which avoids the destruction or complete removal of natural resources.

In 1985, the Intergovernmental Conference for the Single Act had added a declaration to this objective in the Final Act, which stated that Community environmental activities were not to "interfere with national policies regarding

---

[20] Sevenster (note 14 above) gives, p. 100, an indicative list: "Nature conservation, soil protection, waste disposal, town planning, coastal areas, mountain protection, water management, agricultural policy which respects the environment, energy saving and civil protection."

the exploitation of energy resources". This declaration, which had led some authors to conclude that national energy policy has priority over Community environmental policy, has not been repeated by the Maastricht Treaty.[21] It now follows from Article 130s(2) that Community energy policy may also affect Member States' choice between different energy sources and the general structure of its energy supply. Thus, there can no longer be any question of priority of national energy policy on Community environmental policy. Member States' interests are safeguarded by the requirement to take unanimous decisions.

4. Promoting measures at international level to deal with regional or worldwide environmental problems

This objective was inserted by the Maastricht Treaty, on the proposal of the Commission. In substance it does not add much new since international measures could, and were in the past, subsumed under the three previous objectives and, in particular, the objectives of preserving, protecting and improving the quality of the environment. Also in the past, the Commission has constantly promoted measures at international level in order to deal with regional or worldwide measures. For regional measures, action for the Mediterranean, the North Sea, Baltic Sea, Rhine, Danube, Council of Europe Conventions on nature protection and numerous other actions can be mentioned as examples. The most important international environmental conventions of which the Community is a member, are mentioned above.[22] The Community participates in the negotiations of many other conventions, agreements and other international instruments. Thus on the eve of the UNCED Conference of June 1992 on Environmental Development in Rio de Janeiro, the objective might have been inserted into the Treaty in order to legalise international measures as to an existing Community practice.[23]

2.13

5. High level of protection

This provision of Article 130r(2) was introduced into the Treaty by the Maastricht Treaty on European Union; it has some similarities with Article 100a(3) which reads: "The Commission, in its proposals . . . concerning health, safety, environmental protection and consumer protection, will take as a base a high level of protection". However, the two provisions are quite

2.14

---

[21] Other declarations have been repeated, see, for instance the declaration on external competence in environmental matters: [1992] O.J. C191/100.
[22] See, para. 1.50 above.
[23] In the same sense P. Renaudière, *Le droit communautaire de l'environnement après Maastricht.* (Amenagement-Environnement, 1992), 70, 71.

different in their importance. Article 100a(3) is a provision on specific, concrete measures related to the achievement of the internal market. Article 130r(2) concerns environmental policy in general, not necessarily each individual measure. Article 100a(3) requests the Commission to make proposals based on a high level of environmental protection, Article 130r(2) deals with measures taken by the Community in general, thus in particular by the Council; under Article 100a(3) the Council does not have any obligation as regards the level of environmental protection. The function of Article 100a(3), together with Article 100a(4), is to avoid the lowering of the level of environmental protection in a Member State by majority decisions against the vote of that Member State. Article 130r(2) has no such function, but aims generally at the attainment of a high level of protection.

2.15   Neither Article 100a(3) nor Article 130r(2) specify what a high level of protection is. A high level is not the highest level of which one could think. A high level can probably best be determined by looking at environmental standards which Member States that normally have a high standard of environmental protection (Denmark, the Netherlands, Germany) have set, also other industrialised States with a recognised environmental policy at a high level.[24] Policy declaration resolutions and targets can be an important indicator, especially in areas where no standards have yet been set at national or international level. It should also be noted that the overall objective of Community environmental policy is the improvement of the quality of the environment. A high level must therefore aim at improving as far as possible, the existing situation.

The specific reference to a high level of protection no longer permits the adoption of measures which only provide for the lowest common denominator of environmental protection at Community level and let individual Member States which are in favour of better environmental protection, adopt at national level, such measures by virtue of Article 130t. Indeed, the high level is to be achieved by Community, not by national measures.

2.16   The aim to reach a high level of environmental protection must take account of the diversity of situations in the various regions of the Community. This formula repeats almost word for word the requirement which is already (since its introduction in 1987) a requirement of Community environmental policy under Article 130r(3) second indent. In Article 130r(2) the mention of regional diversity mainly signals that Community policy should not take the highest

---

[24] Switzerland, Austria, the Scandinavian States, the United States, Canada or Japan might be quoted.

form of protection aimed at or achieved in one Member State. Furthermore, that the Community policy should allow regions which environmentally lag behind, to catch up. It cannot mean that the aim to achieve a high level of protection is challenged, since this would mean that the principle is entirely put into question.

Whether the Article 130r(2) phrase is enforceable is doubtful. It is not a   **2.17** specific measure in question, but the whole environmental policy. This policy shall aim at a high level of protection, which presupposes that this level is not yet achieved. It would then be difficult to require that an individual measure would also have to aim at a high level of protection. Further, tackling the policy in total with the argument that it was not aiming at a high level of protection, is theoretically possible. In practice, however, such an action could not succeed. Indeed, the policy only "aims at" a high level, which means that one can always argue that it is still on its way towards that aim. The "taking into account" part of the phrase, and the different considerations of Article 130r(3) give so many defence arguments that it cannot be seen how the environmental policy (which is not a common policy) could successfully be attacked under Article 175. Similar arguments apply to the case where, for instance, a Member State would tackle the Community environmental policy with the argument that it did not sufficiently take into account the differences in the various regions.

In contrast to that, the provision of Article 100a(3) is enforceable. Where a Community proposal is not based on a high level of environmental protection, the European Parliament must be able to tackle it before the European Court. This follows from the procedures of Articles 189a and 189b. Indeed the Council can reach a common position which is different from the Commission proposal, only by unanimity (Article 189a), but it can reach a common position which follows a low level of protection as proposed by the Commission by a qualified majority (Article 189b). This common position may only be challenged by an absolute majority of the European Parliament (Article 189b 2c and d). Thus, where the European Parliament wishes to ensure a high level of environmental protection, it has less difficulties where the Commission made a proposal based on a high level, and more difficulties where the proposal is based on a lower level. Therefore the institutional function of the Parliament is affected by the context of the proposals which allows it to take action under Article 173 of the Treaty.

The principles

Article 130r(2) enumerates a number of basic elements for Community   **2.18** environmental policy; some of them are called aims, other principles, or are not named at all; such as the integration requirement. Furthermore, Articles 1

51

to 7 of the E.C. Treaty contain a number of "principles", (hence the title) which outline the founding principles on which the Community is to be built and to operate. Article 130r(2) adds to these general principles others which are specific to the environment, though the wording of Article 130r(2) is less precise—"shall aim at . . . shall be based on"—than that of Articles 1 to 7.

By nature, any principle allows for exemptions or derogations. Consequently, the principles laid down in paragraph 2 are not legally binding rules which must be taken into account as the basis for every Community measure. This follows already from the fact that they apply to the environmental policy as such, not to individual measures. It is true to say that the European Court had ruled that the principles of Article 130r(2) had to be realised for each individual measure.[25] It is doubtful whether this *obiter dictum* which was made under the Single European Act, where Article 130r(2) referred to measures and not to "policy", still applies under the version of the Maastricht Treaty since the emphasis in Article 130r(2) has shifted from "action" to "policy". I remain of the opinion that Article 130r(2) has no direct legal consequence and requires no specific action, but rather sets out general guidelines for policy.[26]

Nevertheless, the principles of Article 130r(2) have some indirect legal significance. They place an obligation on the Community to base its action on these principles and plan its policy and individual measures accordingly. Moreover, observance of these principles could play an important part in deciding, case by case, whether the objectives referred to in Article 130s, paragraph 1, cannot be sufficiently achieved by the Member States, and are therefore capable of being better achieved by the Community (Article 3b), what action is to be taken by the Community, based on Article 130s and whether more stringent protective measures based on Article 130t are compatible with the Treaty.

As mentioned, in Case C-2/90, the European Court used the principle of Article 130r(2): that as a priority environmental damage should be rectified at source, amongst other arguments, to declare a regional import ban for non-dangerous wastes compatible with Article 30 E.C. Treaty.[27] If the court were to confirm this interpretation of the principles also under the present wording of Article 130r(2)—doubts exist insofar as the word "action" has been replaced by "policy"—the consequences could be quite dramatic particularly as regards the compatibility of numerous Community measures in the

---

[25] Case C-2/90, *Commission* v. *Belgium*: [1992] I E.C.R. 4431, [1993] 1 C.M.L.R. 365.
[26] See, L. Krämer, *Focus on European Environmental Law* (London, 1992), p. 62 *et seq.*
[27] Case C-2/90 (note 24 above).

agricultural, transport or energy sector with these principles. For the present I agree with Jans that only in extreme cases, where a systematic disregard of the principles is shown, these principles could be enforced by the European Court.

Paragraph 2 itself specifies no particular order of precedence for the three principles listed. Nevertheless preventive action must take precedence over action to repair damage, since it would be illogical to allow environmental damage to occur and then rectify it at source.[28]

The list of principles and elements of Article 130r(2) is not exhaustive. Consequently, the principles adopted or applied in the past[29] have not been superseded but continue to exist. However, they will become less important than the principles which were expressly laid down in the Treaty. Besides the principles listed in paragraph 2 some other principles will be discussed hereafter.

1. Precautionary principle

The Maastricht Treaty introduced the requirement that Community environ-   **2.19**
mental policy "shall be based on the precautionary principle". Origin and content of the principle are unclear. German legal authors use the precaution-ary and the preventive principle without distinction and see the differentiation

---

[28] Jans (note 14 above), p. 21.
[29] These were the First environmental Action Programme: [1973] O.J. C112/1 (p. 6/7) and Fourth Programme: [1987] O.J. C328/1 annex 1:
  (1)   Pollution or nuisances should be prevented at source, rather than subsequently trying to counteract their effects;
  (2)   Effects on the environment should be taken into account at the earliest possible stage in all the technical planning and decision-making processes;
  (3)   Any exploitation of natural resources or of a nature which causes significant damage to the ecological balance must be avoided;
  (4)   The standard of scientific and technological knowledge in the Community should be improved with a view to taking effective action to conserve and improve the environment and research in this field should be encouraged;
  (5)   The cost of preventing and eliminating nuisances must, in principle, be borne by the polluter;
  (6)   Activities carried out in one state must not cause any degradation in another state;
  (7)   Environment policy must take into account the interests of the developing countries with a view to preventing or reducing the adverse consequences as far as possible;
  (8)   The effectiveness of Community's efforts at internatioanl level will be increased by a clearly defined long-term concept for a European environmental policy;
  (9)   The protection of the environment is a matter for all in the Community and all should therefore be made aware of its importance;
  (10) In each different category of pollution, it is necessary to establish the level of action that befits the type of pollution;
  (11) Major aspects of environmental policy in individual countries must no longer be planned in isolation. The individual national policies should be co-ordinated and harmonised as far as possible without hampering progress at national level.

between the two notions originating in Anglo-American law.[30] British writers seem to see the origin of the precautionary principle—as independent from the prevention principle—in German law.[31] Equally, since no definition exists in the Treaty, this principle is open to broad interpretation. Thus, the precautionary principle is seen to deal with general measures which are independent from an actual, specific problem, such as planning measures; others believe it would justify measures even though scientific research has not yet fully shown the cause of the environmental impairment.

There seems to be no legal situation where Community action would not have been possible under the preventive principle, but is now possible under the precautionary principle. Thus—before the precautionary principle of the Treaty became applicable—the Commission suggested that the Council adhere to the Convention on Climate Change,[32] though the last scientific evidence on the greenhouse effect of human activities is still outstanding.

If there is no legal added value to the insertion of the precautionary principle in the Treaty, then this principle should be read together with that for preventive action which it strengthens. The precautionary principle refers to the environmental policy as a whole, while the preventive principle refers in the wording of Article 130r(2) to the individual action.

2. Preventive action should be taken

2.20 All linguistic versions, other than the English, talk of the principle of "preventive action", without adding "should be taken". The English version highlights the fact that the principle is not of direct, legally binding effect.

The preventive action principle is of overriding importance in every effective environment policy, since it allows action to be taken to protect the environment at an earlier stage. It is no longer primarily a question of repairing damage after it has occurred. Instead the preventive action principle calls for measures to be taken to prevent the damage—in this case environmental pollution—occurring in the first place. Moreover, preventive measures make economic sense, since it is often far more costly to clean up impairment after it has occurred. It is not specified which form the preventive action will take. In the past, Community measures to prevent environmental impairment included the following:

---

[30] Grabitz (note 5 above), para. 31; W. Kahl, *Umweltprinzip und Gemeinschaftsrecht.* (Heidelberg, 1993), p. 21; K. Hailbronner, *Umweltrecht und Umweltpolitik in der europaischen Gemeinschaft* (Linz, 1991), p. 24; see, also, European Council, Dublin declaration (note 1 above) " . . . action by the Community and its Member States will be developed in a co-ordinated basis and on the principles of sustainable development and preventive and precautionary action".

[31] B. Verhoeve, G. Bennett, D. Wilkinson, *Maastricht and the Environment*, (Institute for European Environmental Policy) (Arnhem-London, 1992), p. 17.

[32] [1993] O.J. C44/1.

(a) notification of national legislation in draft form in order to allow the Community to adopt corresponding legislation for the whole of the territory;[33]

(b) an environment impact assessment requirement for important infrastructure projects;[34]

(c) the imposition on industry to take measures in order to prevent major accidents;[35]

(d) obligations to notify public authorities of products, before they are marketed or before they are exported to third countries;[36]

(e) measures to restrict and even to ban the transport of waste within the Community and to restrict the export of waste;[37]

If one bears in mind that even penalties also have a preventive effect[38] it will be clear that the scope for preventive measures is very wide. They also include measure to adapt existing rules to technical progress.

3. Environmental damage should, as a priority, be rectified at source

This principle was inserted into the Treaty by the Single European Act and not changed by the Maastricht Treaty on European Union, though some versions were adapted in style. The principle requires that environmental impairment[39] is tackled as early as possible to avoid the impairment expanding. The principle could gain specific importance in cases of transboundary pollution. Generally it seems difficult to provides for measures which, for instance, rectify the impairment from motor vehicles—air pollution, land use, noise, urban congestion, etc., at source, since this would mean abolishing cars; similar examples could be formed for climate change, high sea pollution or forest decline.

Sevenster is of the opinion that it follows from this principle that the Community should, as a priority, adopt emission standards rather than quality objectives.[40] However, requiring emission standards does not take account of the fact that all human activity affects the environment. Neither does it take account of the environment's capacity of self-regeneration. This self-regeneration would make emission standards unnecessary, where the quality objectives are kept so low that they do not exceed these levels of self-regeneration capacity, and where they are not just used as a method to better

2.21

---

[33] Dir. 83/189: [1983] O.J. L109/8.
[34] Dir. 85/337 (note 2 above).
[35] Dir. 82/501 (note 4 above).
[36] Dir. 92/32: [1992] O.J. L154/1; 90/220: [1990] O.J. L177/15.
[37] Reg. 259/93: [1993] O.J. L30/1.
[38] Seneca: *"Nemo prudens punit, quia peccatur, sed ne peccetur"*.
[39] The English, Italian, Portuguese, and Danish versions talk of "damage", the French, German, Dutch, Spanish and Greek versions of "impairment".
[40] Sevenster (note 14 above), p. 111.

disperse pollutants. Furthermore, it is not clear whether the Treaty really means "impairment" and not "damage", which must be rectified at source. Indeed, it might well be argued that since all human activity causes environmental impairment, it makes no legal sense to have a rule that any impairment is to be rectified; and that therefore this principle only refers to cases where actual damage has occurred.

2.22   Quality objectives allow local, regional or national differentiations. Normally they allow more discharges or emissions to be put into the environment than emission standards. Emission standards create equal competitive situations all over the Community, which favour economically strong Member States. A decisive advantage of emission standards is that quality objectives cannot, or are not, strictly monitored. Control of compliance would require such an administrative effort that in most cases the control of compliance is not effective. If the political will existed, the Community could use this principle in order to tighten emission standards, allowing exceptions, derogations, or transitions for specific circumstances. Since 1987 there has been no tendency which points in that direction. Rather, for particularly dangerous activities or substances, emission standards were tightened—incineration of waste, emissions of volatile organic compounds; for the majority of situations the trend goes towards quality objectives. The principle of rectification of damage at source would need a bold new interpretation to reverse this trend in favour of emission standards; however in law, the principle does not require emission standards, not even as a priority.

The Court has, as mentioned, justified a regional import ban for waste amongst others with this principle[41] which leads, in the Court's opinion, to the necessity to dispose of waste as close to the place of its generation as possible. Whether this apparently result-orientated judgment really will determine future use of this principle, remains to be seen.

In principle, quality objectives have, since 1987, not been less used than emission standards. The Commission's proposals or the Council decisions do not show the slightest sign of having been influenced by this principle. The same applies to the request for using clean technologies in order to rectify environmental impairment at source.

4. The polluter should pay

2.23   This principle was introduced by the Single European Act. Its linguistic versions are quite different. Six versions: the Greek, Italian, Dutch, Spanish, Portuguese and Danish texts state the polluter pays; the French text talks of the "polluter-payer-principle", whereas the German version talks of the causation principle.

---

[41] Case C-2/90, (see note 24 above).

The rather extensive discussion on this principle suffers from the fact that this economic principle is now to be interpreted as a legal rule which causes all sorts of fictions to be made. The principle in substance means that the cost of environmental impairment, pollution damage and clean-up should not be born via taxes by the society, or that the impairment/pollution should not be eliminated at all, but that the person who caused the pollution should bear the cost. Consequently, in principle, no State aid should be paid to clean up environmental pollution, since then, ultimately, the taxpayer would pay that bill. Instead, legally binding rules must define under what circumstances environmental emissions may occur and what could be charged for such emissions. And compliance with Community or national standards should be vigorously enforced, since the failure to observe standards by an undertaking constitutes an economic subsidy for that polluting undertaking.

Community secondary legislation only very seldom invokes this principle and only by general reference. Since the polluter-pays-principle is called a principle, it suffers derogations and exemptions. Jans' opinion that national State aids are incompatible with this principle therefore goes too far.[42] The Commission has, right from the beginning of its environmental policy, admitted that undertakings may receive State aids, and has even set up general rules for such aids.[43] Since the inclusion of the polluter-pays-principle into the Treaty, State aids have increased rather than diminished.[44] The same applies for Community environmental aid which is given to Member States under the Structural Funds, LIFE, the Cohesion Fund or other budgetary titles. Sevenster's observations that this money is given to Member States and not to undertakings[45] is of limited help, since Member States are just a transitory post.

2.24

It seems time to reconsider the whole approach. The protection of the environment is in the general interest of the Community. Despite many measures taken, there is a slow but progressive degradation of the Community environment.[46] The clean-up is a task for public authorities which exists independently from the question of whether a polluter can be identified or not. In cases of groundwater or coastal water contamination, forest decline, erosion, desertification, climate change, smog in urban agglomerations, etc., such an identification is virtually impossible. Thus, the public authorities are often the only ones to ensure a clean-up. As regards new emissions and discharges to the environment, their access should no longer be, in principle,

---

[42] Jans (note 14 above), p. 23; against him also Sevenster (note 14 above), p. 113.

[43] See, Chap. 1, para. 1.55.

[44] COM(91) 28 final of January 31, 1991, p. 37 *et seq.*; see, also, Court of Auditors, [1992] O.J. C245/1, points 1.1 to 1.6.

[45] Sevenster (note 14 above) p. 408.

[46] See, Commission, Fifth Environmental Action Programme: [1993] O.J. C138/5 (p. 11, point 1(i)).

free of costs. Rather, access to the environment should be charged for; the more substances are emitted or discharged or the more the environment is used, the more it should be paid for. At present, it is not the polluter who pays; rather, pollution pays.

5. The integration requirement

2.25   The 1987 version of the Treaty has formulated: "Environmental protection requirements shall be a component of the Community's other policies". This formula was considered too vague and therefore replaced by the present one. Whether this change is for the better is not clear. Indeed, the previous version was clear, precise and unconditional and was thus directly applicable: other policies which did not integrate environmental requirements were not in line with Article 130r(2)(2). The present wording gives a general mandate to the Community institutions for some future action, without specifying time and form of fulfilment of these requirements and without fixing the consequences in the case of non-fulfilment.

Similar integration requirements are now to be found in the Treaty as regards culture[47] and health,[48] which might express the fact that health, culture and the environment are essentials which are omnipresent and cannot be disposed of by sectoral policy considerations.

2.26   The intention of the integration clause is to make sure that environmental aspects are not neglected when other policies are considered, shaped and implemented. The provision is not restricted to the common policies mentioned in the Treaty, nor to the fields of activity which are called "policy" by the Treaty. Instead it expresses the general principle that all the Community's activities must take account of environmental protection requirements. "Environmental protection requirements" are first of all, the different requirements laid down in Article 130r(1), though not all elements of this provision are mentioned. Thus, the specific objectives of Community environmental policy shall also have to be considered within the framework of all other policies. Furthermore, "environmental protection requirements" are also the principles laid down in Article 130r(2). Indeed, it would make no sense to stipulate in the chapter on environmental policy, that the polluter should pay and provide, in the context of agricultural or industrial policy, that the cost of pollution prevention or of clean-up measures should not be borne by the polluter but by the taxpayer. Likewise, it would not make sense to ask of environmental policy, that preventive action should be taken in order to avoid environmental impairment, but to allow in transport, agriculture, or energy policy, the necessity of preventive action to be ignored. Indeed, the

---

[47]   Art. 128 E.C. Treaty.
[48]   Art. 129 E.C. Treaty.

integration principle can only be made operational where the principles of Article 130r(2) are also taken into consideration by other policies, since most of environmental impairment and pollution does not occur through measures in the framework of environmental policy, but by measures in the area of transport, agriculture, energy, industrial development and other policies.

Since the integration principle is a principle and not a legally binding rule for all cases, it would go too far to require that each individual measure in the area of the Community's other policies complies with that principle; Community institutions have a very broad discretion in putting the principle into practice. However, the integration principle requires that these policies "green" themselves and orient their different strategies and measures in order to better comply with the requirements of environmental protection.[49] Since the clause, in contrast to its version of 1987, no longer states a fact, but rather sets an objective to be attained by future Community activity, almost all will depend on the political will of the Community institutions to make the integration clause fully operational. Its enforceability is doubtful. Again, only in extreme cases could it be argued that Community policies did not take into account environmental protection requirements in their definition and implementation. Normally, the wide discretion which is available to Community institutions under Article 130r(2)(2) would not make such an action successful.

2.27

6. Subsidiarity principle

The 1987 Treaty contained, in Article 130r(4), a provision which read: "The Community shall take action relating to the environment to the extent to which the objectives referred to in paragraph 1 can be attained better at Community level than at the level of the individual Member States." This provision, which was, between 1987 and the entering into effect of the Maastricht Treaty, unique in the E.C. Treaty, is now replaced by the Maastricht Treaty which reads in Article 3b(2):

2.28

> In areas which do not fall within its exclusive competence, the Community shall take action, in accordance with the principle of subsidiarity, only if and in so far as the objectives of the proposed action cannot be sufficiently achieved by the Member States and can therefore, by reason of the scale or effects of the proposed action, be better achieved by the Community.

Though the old Article 130r(4) has been very largely discussed in legal and political literature, the author knows of not one single environmental measure where the Council has decided or even discussed whether a measure could be

---

[49] "Reorientation and restructuring of all Community's policies according to the objectives and principles of Article 130r", Pernice (note 5 above), p. 50.

better adopted at Community level than at the level of Member States.[50] A number of Commission proposals were not adopted at all,[51] others only with considerable amendments.[52] However, it was at least never expressed that reasons of subsidiarity played any role in the Council's attitude towards proposals.

The new Article 3b of the Treaty, obviously inspired by the old Article 130r(4) and a preceding draft from the European Parliament,[53] is placed in the Treaty's part on "Principles". It establishes a general rule for all Community activity, even the environment. Much will depend on the interpretation given to the notion whether the objective of environmental protection cannot be sufficiently achieved by the Member States and can thus be better achieved at Community level. The principle of Article 3b is not a rule of competence, but a principle which predetermines the activity of the Community. The Community institutions will, when taking action, have to demonstrate that the conditions put by Article 3b are actually complied with.

2.29   It is not easy to establish general rules to show when environment policy objectives can be attained better at Community level. Member States with an active environment policy of their own may well think that measures at the level of the individual Member States are a better solution. Often the cost of environmental protection measures to industry in the individual Member State plays an important, possibly decisive role. A judge of the German Constitutional Court recently pointed out that the "better" could mean more effective, fairer, cheaper, more efficiently, closer to the citizen or more democratic, without these notions being more expressive.[54]

While taking care to avoid generalisation, it must be pointed out that there is a wide gulf between the individual Member States' national regulations. At the moment three Member States, namely Denmark, the Netherlands and Germany, are far more convinced of the need for environmental protection measures than the others. As a result, while these three Member States have

---

[50] See, also, Renaudière (note 23 above), p. 72: "In practice, this went rather smoothly to a point that the provision could be seen as a simple guideline of a political rather than a legal nature" (author's translation).

[51] Proposals on: mandatory information on draft legislation (Fourth Environmental Action Programme: [1987] O.J. C328/1, point 2.1.7); agricultural measures and environment impact assessment (*ibidem* point 2.3.7); codes of conduct for industry (*ibidem* point 2.3.11); persons in charge of the environment in undertakings (*ibidem* point 2.3.25); state of the environment reports every three years (*ibidem* point 2.6.3); pesticides, fertilizers in water (*ibidem* point 4.2.5); sea pollution measures (*ibidem* point 4.2.6); cadmium and lead in the environment (*ibidem* point 4.3.5); export of industrial processes (*ibidem* point 4.3.7); noise measures (*ibidem* point 4.5.3); soil protection (*ibidem* point 5.2.5), etc.

[52] Reg. 1210/90 on the European Environmental Agency: [1990] O.J. L120/1; Reg. 880/92 on an eco-label: [1992] O.J. L99/1; Reg. 1836/93 on an eco-audit system: [1993] O.J. L168/1.

[53] European Parliament: [1984] O.J. C77/33, Arts. 55 and 59.

[54] D. Grimm, "Subsidiaritat ist nur ein Wort", *Frankfurter Allgemeine Zeitung* September 17, 1992, p. 38.

evolved and are now implementing a strong national environment policy, in other States, such as Belgium, Italy, Greece, Spain, Portugal and Ireland, the environmental protection laws often consist of nothing but the measures taken to implement the relevant Community legislation. Consequently, action at Community level is often a means of ensuring that environmental measures are taken in all 12 Member States. If, instead, it were left to the Member States to take action, it could not generally be guaranteed that all 12 would adopt legislation. And even if they did, the content and timing would rarely coincide. If the Member States take action at different times, once again there is a danger for the Community as a whole, of imbalances, distortion of competition and of patters of trade, and the creation of fresh barriers to trade, etc. In this respect "better" therefore means that the objectives set in Paragraph 1 can be attained faster and more effectively by and in the entire Community or in the "Community eco-system".

When considering the most suitable level for action, it must be borne in mind that some Mediterranean Member States find it difficult, if not impossible, to implement measures to provide effective protection for the environment in general, and for fauna and flora in particular, and that environmental protection measures are perceived to slow down economic development in the Member States with the weakest economies. Considerations such as these demonstrate, once more, that the "better" clause is concerned with how to protect the environment most effectively rather than with who is responsible for protecting it.

"Better" by no means implies that all environmental protection measures will   **2.30** result in greater environmental protection in every Member State or that the Community legislation will raise the standards even higher in the Member States with the best environmental protection record. Instead, it refers to environmental protection in the Community as a whole and, perhaps, even in non-Community countries. In contrast to the Member States' national environmental protection policies which are directed primarily towards the environment in the individual Member State concerned, the Community's environment policy is concerned with the environment everywhere in the Community. Its task is to attain the objective set in Article 130r(1), as successfully as possible, everywhere in the Community and beyond whenever it is appropriate for the Community to take action to protect the environment further afield, for example, the high seas, the air or the environment in non-Community countries.

There is nothing in the subsidiarity clause to suggest that the Community should take action only on issues of concern to the whole of Europe. For instance, a ban on night flights or the establishment of noise abatement areas is undoubtedly a basically local issue designed to protect the local population from excessive noise. Nevertheless measures of this type can, amongst other things, have a considerable impact on flights or on the use of other noisy machinery and on the competitiveness of individual airports. It is perfectly conceivable that the Council might see fit, therefore, to lay down standards for the entire Community. Further examples could be found in almost every other area of environmental policy.

2.31 It must be decided case by case, on the basis of all the facts, whether it is better to take measures at Community or national level to attain any of the objectives set by Article 130r(1). In that process, the aim must be to protect the environment in the entire Community, not just in individual Member States. Due consideration must be given to the differences in the national environmental legislation in the Community, the differing awareness of the environment, the environmental policy infrastructure in the individual Member States, the risk that national environmental protection measures might be differently timed or formulated, the danger of relocating industrial undertakings to countries with less stringent legislation, the possible deflection of trade and the potential changes in competitive position. The decisive concern is to provide the best possible protection for the environment over the broadest possible area.

Though Article B of the Maastricht Treaty provides that the "acquis communautaire" is to be maintained in full, in 1992/93 political approaches were started to review existing environmental Directives in the name of subsidiarity, where Member States were or felt obliged to undertake clean-up investment. These attempts of political influence have not yet really come to an end.

2.32 Sevenster lists, from the old Article 130r(4), a number of reasons where environmental standards can be better set at Community level than at national level.[55]

(a) Community action is, administratively, more effective;
(b) the environmental problem is as such of transboundary nature;
(c) there are external "spillover" effects caused by the problem;
(d) some Member States do not take action to solve a specific problem;
(e) differences in national standards lead to changes in significant investment or to a diminution of quality of life;
(f) differences in national rules cause barriers to trade or distortions of competition;
(g) co-ordination of national activities may result in advantages of scale;
(h) global environmental problems require international or Community-wide co-ordination;
(i) there is a need to protect Community heritage;
(j) Community action leads to a better protection than the lowest protection level at national level.

---

[55] Sevenster (note 14 above), pp. 139 *et seq*.

There are few, if any, examples of past Community measures which would not meet at least one of these criteria. The Commission has, mainly in answers to questions from the European parliament, indicated that it did not see, under the subsidiarity principle, the need to take action at Community level:

- to promote the use of bicycles in cities;[56]
- to combat disco noise;[57]
- to regulate the use of plastic napkins in restaurants.[58]

In contrast to that, for instance, Directive 80/778 on the quality of drinking water[59] at least fulfils the criteria mentioned above as regards (a), (d), (e), (f) and (k); attempts to re-nationalise this area seem more politically motivated than legally justified.

In conclusion, the Court of Justice will certainly rather soon have the opportunity to express itself on the subsidiarity principle and its practical importance. Legally speaking, the environmental policy is not likely to be seriously affected. Politically, the pressure to do less for the environment, in the name of subsidiarity, is likely to grow.

7. The principle of sustainable growth

This principle is not mentioned as such in Articles 130r to 130t. Article B of **2.33** the Maastricht Treaty states: "The Union shall set itself the following objectives: to promote economic and social progress which is balanced and sustainable . . . ". Article 2 of the E.C. Treaty in its version amended by the Maastricht Treaty defines the task of the Community as "sustainable and non-inflationary growth". Article 130u provides that Community policy in the sphere of development co-operation shall foster "the sustainable economic and social development of the developing countries". Finally, Declaration 20 annexed to the Intergovernmental Conference on the Maastricht Treaty states: "The Conference notes that the Commission undertakes in its proposals, and that the Member-States undertake in implementing those proposals to take full account of their environmental impact and of the principle of sustainable growth".

No definition is given in the Treaty of what sustainable growth means and if and what differences there are between sustainable progress, sustainable growth and sustainable development. However, the word "sustainable" does have a specific environmental connotation. Indeed, in 1987 the World Commission on Environment and Development set up in the framework of the United Nations and chaired by Ms G. Brundtland, published a report on

---

[56] Commission, Written Question 3103/91: [1992] O.J. C209/34.
[57] Commission, Writen Question 849/91: [1992] O.J. C202/3.
[58] Commission, Written Question 872/93: [1993] O.J. C301/5.
[59] Dir. 80/778: [1980] O.J. L229/11. Table waters come under that Directive.

"Our Common Future", where it emphasised the need for sustainable development, which was defined as a "development which meets the needs of the present without compromising the ability of future generations to meet their own needs". Thereafter the notion of sustainable development has constantly been used in this way. Its inclusion in the Treaty, together with the other provisions on the environment, signals the commitments to ensure a prudent use of environmental resources in order to also take the environmental interests of future generations into account.

2.34   This is the first time that future generations can see their environmental interests at least mentioned in the legal context of the European Treaty. Whether any legal consequence can be drawn from the notion of sustainability, is more than doubtful. Thus, for example, the use of nuclear energy which includes the generation of nuclear waste, (for which no worldwide, safe technology yet exists for final disposal), must certainly affect future generations and is therefore not sustainable. Another example could be the contamination of groundwater which often shows its effects only decades later, when the groundwater is used. Generally, it is almost impossible legally to determine if and when precisely future generations—which generations?—are unable to meet their own needs. In the last instance, any town siting, any new road construction, affects future generations' right to determine their own needs. For the time being, thus, it is difficult to draw any legal consequence out of this principle, though in theory there might be some. Rather, the principle should be seen as a guideline for Community action which supports and strengthens the requirement of Article 130r(1) that there should be a prudent and rational utilisation of natural resources.

8. The principle of optimising the protection of the environment

2.35   This principle is not expressly found in the Treaty. German legal writers have developed it, since 1987, out of several provisions and principles of the Treaty, in particular Articles 130t, 100a(4), 100b(2), 130r(2)(2), and declared it a legal principle of the Treaty. Its definition varies. Zuleeg, who first talked of this principle, defines it as "the right of Member States to maintain or introduce more protection for the environment, even where the Community has adopted a measure to protect the environment".[60] Other authors, while following Zuleeg in this approach, even go further and suggest to abstract from this principle the general need to use, as a legal basis for Community environmental measures, those provisions which optimise environmental protection; this legal basis would be Article 130s.[61]

---

[60] M. Zuleeg, "Vorbehaltene Kompetenzen der Mitgliedstaaten der Europaischen Gemeinschaft auf dem Gebiet des Umweltschutzes". Neue Zeitschrift fur Verwaltungsrecht, 1987, p. 280.
[61] Schroer, "Die Kompetenzverteilung zwischen der EWG und ihren Mitgliedstaaten auf dem Gebiet des Umweltschutzes". (Berlin 1992), p. 49, Kahl (note 30 above), p. 10.

There is no room here to discuss this legal theory in detail. It appears that this theory is only discussed and approved in German legal publications. In the author's opinion such a legal principle:

(a) would have need a clearer expression in the Maastricht Treaty which had the opportunity to provide expressly for such a principle, but has not done so;

(b) privileges environmental protection beyond other principles and policies, such an uniformity of standards, suppression of competition distortions, etc.;

(c) would generalise the application of Article 130t to all policy areas. Again, the Maastricht Treaty could have provided for that but has not done so;

(d) is not likely to be very helpful to the environment, since a counter-reaction could be that all environmental provisions are only fixed on a low common denominator;

(e) is counterproductive as regards the general objective of the Treaty to promote Community integration as regards all aspects of Articles 2 and 3;

Neither do the legal arguments convince nor can the political and economic consequences of this theory justify the acceptance of such a principle. There is no reason to limit such a principle just to the protection of the environment. Why could it not be applied in order to protect human health, which is also of paramount importance, or to the respect of human rights and fundamental freedoms in all Member States? It should also be noted that no federal State in the world has adopted such a principle, and certainly not Germany in favour of its Lander. The principle seems to be more motivated by concerns on national sovereignty than on environmental optimisation, since it cares little for the numerous Member States which do not have an elaborated, consistent, national environmental policy.[62]   **2.36**

Article 130r, paragraph 3, conditions to be taken into account

Paragraph 3 was inserted into the Treaty by the Single European Act. It   **2.37**
started with the words: "In preparing its action relating to the environment
. . . " This part was revised by the Maastricht Treaty and now reads: "In preparing its policy on the environment . . . " The rest of the paragraph has remained unchanged. The change in the beginning of the paragraph clarifies

---

[62] See, also, L. Krämer, Common Market Law Review (1993), p. 1076.

that the criteria do not have to be taken into account when individual measures are prepared, but rather, when the Community prepares its policy. This means that not every draft of a directive or a regulation must satisfy all these criteria. The paragraph in no way sets preconditions for action by the Union. This is clear from the wording alone which requires that account must be taken of the different criteria, without giving details of which conditions are to be attained or which level of regional development or data would require action.

The four parameters could usefully be mentioned in the recitals of a Community legal instrument and in the explanatory memorandum of Commission proposals, without being made a precondition for application of the measures along the lines of, say, Article 190 of the Treaty.

Available scientific data

2.38   This criterion was inserted in paragraph 3 at the request of the United Kingdom on the grounds that the Community should base its measures on scientific and technological knowledge. In particular, no scientific proof has yet been produced that the United Kingdom is to blame for acid depositions in Europe, but such evidence would have to be presented if the Community wished to taken action.

This provision expresses the obvious and demands only that account be taken of the available data. The Community need not even order its own studies before taking measures but can simply draw on the data available. Nor is there any need to produce "proof" that the environment could be or already has been damaged or that the measures planned by the Community would be effective. It would be going much too far to demand scientific proof that action needed to be taken.

Indeed, the principles of Article 130r(2) that precautionary and preventive action should be taken would lose much of its force if unequivocal scientific data has to be produced before any measures could be taken. For example, until the end of 1993 there was no scientific certainty about the causes of forest decline in Western Europe, or the impact of the greenhouse effect on climate change. The longterm effect of deliberate release of genetically modified organisms into the environment are in the same way unknown as the evolution of groundwater contamination or the question of which fauna and flora species are to disappear in the next decades. Asking for full scientific evidence before action is taken is based on the traditional assumption that emissions and discharges to the environment are free and unrestricted and should remain so, unless their damaging nature is proven.

As regards scientific data, by 1978 the Commission had already set up, a Scientific Committee on the Toxicity and Ecotoxicity of Chemicals.[63] This

---

[63] Commission, Decision of June 28, 1978: [1978] O.J. L198/17.

Committee is in charge of assessing scientific data on chemicals and thus gradually contributing to form a Communitywide scientific consensus. Its opinions are published, but are only accessible with difficulties. The Committee does not seem to have acquired a generally accepted scientific reputation and its opinions are not well known.

The European Environmental Agency, set up in 1990,[64] is in charge of collecting, processing and distributing data on the environment, in order to improve knowledge of scientific and technical data. Its operations were delayed for more than three years since Member States could not agree on the seat of the Agency. On November 1, 1993 the Regulation setting up the Agency came into effect, the Agency was to be located in Copenhagen.[65] The Commission has started to systematically collect statistical data on the environment, encouraged in doing so by a Council decision on a multi-annual programme on environmental statistics.[66]

So far, the Commission has published four reports on the State of the environment which are, however, not very informative and not always entirely reliable.[67]

Overall, the lack of economical, ecological, scientific and technical data on the ecosystem of the Community is desperate.

"Environmental conditions in the various regions of the Community"

This provision is worded more or less identically in every language. It too was inserted at the express request of the United Kingdom. It stems from a controversy exposed by Directive 76/464.[68] The United Kingdom opposed the imposition of Community-wide limit-values for pollution of the aquatic environment on the grounds that its rivers were short and fast-flowing and that the seas around the country had ample absorption and regenerative capacity. These natural advantages of industrial sites in the UK must not be legislated away by uniform Community limit-values. Insularity could not be "harmonised" any more than the shorter journey times enjoyed by French and German transporters or the climatic advantages held by citrus fruit growers in the Mediterranean countries. In a different context but in a similar vein, Spain argued that since the environment was cleaner and air pollution levels were lower in Spain than in Northern European countries there was no need for Spain to take stringent protective measures.

2.39

---

[64] Reg. 1210/90 (note 52 above).
[65] [1993] O.J. L294/29; see, also, [1993] O.J. C323/1 where Copenhagen has been fixed as the seat of the Agency.
[66] Decision of July 22, 1993: [1993] O.J. L219/1.
[67] (1) "State of the Environment. First Report" Bruxelles-Luxembourg 1987; (2) "State of the Environment. Second Report". Bruxelles-Luxembourg 1979; (3) "The State of the Environment in the EEC". Luxembourg 1986; (4) The State of the Environment in the European Community, COM(92) 23 final, Vol. III of April 3, 1992.
[68] Dir. 76/464: [1976] O.J. L129/23.

The first example of different arrangements for different regions based on this criterion was Directive 88/609 on the limitation of emissions from large combustion plans,[69] where Member States have to reach different reductions of SO_2 and NOx-emissions from large combustion plants by 1993, 1997 and 2003; Portugal, Spain and Greece are even allowed to increase their air emissions by that time.

Environmental conditions means every indicator of the state of the environment, particularly water, air and soil pollution levels, the load which can be borne by each part of the environment and the functions of the site, for example, as a habitat. Economic factors, on the other hand, do not count as environmental conditions.

"Regions" can be interpreted only in the layman's sense. The Community's regional policy divides the Community into some 170 regions. It would cripple the Community's environment policy if account had to be taken of environmental conditions in everyone of them. Instead, this provision is designed to make sure that account is taken of the different geographical conditions in the Community and, if necessary in the Member States.

Potential benefits and charges

2.40 Originally the Commission had suggested to include a reference to costs and benefits into paragraph 3. The Intergovernmental Conference in 1987 found, however, that this term—"coûts et bénéfices" in French—was too narrow and changed it to "advantages and charges" (avantages et charges) in all linguistic versions; only the English text kept the term "benefits and costs", since the Conference was of the opinion that "costs" included all elements of "charges", in particular the social costs.

The Maastricht Intergovernmental Conference added a declaration to the protocol which notes the Commission's undertaking to evaluate the costs and benefits of its legislative proposals to the public authorities and all parties concerned.[70] This declaration—which is not limited to environmental matters—thus does not refer to the societal charges and advantages of lack of action in the environmental sphere. It does therefore not enlarge in anyway the obligation which the Commission has at present under Article 130r(3).

The Community must weigh up the advantages and disadvantages of Community rules before drafting and adopting measures. This appraisal must include *inter alia*, economic considerations. This is clear from the fact that the other language versions avoid the words "costs" and "benefits" but talk of "charges and advantages". Even the English wording fits in with this interpretation since "costs" in the sense of "social costs and benefits" are not always economically quantifiable. Consequently, this provision cannot be

---

[69] Dir. 88/609: [1988] O.J. L336/1.
[70] Maastricht Treaty on European Union: [1992] O.J. C191/1; Declaration No. 18.

interpreted as requiring a cost-benefit analysis for every Community measure relating to the environment.

Often cost-benefit analyses are over-restricted to production costs and take little or no account of the costs of environmental pollution, *e.g.* contamination of the sea or air, loss of forests or of diversity of fauna and flora, especially since there are no recognised methods of measuring environmental pollution costs, as compared with the long-term use of a cleaner environment.

Instead, as far as possible the Community must consider the full range of short—medium—and long-term measures and attempt to assess the effect of taking action or of failing to do so. At the end of this appraisal if doubts still persist as to whether the measures will be sufficiently effective, the preventive action principle comes into play, plus the fact that one of the objectives of the action taken by the Community relating to the environment is not only to preserve the quality of the environment but also to improve it.

The provision gives no details of the ways and means of taking account of the potential charges and advantages. In this respect, the political resolutions adopted by the Council and the Community Action Programmes on the Environment assume greater importance: if the Community institutions adopt a package or programme of environmental measures that will usually be sufficient proof that implementation of the measures forming part of the overall strategy will be beneficial on the whole.

Often, however, Community measures have advantages for some areas or branches of industry but perhaps disadvantages for others. In this case the next criterion requires the Community to proceed with an overall assessment to consider whether the measures will protect, preserve or improve the "Union eco-system".

The economic and social development of the Community as a whole and the balanced development of its regions"

This criterion takes account of the less developed Member States' concern that   **2.41** environmental protection regulations should not be imposed at the expense of economic growth. Once again the 1984 Commission proposal on emissions of certain pollutants from large combustion plants provides an example.[71] Several Member States argued that an identical reduction in emissions throughout the Community would fail to take account of the genuine differences, since air pollution levels were not the same everywhere and the effects too—for example on forests—varied from one Member State to another. The Directive finally differentiated according to national, not regional criteria.[72] This clause is so broadly worded that it covers virtually all economic and social development. Every Community-wide rule inevitably

---

[71] [1984] O.J. C49/1 and [1985] O.J. C76/1.
[72] Dir. 88/609 (note 69 above).

implies a degree of standardisation and cannot, therefore, take account of the level of development in every individual region. Similarly, perhaps the same scientific and technical data are not available in every region. The rules can bring greater advantages for some regions than for others. Measures may be essential in some areas but unnecessary in others.

The Community institutions must weigh up all these factors and produce an overall assessment. In the process differences are bound to arise between the Community and the Member States or regions. These will have to be resolved in the course of the decision-making procedure provided for by Article 130s.

Once again the broad wording of this clause is tempered by the opening words of paragraph 3 which state that the Community shall just "take account of" the impact of the measures on the Community as a whole and on individual regions. It is left to the discretion of the institutions to decide how far these considerations influence the wording of the Commission proposal or Council resolution.

THREE

The Decision-Making Procedure

Introduction

The decision-making rules in environmental matters are fixed in Article 130s.   **3.01**
Besides this provision, matters of environmental policy may also be based on
other provisions of the Treaty, in particular on Articles 43, 84, 99, 100a, 113
and 130o. The decision, on which a specific directive or regulation is to be
based is rather difficult, since on the one hand, the Treaty does not give precise
indications and, on the other hand, the decision-making process and the
consequences for Member States' possibilities to legislate in the area covered
by the directive or regulation in question are different.

Article 130s was first introduced in the Treaty in 1987. Under the version
which applied between 1987 and 1993, decisions were taken by unanimity.
The Council could unanimously decide to take decisions by majority. The
present wording of Article 130s considerably enlarged the previous version. It
provides for majority decisions, according to Article 189c, as a rule (paragraph
1); such majority decisions may contain specific provisions for certain
Member States (paragraph 5). In a number of specifically enumerated cases,
decisions are taken unanimously (paragraph 2); the Council may unanimously
decide to take majority decisions. General environmental programmes shall be
adopted by co-decision majority decisions under Article 189b (paragraph 3).

Article 130s stipulates who decides, and how, on the action to be taken by
the Union on environmental issues. Consequently, European rules on
environmental issues under Title XVI must be based on Article 130s. The
decision-making body on all environmental issues is the European Council. Its
decisions can be challenged before the Court of Justice, following the
procedures provided for in the Treaty, particularly in Articles 169 *et seq.*

Majority decisions [Article 130s(1)].

Article 130s(1) provides that, as a general rule, decisions by the Council are   **3.02**
taken by majority decision, according to Article 189c. The majority must be a

qualified one; under Article 148 of the Treaty, at present 54 votes out of the 76 votes must thus be given for such a qualified majority to be reached.

The words introduced at the end of paragraph 1, that the decision must be taken "in order to achieve the objectives referred to in Article 130r" is mainly of stylistic value. It clarifies that a measure which aims at achieving the objectives of, for instance, Article 39, could not be based on Article 130s. But it does not indicate, whether Article 130s tries to achieve the objectives of Articles 130s and 39 jointly. This question will be discussed below. The Council must in all cases be in presence of a proposal by the Commission before it can take action. This applies where a resolution or another non-binding measure is to be adopted; it is true, though, that there has been some tendency during the last years to see Council resolutions adopted without a corresponding proposal from the Commission. Since resolutions, though not mentioned in Article 189 of the Treaty, influence the orientation of Community environmental policy, the strategy to adopt and the lines to follow, they form part of the measure to achieve the objectives of Article 130r. Thus the Commission's right of initiative also exists in such cases.

The Commission's proposal must, according to Article 130r(2) contribute to aim at a high level of protection, while taking due account of Community reality. As stated above, it would go too far to request a high degree of protection for each individual proposal.[1] Instead, the Commission has a very large margin of discretion on how to reach the objectives of Article 130r(1) and is, furthermore, expressly asked to take account of Community diversity. Whether the high degree is achieved by one piece of legislation or progressively by a number of successive directives,[2] must be left at the discretion of the Commission. The individual measure, though, must integrate itself into the overall objective to improve the quality of the environment.

3.03 Parliamentary opinion is necessary under the procedure of Article 189c, first on the proposal of the Commission and then on the common position of the Council.

The European Parliament is particularly active in the area of the environment policy. Its committee on environment, public health and consumer protection, set up in 1972, is not only one of the biggest, but also one of the most active of all parliamentary committees, as regards written and oral questions, initiatives for opinions and resolutions and as regards the attempts to integrate the environmental dimension into other opinions of the Parliament. Its opinions on Commission proposals are generally thorough, well

---

[1] See above, para. 2.18.
[2] See, for instance Dir. 67/548 on chemical substances: [1967] O.J. 196/1, which was amended seven times by the Council and some 20 times by the Commission between 1967 and 1993; Dir. 70/220 on exhaust emissions from cars: [1970] O.J. L76/1, which saw the emission values from cars amended 10 times between 1970 and 1993.

considered and undertake to provide for more protection for the environment than the Commission had suggested. The impact of these opinions on the Council is, however, limited, even where the Commission agrees to amend its proposal under Article 189a—the old Article 149—of the Treaty. One reason for this is that the Council not infrequently starts discussing the Commission's's proposal in working groups before it disposes of Parliament's opinion.

The consultation of the Economic and Social Committee (ECOSOC) is equally **3.04** mandatory. ECOSOC is thought to represent the different interests within the Union, although the environment is not expressly mentioned in the Treaty. At present, only one member of ECOSOC has indicated specific interests in environmental questions. The consultation of the Committee of the Regions, set up under the Maastricht Treaty, is not mandatory in environmental matters. However, this Committee may deliver an opinion where it is of the opinion that specific regional interests are involved.[3] This possibility will certainly gain some importance in future, since environmental matters regularly affect the interests of the regions.

Council decisions can either take the form of specific protection measures, in particular directives or regulations, or be more general in nature, which then state, for instance that the Community should take new action in areas which are "new", such as soil protection or global warming. The form of Council decisions is not fixed in Article 130s(1). The Council may thus adopt directives, regulations, decisions, recommendations, resolutions or agreements.

Article 130s(1) is completed by Article 130s(5). This provision was introduced **3.05** into the Treaty by the Maastricht Treaty. A provision with a similar objective is to be found in Article 7 of Directive 92/43 on fauna and flora habitats.[4] The provision has its origin, as stated, in the idea pronounced in particular by less wealthy Member States, that if the protection of the environment is in the general interest of the Community, the Community should pay for measures which protect the environment. Spain in particular was reluctant to designate habitats and take conservation measures, unless the Community assisted financially.

The provision states that it is the Council which must, together with the measure which it adopts, decide on the specific measures. The following conditions must be fulfilled:

(1) The Community measure must be adopted by virtue of Article 130s(1). This condition excludes that one single Member State could veto the

---

[3] See Art. 198a to 198c E.C. Treaty.
[4] Dir. 92/43: [1992] O.J. L206/7.

adoption of a Community measure until it has got satisfaction for a temporary derogation or a financial contribution.

(2) There must be a request from a Member State stating that costs are disproportionate. This condition leads to an examination of the request by the Council, *i.e.* by all the other Member States and the Commission. Thus, frivolous requests will more easily be detected. The request may be made by any of the Member States, not just by those which are at present entitled to accede to the Cohesion Fund.[5]

(3) The costs must be deemed inappropriate for the public authorities. It is thus not the cost of the measure itself which will be examined, but rather the cost impact on public authorities. Where these authorities have the possibility to charge private undertakings with costs—where they can in particular make the polluter pay—the provision is not applicable.

The Council decision, which needs a qualified majority, may consist of temporary derogations or financial support from the Cohesion Fund. It is not quite clear why the possibility of temporary derogation was mentioned, since this possibility existed well before the Maastricht Treaty and has also been used in a number of cases. At least this formula demonstrates that the non-application of environmental legislation brings an economic advantage to the non-complying Member State.

The financial support from the Cohesion Fund is not further specified. It might consist in a lump sum or in regular payments over a longer period, or in the financing of an investment programme. Paragraph 5 is introduced with the words "without prejudice to the principle that the polluter should pay". It might well be argued, in view of this wording, that the non-compliance with Community environmental legislation is a breach of the polluter-pays-principle.

Unanimous decisions [Article 130s(2)]

3.06   Article 130s(2) was inserted into the Treaty by the Maastricht Treaty. It is expressly marked as a derogation of the normal decision-making procedure. It does not apply to Community decisions which are adopted by virtue of Article 100a and which aim thus at the achievement and the functioning of the

---

[5] According to a Protocol, annexed to the E.C. Treaty in its Maastricht version, the Cohesion Fund provides "Community financial contributions to projects in . . . Member States with a per capita GNP of less than 90 per cent. of the Community average . . . ". By the end of 1993, Greece, Spain, Portugal and Ireland had fulfilled these conditions.

common internal market. The consultation of the European Parliament and the Economical and Social Committee is mandatory.

The list of provisions for which unanimous decisions are required, is a compromise list, where, during the discussions of the Maastricht Treaty, Member States had joined their requests for derogating from the principle of majority decision-taking.

It should be remembered that there is a general rule of the E.C. Treaty that the Council may only decide by unanimity when it changes a proposal from the Commission (Article 189a). In such a case, therefore, it is enough for the Commission to find one Member State as an ally, in order to be able to veto a Council decision. This possibility might become particularly relevant, where the Council wants to lower the degree of environmental protection with regard to the Commission's proposal.

(1) PROVISIONS PRIMARILY OF A FISCAL NATURE

Provisions of a fiscal nature come, at present, under Article 99 of the Treaty which expressly provides for unanimous decisions. Nevertheless, Article 99 does not make the provision of Article 130s(2) superfluous. Indeed, Article 99 expressly allows harmonisation of fiscal legislation to the extent that this is necessary for the establishment and the functioning of the internal market. Article 130s(2) clarifies that fiscal measures are also possible in order to achieve the objectives of Article 130r(1). For a number of years, the Community has announced its intention to adopt fiscal and economic measures in the area of the environment.[6] Until now, only one proposal for an environmental tax has been made, on the introduction of a combined CO_2—energy tax. This proposal was based on Article 99 and 130s jointly.[7]   **3.07**

Fiscal questions touch the core of national sovereignty. It is therefore understandable that Member States, who did not accept, in the discussions on the Single European Act or on the Maastricht Treaty, majority decisions in Article 99, were not either ready to accept such decisions in environmental issues.

Environmental provisions which are not primarily of a fiscal nature, may be the subject of majority decisions, even where they contain fiscal rules. An example is provided by the Directives on car emissions, which fix standards for these emissions and allow, as an accompanying measure, Member States to

---

[6] See, for instance Fourth Environmental Programme: [1987] O.J. C328/1 point 2.5.
[7] Commission: [1992] O.J. C196/92.

grant fiscal or financial incentives in order to accelerate the introduction of new standards.[8]

(2) TOWN AND COUNTRY PLANNING, LAND USE

3.08 Town and country planning and land use measures affect rather directly the way in which Member States use their territory for infrastructure projects such as roads, railways, cities, ports, airports, etc. Decision on such matters by the Community legislator could all too easily affect Article 222 of the Treaty.[9] Thus, it is understandable that Member States wished to retain a right to veto any Community legislation in the area of town and country planning and land use, which is practically ensured by the requirement of unanimous decisions. It should be noted that the non-binding guidelines for the setting-up of trans-European networks in the areas of transport, telecommunications and energy infrastructures, while being adopted, under Article 129d of the Treaty, by majority decisions, require the approval of the Member State concerned.[10] Article 129d thus expresses the basic idea that the use of soil in a Member State should not be decided upon without the consent of that Member State. This principle is to be approved of, even if one should have little illusions about the persuasive power of the Union's institutions to reach a consensus on town and country planning, measures, or land use.

Waste management and measures of a general nature affecting the use of land are exempted from the requirement of unanimity. Directives on landfill or on other aspects of waste management thus follow the general rules of decision-making which are either Article 130s(1) or Article 100a.

General measures are in particular measures such as the requirement of an environment impact assessment for infrastructure projects[11] or even for policies, plans and programmes,[12] but also measures aiming at the protection

---

[8] See, for instance Dir. 91/441 amending Dir. 70/220 (note 2 above): [1991] O.J. L242/1, Art. 3: "Member States may make provisions for tax incentives for the vehicles covered by this Directive. Such incentives shall meet the provisions of the Treaty as well as the following conditions:
— they shall apply to all domestic car production and to vehicles imported for marketing in a Member State and fitted with equipment allowing the European standards to be met in 1992 to be satisfied ahead of time,
— they shall be of value, for each type of vehicle, substantially lower than the actual cost of the equipment fitted to meet the values set and of its fitting on the vehicle.
The Commission shall be informed of any plans to introduce or amend the tax incentives referred to in the first subparagraph in sufficient time to allow it to submit comments."

[9] Art. 222 E.C. Treaty. "This Treaty shall in no way prejudice the rules in Member States governing the system of property ownership".

[10] Art. 129d(2) E.C. Treaty: "Guidelines and projects of common interest which relate to the territory of a Member State shall require the approval of the Member State concerned".

[11] Dir. 85/337: [1985] O.J. L174/40.

[12] See, Commission Legislative Programme for 1993: [1993] O.J. C125/9, point 241; Legislative Programme for 1994, COM(93)588 final of November 24, 1993, point 241.

of fauna and flora habitats or measures concerning the urban environment. As regards the environment impact assessment, it remains a Member State's decision if and where a specific project is to be realised or—should legislation on environment impact as assessment of policies, plans and programmes be adopted—how the plans and programmes are actually implemented; the requirement of an assessment is thus only a formal one and does not really affect the use of the land.

Slightly more complicated is the question, whether the protection of habitats **3.09** is a general measure or a measure for land use. Until now, the Community has legislated twice in this area: Directive 79/409 on the conservation of wild living bird provides in Article 4, for the protection of bird's habitats.[13] And Directive 92/43, which aims at the protection of fauna and flora generally, contains detailed rules on the identification, designation and protection of habitats.[14] Both Directives were adopted unanimously, prior to the coming into effect of the Maastricht Treaty; the essential question is therefore, whether amendments to these Directives will have to be based on Article 130s(1) or 130s(2).

In my opinion, both Directives are, in future, to be based on Article 130s(1). They are measures of general nature for land use. As regards Directive 79/409, its objective is an overall, general protection of birds and living animals. Such a general protection scheme must include the protection of biotopes and habitats. However, the principal objective, the "centre of gravity", remains the protection of birds and not the rules on habitat designation or on the use of land within the habitats. Similar considerations apply to Directive 92/43. The designation of habitats and the conservation measures flowing out of such a designation are not an end in itself, but aim at achieving the objective of fauna and flora protection, which is the centre of gravity of the Directive's provisions. Rules on the designation of habitats are no more rules on "land use" than rules on the designation of trans-European networks. Furthermore, it is normally the Member States which designate habitats that come under European provisions. Only in exceptional circumstances may a Member State be in breach of its obligations by not designating a specific habitat. Such cases occur, where there is European and international common scientific opinion that the habitat in question belongs to the group of habitats, the conservation of which is of paramount ecological importance. In such cases, Community mechanisms might intervene, which lead to the

---

[13] Dir. 79/409: [1979] O.J. L103/1.
[14] Dir. 92/43: [1992] O.J. L206/7.

designation of a habitat by the Community. Even in such cases, though, is a unanimous Council decision necessary.[15]

(3) MANAGEMENT OF WATER RESOURCES

3.10   Are unanimous decisions also required for directives on water quality such as drinking water, bathing water, groundwater, discharge of dangerous substances into water etc; or does the provision of the Article 130s(2) only refer to quantitative measures on water supply such as dams, irrigation, water supply systems, etc?[16]

The Treaty does not give much clarification on this point. The different notions "Bewirtschaftung der Wasserresource", "gestion des ressources hydrauliques", "waterbeheer"—do not really help answering the question. The Dutch version of the text is the only one which adds an adjective "quantitative" before the noun ["waterbeheer"].

Where the first, third and fifth Community Environmental Action Programmes mentioned the management of resources or of water resources, they included both quantitative and qualitative aspects. The Fifth Action Programme, submitted to the Council in March 1992, shortly after the signature of the Maastricht Treaty, dealt under no. 5.4 with "management of water resources" and included under that heading questions of quantity and quality of water.[17] Decision 85/338 on the CORINE project differentiated, as far as water was concerned, between water quality and water resources.[18] Regulation 1210/90 on the European Environmental Agency differentiated in Article 3(2), between "water quality, dangerous substances and water resources".[19]

3.11   Limiting the notion of "management of water resources" to quantitative aspects would certainly bring this notion closer to the notion of land use, since it would then rather be a question of "water use". It is, however, doubtful, whether quantitative and qualitative aspects can really be so clearly separated from each other. Another underlying reasoning of Member States may have been that water legislation might have considerable financial consequences. Indeed, it is still quite frequent that rivers, coastal waters and seas are used as sewers for domestic and industrial waste waters or as waste dumping sites.

---

[15] See, Art. 5 of Dir. 92/43 (note 12 above): see, also, Case C-355/90, *Commission* v. *Spain*: [1993] I E.C.R. 4221, where the Court held that Spain had breached its obligations under Dir. 79/409 by not designating a specific are under Article 4 of that Directive.

[16] In this sense P. Renaudière, *Le droit communautaire de l'environnement après Maastricht* (Aménagement-Environnement, 1992), p. 70. B. Verhoeve, G. Bennett, D. Wilkinson, *Maastricht and the Environment* (Institute for European Environmental Policy) (Arnhem-London, 1992), p. 29.

[17] Fifth Environmental Action Programme: [1993] O.J. C138/1, 50.

[18] [1985] O.J. L176/14.

[19] [1990] O.J. L120/1.

The decisive point is, in my opinion, the following: it would have been easy to refer in Article 130s(2) to water legislation, as well as one had earlier referred to waste legislation. The sophisticated wording "management of water resources" in fact shows that only a specific sector of all water legislations was to be covered. This analysis matches well with the fact that the text was drafted by the Dutch presidency of the Council; and in the Netherlands, there is a Department for Transport and Waterstaat which deals with quantitative water aspects, whereas the Department for the Environment deals with qualitative water aspects. The addition of the world "quantitatief" in the Dutch version of the Treaty points to the fact that the text of the Treaty meant to maintain a borderline between quantitative and qualitative aspects. These have been sufficiently clearly expressed in the text in order to allow the conclusion that mere qualitative aspects of water policy are to be decided by majority decision. "Management of water resources" is thus equivalent to "water use".

(4) CHOICE OF ENERGY SOURCES; ENERGY SUPPLY

The last category of measures where unanimity is required, concerns the energy sector. There is no specific chapter on energy in the Treaty. Measures on energy aspects of the environment are therefore, at present, based on Article 130s or Article 235. Unanimous decision is required for measures "significantly affecting a Member State's choice between different energy sources". An example for this kind of measure would be the abandonment, for environmental reasons, of nuclear energy or of lignite which contains too much sulphur. Unanimous decisions are also necessary where a Member State's general structure of energy supply is significantly affected. This provision concerns, for instance, a Community decision not to import petrol from third countries or to rely primarily on nuclear energy all over the Community territory.   **3.12**

Questions have been raised, whether the adherence, by the European Community, to the United Nations Convention on Climate Change[20] would not require unanimous decision, since the Community discusses, amongst other measures, the introduction of a CO_2-energy tax in order to achieve the targets fixed by that Convention, in particular a stabilisation of CO_2-emissions.[21] However, the Convention does not impose, legally, the introduction of a tax; the stabilisation of CO_2-emissions could also be achieved by, for instance, a serious energy-saving programme, by imposing stringent standards on car and truck manufacturers, etc. Evidence of the absence of a legal

---

[20] [1994] O.J. L33/11.
[21] See, Commission proposal of 1992 (note 7 above).

79

link between the Convention and a tax might also be that neither the USA nor Japan, which both signed the Convention, intend to introduce such a tax.

The Council adhered to the Convention. It decided by unanimity, but applied Article 130s(1). The United Kingdom, which had pleaded for the application of Article 130s(2), abstained, in order to not create a precedent.

3.13   The Council may unanimously decide that decisions on the above-mentioned aspects are no longer taken by unanimity but by qualified majority. This provision was already part of Article 130s (old version). Between 1987 and 1993 it did not gain any importance. Member States were reluctant to decide to move over to majority voting. In the area of water, a Commission proposal from 1990 to decide by majority on the discharge of dangerous substances into waters was not adopted by the Council and was withdrawn in 1993.[22]

An example, where Article 130s(2) (old version) was applied, is Article 9 of Regulation 1734/88 on the export and import of certain dangerous chemicals; this provision allowed a decision to be made on the adaptation of the list of chemicals coming under that Regulation with qualified majority.[23] Another example is Directive 88/609 on large combustion plants, Article 3(5), where the Council may adopt, in urgency cases, an amendment of limit-values or dates, provided a Member State has appealed to the Council against a corresponding decision by the Commission.[24]

Past experience does not suggest that the provision of Article 130s(2) second sub-paragraph will gain much relevance in the future. Even if the Council decided to recur to this sub-paragraph and adopt a measure by qualified majority, the procedures under Article 189b or 189c would not apply. The provision in the sub-paragraph is clear and non-ambiguous in that regard. There is no systematic link in the Treaty between majority decisions and the procedures under Articles 189b and 189c. Thus, the European Parliament will only need to be consulted, but has no co-operative or co-decisional powers.

Decisions on programmes [Article 130s(3)]

3.14   Paragraph 3 of Article 130s was also introduced by the Maastricht Treaty on European Union. It provides for the adoption of "general action programmes setting out priority objectives to be attained", which shall be adopted by the Council by way of the co-decision procedure under Article 189b. This new rule aims at increasing Parliament's influence on the Community decisions and on the policy in general: Details of the procedure are laid down in Article

---

[22] Commission proposal: [1990] O.J. C114/9; withdrawal: [1993] O.J. C228/13.
[23] Reg. 1734/88: [1988] O.J. L155/2.
[24] Dir. 88/609: [1988] O.J. L336/1.

189b. The co-decision procedure in the area of the environment applies only to the adoption of the above-mentioned programmes and to the environmental decisions based on Article 100a.

Programmes which come under paragraph 3 are programmes "in other areas". It is not clear what is meant by this formula. An interpretation, that other areas than those listed in paragraph 2 are meant, seems impossible, since paragraph 3 sub-paragraph 2 indicates that areas of paragraph 2 may well be covered by such programmes. Despite this difficulty, the reference to "other areas" refers well, in the author's opinion, to the areas mentioned in paragraph 2. Indeed, the co-decision procedure of paragraph 3 is a majority decision. If the areas of paragraph 2 were not excluded in paragraph 3, general action programmes could be adopted by majority decisions in areas which are subject to unanimous decisions under paragraph 2. It is true that such general action programmes would need implementation measures and that these, as far as areas of paragraph 2 are concerned, must be adopted by unanimity. However, even the existence of a binding action programme, adopted jointly by the Council and the European Parliament and published, could be considered to constitute a form of undue pressure on a Member State, in order to accept Community decisions in such areas.

The only alternative to this interpretation would be to ignore the words 'in other areas" and allow general action programmes to be adopted by the co-decision procedure in all areas of environmental policy. For the reasons just explained, such an interpretation seems to go too far. **3.15**

"General action programmes" are programmes which group a number of actions to be undertaken in order to reach the objectives of Article 130r(1) and which contain a timetable within which these actions are to be taken.[25] Programmes to ensure the implementation of a specific Directive are not "general" programmes.

In the environmental sector the Community has, for more than 20 years, worked with action programmes. However, these programmes have never been approved by the Council alone, but also by Member States meeting in Council.

The Fourth and Fifth Programmes date from 1987[26] and 1993[27] respectively, *i.e.* after the entry into force of the Single European Act. They, again, were approved by the Council and the representatives of the Member States in 1987, probably as a follow-on from the tradition of the previous decisions. In **3.16**

---

[25] In the same sense Renaudière (note 16 above), p. 73.
[26] Fourth Environmental Action Programme: [1987] O.J. C328/1.
[27] Fifth Environmental Action Programme: [1993] O.J. C138/1.

1993, when the Maastricht Treaty had not yet entered into force, the discussion on subsidiarity and Member States' competence in environmental and other issues played an important role. Presumably, Member States wished to avoid the impression that an approval of the Fifth Programme by the Council alone would signify some supplementary transfer of competence to the Community. Legally, there is no longer any basis for such method of approval, following the incorporation of Articles 130r to 130t into the Treaty. Indeed, numerous action programmes, for instance in the field of energy policy, transport policy, social policy, regional policy, etc., have been adopted by the Community without the Community increasing or even claiming to increase its competence to the detriment of Member States. The fact that the Fourth Programme was approved by the Council and Member States jointly was not of any legal significance and has not played any practical role at all between 1987 and 1993.

3.17   The action programmes of the past were political declarations of intent which took all the measures planned for a certain period, placed them in a overall context, set priorities and, if necessary, introduced or explained changes in course. They did not constitute a legal basis for Community environment measures. Nevertheless, they do represent more than a voluntary undertaking by the Council and the Member States to endeavour to implement the objectives stated in the programmes. In the context both of Articles 100 and 100a and of Article 130s, the question of whether a measure is necessary for the establishment and functioning of the internal market (Article 100a), or whether the objectives of Community environment policy can be attained "better" at European level than at the level of the individual Member State (Article 3b), is of paramount significance in drawing the dividing line between the Union's powers and those of the Member States. To answer these questions, a number of political, legal, economic and social aspects have to be carefully considered.

The process of discussing and deciding on Community action programmes translates the general wording of Articles 100a and 130r into concrete policy initiatives for the environment sector. If an environment programme states that certain measures are necessary to protect the environment, the European Community institutions are thereby documenting their political view that action should be taken at European level. This provides an important pointer for the assessment of whether a certain measure is necessary to protect the environment and/or complete the internal market. At the same time it influences the debate on the allocation of financial and manpower resources to the Community institutions in the context of the annual budget discussions. Finally, a Council decision to adopt a programme also implies a decision to take action on environment matters at European level pursuant to Article 130s. All in all, then, the environment programmes and accompanying Council decisions do have a legal significance.

The Court reached a similar conclusion in Cases 91/70 and 92/79 concerning   **3.18**
the legal force of Directives on detergents and the maximum sulphur content
of liquid fuels.[28] The Court affirmed the Directives' validity, as they had been
adopted under the Community programmes to eliminate technical barriers to
trade and to protect the environment, and declared: "in this sense it (the
Directive) is validly founded upon Article 100".

The correct interpretation of the Court's judgments must therefore be that,
if the Community by adopting action programmes has documented its
political view on the measures that are to be the subject of Community
legislation, there is no need for further proof of the necessity for Community
action.

In the past, the action programmes were never formally adopted. Independ-
ently of the question, whether a resolution may contain a legally binding
obligation, the wording of the resolution was always extremely prudent; thus,
Council and Member States Representatives declared, as regards the Fifth
Action Programme, "(they) approve the general approach and strategy of the
programme 'Towards Sustainability' presented by the Commission".[29]
Further, the wording of the programme, as it was submitted by the
Commission,was not in any way changed by the Council or by Member States.

Article 130s(3) now expressly requires the adoption of the environmental
action programme. The legal form is that of a decision as other programmes,
such as the environmental research programmes were already formally
adopted by Council decisions.[30] Since a decision is legally binding, there is
therefore a binding commitment by the Council and the European Parliament
to contribute to the implementation of the programme. At the same time, the
Commission is bound to submit the necessary proposals to the Council in
order to allow such implementation. The Commission's right of initiative can
thus be considerably narrowed down. Where, for instance, an Action
programme provides for the adoption of Community legislation on environmental liability, the Commission is obliged to submit, within a reasonable
time-span, a proposal for such legislation, in order to allow its final adoption.

Failure to take the necessary steps towards implementation of a programme
may be tackled, in particular by the European Parliament or a Member State,
under Article 175 of the E.C. Treaty before the European Court. Also the
Council could be exposed to such a procedure under Article 175, if it fails to
adopt the envisaged measure within reasonable time.

---

[28] Case 91/79, *Commission* v. *Italy*: [1980] E.C.R. 1099; Case 92/79, *Commission* v. *Italy*: [1980]
E.C.R. 1115, [1981] 1 C.M.L.R. 331.
[29] See, Resolution of February 1, 1993: C138/1, 4.
[30] See, Council Decision 86/234: [1986] O.J. L159/31, adopting an environmental research
programme 1986 to 1990; Decision 91/354: [1991] O.J. L192/29, adopting an environmental
research programme 1990 to 1994.

3.19   Besides the Environmental Action Programmes, the Community has also adopted action programmes on cadmium pollution[31] and the reduction of pollution by hydrocarbons at sea.[32] These programmes are certainly also "general action programmes". Indeed, it depends on the political will, whether action programmes for specific pollutants or specific sectors, such as waste, or media—soil or nature—are formulated at European level. Where an action programme is adopted by co-decision procedure it will, at a later stage, be rather difficult to argue that under a subsidiarity clause a specific action mentioned in such a programme should instead be dealt with at national level.

Co-operation with other countries [Article 130r(4)]

3.20   The provision of Article 130r(4) was inserted in the Treaty in 1987, at the same time as Article 130r(5). Since the Maastricht Treaty removed the old Article 130r(4), the provision was renumbered. Its wording was not changed. However, Article 228, to which the provision refers, was considerably changed.

Article 130r(4) gives express competence to the Community to conclude international environmental agreements, which then are binding on the institutions of the Community and on the Member States (Article 228(7)).

Agreements are negotiated by the Commission, which needs an express negotiating mandate by the Council. The Commission, during the negotiation period, continuously consults with a special committee composed of Member States' representatives. In practice, Member States also participate in the negotiation of the environmental agreements. Agreements are concluded by the Council upon proposal of the Commission. The Council may empower the Commission to approve later modifications on behalf of the Community, where the agreement provides for them to be adopted by a simplified procedure or by a body set up under the agreement (Article 228(4)). This kind of procedure might gain importance in future, since international environmental agreements seem more and more to work with a basic agreement and subsequent protocols, which are adopted by a simplified procedure.

The main problems of international agreements on the environment are whether they are to be concluded by the Community alone or whether also Member States shall conclude them and furthermore, what the consequences of the conclusions of an international agreement by the Community are; this latter problem will be dealt with below.

---

[31] Council Resolution of January 25, 1988: [1988] O.J. C30/1.
[32] Council Resolution of June 26, 1978: [1978] O.J. C162/1.

The Community alone concludes international agreements, where it has **3.21** exclusive power to do so. Such exclusive power can be laid down explicitly in the Treaty, though, as far as the environment is concerned, this is certainly not the case of Articles 130r and 130s. The Court of Justice has ruled that exclusive competence for concluding international agreements can also flow out of the adoption by the Community, of Community-wide provisions in an area of Community policy.[33] In such a case Member States may not conclude international agreements which affect or amend Community rules.

As stated earlier, the Community has adopted an important number of Directives and Regulations in the area of environmental protection.

To the extent that these instruments were based on Article 130s, it follows from Article 130t that the Community competence, in such a case, is never exclusive, since Member States have kept the right to take more stringent protective measures.[34] The same reasoning applies, where such instruments were, prior to the introduction of Articles 130r to 130t into the Treaty, based on other provisions than 130s, but would now come under this provision. Finally, the same reasoning applies where a Community legal instrument expressly authorises Member States to take more stringent protective measures than those laid down by the Community, which was very often the case prior to 1987.

In all these cases, the Community competence is not exclusive. The Member **3.22** States are entitled to conclude international agreements. Doubts exist where Community legislation is based, for instance, on other provisions of the Treaty. An illustrative example for this is Directive 84/631 on the transfrontier shipment of dangerous waste, which regulated transport of dangerous waste between Member States and export of such waste to third countries.[35] The Directive was based on Articles 100 and 235. The Court ruled in Case C-2/90 that the Directive contained a complete set of rules in this area and had left Member States with no residual competence.[36] Following from that and applying the general rules on exclusive competence, it should have been the Community that concluded the Basle Convention on the transport of hazardous waste. However, Member States used two marginal provisions in the Basle Convention on technical assistance and on research, to argue that the convention did not come into the sphere of exclusive competence of the Community, but that it was a mixed agreement—*i.e.* that it contained provisions for which the Community was responsible and others which were

---

[33] Court of Justice, Case 22/70, *Commission v. Council*: [1971] E.C.R. 263, [1971] C.M.L.R. 335.
[34] Court of Justice, Opinion 2/91 [I.L.O.], delivered on March 19, 1993: [1993] 3 C.M.L.R. 800.
[35] Dir. 84/631: [1984] O.J. L326/31. This Directive is now replaced by Regulation 259/93: [1993] O.J. L30/1.
[36] Case C-2/90, *Commission* v. *Belgium*: [1992] 1 E.C.R. 4431, [1993] 1 C.M.L.R. 365.

of the competence of Member States. Thus, Member States signed and notified the Convention themselves, next to the Community.[37]

One should be aware that in the legal practice, Member States have on no occasion, recognised in environmental matters, an exclusive competence of the Community to conclude international agreements. All environmental agreements are thus mixed agreements which are negotiated and concluded by the Community and, at the same time, by Member States.

Decisions based on other Treaty provisions

3.23　All human activity affects the environment in one way or the other. European Union decisions are not excluded from this trivial remark. Since the Union acts within the limits of the powers conferred upon it by the Treaty, its different acts must be based on specific Treaty provisions. These Treaty provisions differ as to conditions, procedures and consequences. It is therefore important to establish the legal basis for environmental measures which are taken by the European Union.

The environmental provisions were first inserted into the Treaty in 1987, by the Single European Act. The Court of Justice stated that this insertion has not meant that provisions which earlier were based on specific provisions of the Treaty should now be based on Article 130s only.[38] No attempt will be made in the following to develop a legal theory on legal bases and their interrelationship under the Treaty. As regards environmental matters, the main provisions, which are applicable are Articles 43, 84, 100a, 113, 130o and 130s. A number of other provisions may, as the case might be, constitute the basis for measures that affect the environment, such as Article 99 on taxation, 118a on the working environment, 129a on consumer protection and 130e on economic and social cohesion. The decision, whether one of these provisions or Article 130s is to be applied in a concrete case, does not seem, however, to raise significant problems.

ARTICLE 43

3.24　Article 43(2) provides that the Council, in working out and implementing the common agricultural policy, adopts legislation in accordance with Articles 38 *et seq.* by qualified majority. Numerous measures in the area of agricultural policy affect—positively or negatively—air and soil, water, fauna, flora and landscapes. Examples include animal husbandry, use of fertilisers and

---

[37] Council Decision 94/98: [1993] O.J. L39/1.
[38] Case C-62/88, *Greece* v. *Council*: [1990] I E.C.R. 1527, [1991] 2 C.M.L.R. 649.

pesticides, drainage or irrigation measures, land use, discharges, the production and marketing of agricultural products, etc. The objective of the rules
adopted by virtue of Article 43(2) is the establishment of a common
agricultural policy among Member States, which includes the production of
uniform products and inform production and marketing conditions. As
emerges from Article 38(2), Article 43(2) has precedence over the provisions
of the Treaty on the establishment of the common market or, to use modern
terminology, completion of the internal market. For a long time, it was
disputed whether measures under Article 43(2) could also include aspects on
human health or whether such measures had to be based (also) on Article 100
of the Treaty, which requires unanimous decisions. The question was decided
by the Court in 1988 in a case concerning the ban of hormones in animal
feeding stuff; the Court ruled that such a measure could be based on Article
43(2) alone, though it was also destined to protect human health.[39] This
judgment might have been influenced by the fact that since 1987, Article 100
was superseded by Article 100a, which provided for majority decisions also in
matters relating to human health.

The Court's decision also affects the relationship between Articles 43 and
130s. It follows from it that environmental-agricultural measures may be
based on Article 43(2).

Furthermore, in Case C-405/92 the Court of Justice held that Regulation
345/92[40], which prohibits the use of drift-nets, was rightly based on Article 43,
since its principal objective was the protection of marine resources, which was
part of a fishery policy.[41] The fact that the Regulation in question also aimed at
the protection of the environment could not, so the Court, be decisive since it
followed from Article 130r(2)(2) that provisions which affect the environment
may also be based on other provisions of the Treaty than Article 130s. This
judgment is already the third with such a conclusion and may thus be
considered to be in a consistent line of decisions by the Court.

A number of legal acts concerning forest protection against fire or air
pollution were adopted on the basis of both Article 43 and 130s, since Articles
38 to 47 do not cover forest measures.[42]

In legal literature, only Schroer pleads for Article 130s as the legal basis of   **3.25**
most of these provisions,[43] in particular of Directive 91/414 on the authorisation of the marketing of pesticides.[44] His arguments are based on the

---

[39] Case 68/86, *United Kingdom* v. *Council*: [1988] E.C.R. 855, [1988] 2 C.M.L.R. 543
(hormones).
[40] Reg. 345/92, [1992] O.J. L42/15.
[41] Case C-405/92, *Mondiet* v. *Islais*: [1993] I E.C.R. 6133.
[42] See, Reg. 3529/86: [1986] O.J. L326/5, with later amendments.
[43] T. Schroer, *Die Kompetenzverteilung zwischen der Europaischen Wirtschaftsgemeinschaft und ihren
Mitgliedstaaten auf dem Gebiet des Umweltschutzes.* (Berlin, 1992), 140 *et seq.*
[44] Dir. 91/414: [1991] O.J. L230/1.

assumption that the Treaty provides the optimisation of environmental protection and that any Community legislation which significantly aims at achieving the objectives of Article 130r(1) should be based on 130s. In my opinion, Article 43(2) has correctly been chosen as the legal basis of Directive 91/414. The licensing of pesticides is a provision which aims at setting common standards for agricultural production. The need to reach common rules for agricultural products and production was, since the beginning of the Treaty, considered so important that majority decisions were thought to be necessary. While this element has now lost some of its importance, since Article 130s also provides for majority decisions, there is no reason not to consider Article 43(2) an appropriate legal basis, all the more since, according to Article 130r(2)(2), agricultural measures must take into account the provisions of Article 130r(1) and (2).

The real question at issue is whether the provisions of Article 130t apply, in other terms, whether Member States may prohibit at national level, a pesticide which was admitted at Community level. The Court has not yet given a ruling on this question. Where legal authors hold that there is a legal principle of optimising environmental protection,[45] they also come to the conclusion that Article 130t applies all over the Treaty. In contrast to that, I cannot see any convincing argument to apply the principle of Article 130t to provisions adopted under Article 43(2), for reasons explained elsewhere.[46] A common agricultural policy with different national bans for products used in agriculture cannot function. Therefore, a national prohibition of a pesticide which is authorised Community-wide is not possible.

This observation does of course not exclude the prohibition of use of certain pesticides in order to protect the local or regional environment of a Member State, such as habitats or water protection areas.

ARTICLE 84

3.26 The common transport policy (Articles 74 to 84) tries to set common conditions for transport within the Community and beyond; such conditions may have a very considerable impact on the environment.

Both Articles 75 and 84 now provide, as a rule, majority decisions by virtue of Article 189b. However, they require unanimous decisions where a measure "would be liable to have a serious effect on the standard of living and on employment in certain areas and on the operation of transport facilities."[47] Normally thus, environmental-related transport provisions are the subject of majority decisions. Hence, the question of whether Article 75/84(2) or 130s is

---

[45] See above, para. 2.35.
[46] See, L. Krämer, 30 C.M.L.Rev. p. 1076 (1993).
[47] Art. 75(3) E.C. Treaty.

applicable, is mainly of relevance as regards Article 130t. Reference is made to what was said above. The legal bases of the acts adopted so far by the Community seems correct.

ARTICLE 100a

Article 100a serves "the achievement of the objectives set out in Article 7a", **3.27** *i.e.* progressive establishment of the internal market. In its proposals in the context of Article 100a concerning environmental protection in addition to other sectors, the Commission has to take as a base a "high level of protection". In the case of majority decisions a Member State may under certain circumstances pursuant to paragraph 4 apply national measures to protect the "environment" which are more stringent than the Community provisions adopted. It is clear from these provisions that environmental protection measures can also be based on Article 100a of the Treaty. Otherwise the mention of environmental protection in both Article 100a(3) and (4) would be pointless. Measures to approximate laws and regulations for the purpose of completing the internal market can, in addition, serve the objectives of environmental protection just as measures to promote environmental protection can further the aims of the internal market. It had already been clarified by Court rulings before the entry into force of the Single Act that environmental provisions could be based on Article 100;[48] there is nothing to suggest that the changeover to decisions by qualified majority in Article 100a has changed this position in any way.

The Treaty does not contain any criterion for making a clear distinction between Articles 130s and 100a. Article 100a is designed to bring about completion of the internal market for goods and services, persons and capital. Articles 130r to 130t, on the other hand, do not contain anything explicit that could be allocated to the sector "free movement of goods". On the contrary, Article 130t explicitly indicates that different measures are both possible and necessary to protect the environment in the Community.

As Article 100a is concerned with goods and services, provisions affecting trade in these goods and services should primarily be allocated to Article 100a; by contrast provisions contributing to the attainment of one of the objectives specified in Article 130r should primarily be assigned to Article 130s. However, this rough classification is of little value.

It would be conceivable to take as a yardstick the objective of a provision and, **3.28** in the event of different objectives, the overriding objective of the provision. Thus, a provision would have to be assessed to ascertain whether its main purpose was to protect the environment or complete the internal market. It is

---

[48] Cases 91/79 and 92/79 (note 28).

worth remembering in this connection that the basic Directive on emission standards for motor vehicles was adopted as part of the Community programme to eliminate technical barriers to trade,[49] *i.e.* for the purpose of establishing a common market for motor vehicles. The fact that a Member State presses for more stringent standards at national level for environmental protection reasons does not exclude that the Community provision is primarily designed to maintain the free movement of goods, and lays down stringent environmental standards to prevent a collapse of the internal market. However, it may equally be the objective of a Community provision to take on board the motives of the environmentally conscious Member State and improve the quality of the Community environment. These reasons for a Community provision may be supplemented by others, such as protection of consumers, protection of the national or European motor industry, an attempt to shut out imports from third countries, or economic transport or commercial policy objectives.

3.29   Case 302/86 illustrates a further example.[50] Denmark had prohibited the use of metal cans as containers for drinks. The objective of the ban was apparently primarily to protect the environment, especially since Denmark had at the same time adopted other measures to avoid waste arising from packaging materials. The Danish ban, however, undoubtedly implied competitive advantages particularly for suppliers of beer and soft drinks from other Member States, as cans are lighter and cheaper to transport. The Danish drinks industry was therefore the main beneficiary. It appears impossible to ascertain with certainty what the specific objective of the Danish measure was, as tax, health and other considerations may also have played a part. In the same way, a Community measure prohibiting cans could also have several objectives, such as the maintenance or restoration of uniform provisions on cans within the Community, the rectification of a solo initiative by a Member State, protection of the environment from tin cans, promotion of the glass industry, a reduction in dependence on raw material imports, economic policy reasons, etc.

3.30   In Case C-300/89[51] relating to Directive 89/428[52] on the harmonisation of programmes for the reduction of waste from titanium dioxide industry, both the Council and the Commission agents based their arguments before the Court on the primary objective of Directive 89/428,[53] which was to determine the decision on the legal basis. However, while the Commission agent saw the

---

[49] Dir. 70/220 (note 2 above).
[50] Case 302/86, *Commission* v. *Denmark*: [1988] E.C.R. 4607, [1989] 1 C.M.L.R. 619 (Danish bottles).
[51] Case C-300/89, *Commission* v. *Council*: [1991] I E.C.R. 2867 (Titanium dioxide).
[52] Dir. 89/428: [1989] O.J. L201/56.
[53] See, L. Krämer, *European Environmental Law Casebook* (London, 1993), pp. 25 *et seq.*

primary objective of the Directive in the creation of equal competitive conditions for the industrial sector in question, the Council agent saw as its primary objective the protection of the environment. The Court did not recur to the theory at all, but argued on other grounds in favour of Article 100a.

In Case C-155/91[54] the Court had to deal with the question of the legal basis of Directive 91/156 on waste.[55] In this judgment, the Court recurred to the theory of primary objective. It saw the Directive as primarily aiming at the protection of the environment and only in an accessory way dealing with aspects of the internal market. Consequently, the Court held that Article 130s was the appropriate legal basis. This jurisprudence was further confirmed in Case C-405/92.[56]. Thus, it is to be expected that the Court will now continuously apply the theory of the primary objective of a Community measure, in order to determine the appropriate legal basis.

My problem with the Court decision is not the application of the theory of the primary objective of a measure. There seems to be no better yardstick. The problem is that in my opinion the distinction between Articles 100a and 130s should be made according to objective criteria which are accessible to verification by the Court and which give, at the same time, legal security to Community institutions as well as to economic agents. These objective criteria cannot only, it is submitted, be found in the recitals and the articles of a Directive or a Regulation. To give some examples: (a) the introduction of Community car emission standards which required the introduction of catalytic converters was motivated by increasing air pollution. This was the stated reason in the Directives;[57] mentioning was also made of internal market considerations, however, in a more marginal form. (b) Following German national legislation, the Community severely restricted the use of Pentachloro-phenol within the Community. Directive 91/173 stated that its main objective was to reduce the environmental and human health risk caused by Pentachlor-ophenol.[58] (c) Directive 91/157 deals with batteries and accumulators containing dangerous substances, and limits the content of such substances. Its main objective, as it appears in the recitals and in the text itself, is the reduction of dangerous substances in the environment.[59]

In all three cases the Council had based the Directives on Article 100a, in my opinion correctly. If one were taking the theory of the primary objective seriously, all three Directives would have had to be based on Article 130s, since their primary objective, as indicated in their text, was the protection of the environment. Where a substance or a product is banned from use, it is

---

[54] Case C-155/91, *Commission* v. *Council*, judgment of March 17, 1991, not yet reported.
[55] Dir. 91/156: [1991] O.J. L78/32.
[56] Case C-405/92 (note 41 above).
[57] Dir. 88/76: [1988] O.J. L36/1; 88/436: [1988] O.J. L214/1; 89/458: [1989] O.J. L226/1; 91/441: [1991] O.J. L242/1; 93/59: [1993] O.J. L186/21.
[58] Dir. 91/173: [1991] O.J. L85/34.
[59] Dir. 91/157: [1991] O.J. L78/38.

almost always a mere fiction to talk of the primary objective being the setting of uniform rules for the whole of the Community.

3.31   The wording of the recitals and the articles of a legal act cannot therefore, alone be decisive. The relevant criterion is rather—independently from the wording of a legal act—whether uniformity is necessary in order to achieve the Treaty objectives or not. Indeed, the Community has the objective to achieve the free movement of goods and services in particular (Article 7a). This objective requires uniform rules. For this reason, Community instruments laying down common product standards must come under Article 100a. This provision also applies when the measures contain common provision of a restrictive nature, prohibitions and maximum limitations, etc. If such measures were based on Article 130s, the effect, flowing out of Article 130t, would be that the Community's objective of achieving freedom of trade for goods or, more generally, completing the internal market, would never be attained. The legal basis of a measure should therefore be chosen with a view to permitting achievement of both objectives, namely completion of the internal market—Article 7a—and improvement of the quality of the environment—Article 130r(1). Since the requirements of the environment must be integrated into other Community policy measures—Article 130r(2)(2)—there is not really a risk for the environment, if Article 100a is chosen as a legal basis.

3.32   Against this approach it might be objected that the Council could decide not (yet) to have uniform product standards and thus base product-related measures on Article 130s, which, as can be seen from Article 130t, allows different national rules to exist. Therefore the council could, for products, take the following line:

(a)   No Community Legislation

Articles 30/36 apply, Member States take environmental measures;

(b)   Harmonisation under Article 130s

Member States have the possibility to maintain or introduce more stringent national measures (Article 130t);

(c)   Harmonisation under Article 100a

Member States may apply (existing) environmental measures (Article 100a(4)).

In other terms, Article 130s is taken as a degree of harmonisation for product-related measures, which the Council may adopt in cases, where it does not wish to proceed to total harmonisation; whether Article 130s or 100a is chosen, depends on the content of the Articles and the recitals, but is finally dependant on how the Council drafts the text in question.

Against this concept—which seems at present to be that of the Council—Article 7a of the Treaty is to be mentioned, which expressly requests measures that lead to the achievement of the internal market by end of 1992. This provision, which is supported and strengthened by Articles 100a and 100b, (provisions which aim at the target-date end 1992 to be respected) is so clear and unambiguous that there is no room for having product-related standards adopted under Article 130s. Article 7a and, more generally, the whole Treaty, is also binding on the Council.

I am therefore of the opinion that all product-related measures adopted by the Council must be based on Article 100a and that, for instance, Regulation 594/91 on the manufacture and use of ozone-depleting substances[60]—obviously a product-related Regulation—should have been based on Article 100a and not on Article 130s.

A specific problem is waste. Wastes are physical goods and as such capable of circulating between Member States. The Court has considered waste to come under Article 30 of the Treaty, whether it is recyclable or not.[61] Nevertheless, it has argued that Directive 91/156 on waste was rightly based on Article 130s.[62] It came to this conclusion by analysing the recitals and the articles of the Directive from which it concluded that the Directive's primary objective was the protection of the environment. As stated above, this opinion is contested here. However, in practice, it is more than likely that the Court will not change its approach, until the Council itself changes its approach and bases its waste legislation on Article 100a.

3.33

The Council did base Directive 91/157 on batteries[63] on Article 100a. This approach seems to suggest that the Council considers Articles 130s and 100a being equally accessible for product-related waste standards, according the relative emphasis on the free circulation or the protection of the environment which is expressed in the Directives. However, in my opinion, the Treaty provisions are not at the disposal of the Community legislator. And the existence of the requirement to achieve the internal market as quickly as possible excludes the recurrence of product-related measures to Article 130s at the discretion of the Council. Advocate-General Tesauro was of the opinion, that waste directives which concern specific terms of waste, such as batteries and their waste, waste from titanium dioxide industry—are to be based on Article 100a, since in such cases the competitive elements of a regulation at Community level is high. In contrast to that, waste directives which tackle the problem generally, are to be based on Article 130s, if and since their primary

---

[60] Reg. 594/91: [1991] O.J. L67/1.
[61] Case C-2/90 (note 30 above).
[62] Case C-155/91 (note 54 above).
[63] Dir. 91/157 (note 59).

objective is the protection of the environment.[64] It is not quite clear, whether the Court, in Case C-155/91, adhered to that concept. It has, to my mind, the disadvantage that the impact of a general directive on a specific branch of industry or waste industry might be as big as the impact of a specific directive; the borderline between general measures and specific measures is not clear at all.

3.34   Provisions on environmental production standards and production-related standards also pose certain problems. Such measures concern air emissions or water discharges from installations, conditions for landfill sites, accident prevention measures in installations, etc. Industrial installations do not circulate freely within the Community, but the products produced in them do. Environmental specifications may have an impact on costs and affect the competitive position of a manufacturer. This is therefore relevant to the establishment and functioning of the internal market which, as emerges from Article 100a(4) Phase 2, also includes competition free from distortions. This risk of distortions of competition increases as environmental standards become more stringent, unless uniform provisions prevail throughout the Community. If the objectives "completion of the internal market" and "improvement of the quality of the environment" are to be attained simultaneously everywhere in the Community if possible, provisions relating to production or plant must be based on Article 100a.

Similar considerations appear to have governed the Commission's approach in the case of the Directive on waste from titanium dioxide production. Article 9 of Directive 78/176 required Member States to communicate to the Commission programmes for the reduction of waste from titanium dioxide production.[65] The Commission was to put before the Council a proposal for a Directive on harmonisation of the programmes, in order to improve the competitive situation of the whole sector. The proposal tabled in 1983 was based on Articles 100 and 235.[66] The Commission changed the legal basis to Article 100a when the Single Act came into force. Directive 78/176 already required Member States to reduce quantities of waste arisings. The purpose of the new proposal, as was clear also from the recitals, was not to reduce environmental pollution, but to iron out the difference in conditions and competition. The Council based the Directive on Article 130s.[67]

The Court of Justice held that the Directive should have been based on Article 100a.[68] The Council thus adopted a new Directive, 92/112, based on Article 100a which, however, provided for minimum standards only.[69]

---

[64] Advocate General.
[65] Dir. 78/176: [1978] O.J. L54/19.
[66] [1984] O.J. C138/5.
[67] Dir. 89/428 (note 52 above).
[68] Case C-300/89 (note 51 above).
[69] Dir. 92/112: [1992] O.J. L409/11.

Apart from this judgment and in particular since the judgments in Case C-155/91 on Directive 91/156, where the Court applied the doctrine on the primary objective of a Directive, the Council bases all production-related Directives on Article 130s and the Commission, in its proposals, now follows the same line.

This practice, which leads in substance to setting aside the judgment in Case C-300/89, is doubtful. Indeed, as the Court has stated, an internal market also requests that competition is not distorted. Different environmental standards for the production—air emissions, water discharges, accident prevention schemes, etc.—will lead to different competitive situations and the more cost-intensive such standards are, the greater the competitive distortion becomes. It might be acceptable to have differences from one Member State to the other of one or two per cent. in the production costs which are due to different environmental standards. However where such costs reach five, ten, or as in the case of titanium dioxide industries,[70] twenty per cent. of the production costs, these differences must be eliminated through the adoption of uniform standards—thus on measures that are based on Article 100a. In other terms the limit between Article 100a and 130s is not fixed once and for all, but is flexible and the more stringent the environmental standard is (it should not be forgotten that the Community is committed to environmental standards at a high level (Article 130r(2)) the more it is necessary to base the measure on Article 100a.

3.35

Basing product-related measures on Article 130s bears the political risk that Member States with a low priority for environmental issues will inevitably try to fix low standards at Community level, arguing that Member States with a developed environmental policy could always under Article 130t, adopt more stringent protective measures. This risk has even increased after the coming into effect of the Maastricht Treaty, because there are now also majority decisions possible to lower existing standards. Such a general tendency is bound to increase discrepancies on environmental standards within the Community and will thus be, from an environmental point of view, counter-productive, since even environmentally conscious Member States will be reluctant to adopt stricture measures that would lead to a competitive disadvantage of installations on their territory. Finally, it should be realised that the debates at European level about environmental standards, such as for air or water quality, or emission standards never centre on the issue of how much pollution of one or the other contaminant the environment can tolerate, but on the issue of what standards can reasonably be imposed on the polluting industries or other economic agents.

---

[70] Case C-300/89, *Commission v. Council* (note 51 above), Advocate General Tesauro's Opinion para. 7.

As regards waste disposal installations, in my opinion no specific observations are necessary. Measures which fix high standards for disposal must be based on Article 100a. However, the Council, as stated, bases all waste (disposal) installations measures on Article 130s.

It should be added that the transition, made by the Maastricht Treaty, to majority decisions under Article 130s might have eliminated much of the emotions of the past discussions. The remaining difference in the choice of the legal basis is the application of Article 130t. This question is almost political and amounts to asking how much of an integrated Community is in reality provided for under the Treaty.

3.36   The Council's practice might be resumed as follows:

(*a*)   *water*

All measures adopted under Article 130s

(*b*)   *air*

Air emissions from cars, motorcycles etc: Article 100a
Content of petrol, gasoil: Article 100a
Limit-values, emission limits from installations: Article 130s.

(*c*)   *noise*

Noise from cars, motorcycles, machines: Article 100a
Noise from aeroplanes Article 84(2)

(*d*)   *chemicals*

Substances and products: Article 100a
Ozone-depleting substances: Article 130s
Biotechnology: market standards: Article 100a
   research standards: Article 130s
Accident prevention of installations: Article 130s
Eco-audit, labelling schemes: Article 130s
Bans, restrictions for use: Article 100a
(exception: ban of CFCs)

(*e*)   *nature*

Bans, restriction of trade in species: Article 130s
Habitat conservation, other measures: Article 130s

(*f*)   *Waste*

Measures related to specific wastes: Article 100a
All other measures: Article 130s

(g) Measures of general nature

Access to information, environmental impact assessment etc.: Article 130s

ARTICLE 113

The decisions in the area of commercial policy—Articles 110 to 115—are taken   **3.37**
by the Council by qualified majority under Article 113. Commercial measures
might have an impact on the environment. The provisions of Articles 110 to
115 establish exclusive Community competence. In the past, however, the
importance of Article 113 for environmental issues, was diminished as a
follow-up of divergencies on its meaning. Whereas the Commission considered Article 113 as relevant for all commercial provisions and international
agreements, the Council applied Article 113 only in those cases where the
measure in question did not pursue any other objective. Thus, where a trade-
related measure also aimed at the protection of the environment, Article 113
was, according to the Council, not of relevance; instead, other provisions
applied, in particular Article 130s. Therefore in practice, Article 113 was only
rarely applied.

The fact that Article 113 gives exclusive competence to the Community,
whereas, under Article 130r(4) and 130s the competence is shared between the
Community and Member States, might have influenced the respective
interpretation. The supplementary aspect that measures under Article 113
were adopted by qualified majority, whereas measures under Article 130s or,
prior to 1987, under Article 235 required unanimity, has lost its importance
now, since the Maastricht Treaty introduced majority decisions also for
Article 130s.

Jans points out rightly that modern commercial agreements often include   **3.38**
environmental rules, which may also contribute to the "harmonious development of world trade" (Article 110) and that there is no reason to be so unduly
restrictive in the interpretation of Article 113 as the Council.[71] He finds a
number of arguments in different court judgments for a more frequent
application of Article 113; to these it might be added that the Council adheres,
as regards the borderline between Article 100a and 130s, to the theory of
"primary objective" and "accessory objective".[72] There is little reason then
not to follow this theory as regards the borderline between Article 113 and
130s.

The Court of Justice ruled in Case 62/88 that the fact that a commercial
regulation also aimed at the protection of the environment was no reason to
base it on Article 130s, since environmental requirements were component of

---

[71] Jans, *Europees milieurecht in Nederland* (Groningen, 1991), 42 *et seq.*
[72] See above, para. 3.30.

other policies.[73] The Court therefore upheld the Council decision which had based Regulation 3955/87 on trade in radioactively contaminated agricultural products on Article 113.[74] This judgment seems to confirm the Commission's points of view.

However, these legal considerations have not (yet) influenced the Council's decision practice in the past and it is not likely that they will do so in the future. Commercial measures and international agreements which also aim at the protection of the environment, will probably continue to be based on Article 130s.

ARTICLE 130o

3.39 The single European Act incorporated provisions on research and development in to the Treaty. This title became, under the Maastricht Treaty, "research and technological development", Articles 130f to 130o. Article 130i provides for the adoption of a multiannual framework programme, to be adopted under the procedure of Article 189b. Article 130o, the old Article 130q, provides that the Council decides unanimously on measures under Articles 130n (the establishment of joint undertakings or any other structure for the execution of Community research, technological development and demonstration programmes) and by majority decisions under Article 189c on measures for the implementation of the multiannual programme.

Decisions on research and technological development programmes on the environment are taken on the basis of Article 130o, not of Article 130s, as stated by Article 130f(3): "all Community activities including demonstration projects, shall be decided on and implemented in accordance with the provisions of this Title".

[73] Case 62/88, (note 38 above).
[74] Reg. 3955/87: [1987] O.J. L371/14.

FOUR

Community law and national law

Introduction: the effect of Community law

European Community environmental law is not the only law which organises   **4.01**
the preservation, protection and improvement of the quality of the environment. The environmental law of the Member also exists. The Treaty contains
a number of explicit provisions which deal with the interrelationship between
E.C. and national environmental law. There are, furthermore, other general
provisions which affect this relationship.

This chapter will first discuss the Treaty provisions of the relationship
between the European Community and the national system of law, Articles
130t and 100a(4). It then discusses the specific safeguard rules of Articles
100a(5) and 130r(2)(2). Finally, the chapter will examine Member States'
possibilities to legislate in environmental matters which are not or not yet
covered by E.C. legislation, in particular Articles 30 and 36.

Article 130t

Article 130t was introduced into the Treaty by the Single European Act. The   **4.02**
Maastricht Treaty slightly changed the wording and added that national
measures, which were maintained or introduced, had to be notified to the
Commission. The Article balances the Member States' right to adopt
measures to protect the environment against the Community provisions.
Article 118(a)(3) in the social policy section and Article 129(a)(3) in the
consumer policy section contain similar provisions, which thus express the
need to protect diffuse interests within the Community.

Many of the environmental Directives and Regulations adopted by the
Community before the Single European Act entered into force included a
clause to the same effect as Article 130t. Only the rules on specific products
contained no such clause.

Article 130t governs action by the Member States, though only on matters where the Community has adopted rules unanimously or by a qualified majority under Article 130s. If the Community has adopted no rules on the subject, the balance between Community and national legislation is governed by the general rules laid down in the Treaty, notably Articles 30 to 36.

4.03 Article 130t lays down the preconditions for the Member States to adopt legal measures on subjects on which the Community has adopted rules. In other words, the Article sets out from the premise that such national measures are permissible. Consequently, it is not true to say that Articles 130r to 130t transfer responsibility for protecting the environment from the Member States to the Community. On the other hand neither can the respective responsibilities of the Community and the Member States be described as complementary, since this would imply that the Community legislation supplements the national legislation or vice versa. Both are possible in individual cases. But by no means is the Community not empowered or required to take action on any given subject unless one or more Member States have done so already. Similarly, Articles 130r and 130t by no means imply that any Member State needs to wait for the Community to take action before it can adopt measures to protect the environment.

4.04 The Community may, therefore, take measures to attain the objectives set by Article 130r(1) even if none of the Member States has adopted any similar legislation. In this case, the principles laid down in Articles 130r and 130s apply. All in all, the Community's powers over the environment can be summarised as follows:

Protection and preservation of the environment is a fundamental objective in the general interest of the Community and of Member States. Like the non-commercial assets listed in Article 36, the environment cannot be left unprotected. For such time as the Community fails to take action on a given environmental issue, the Member States retain their powers to adopt rules to preserve and protect the environment, provided their measures are compatible with the general rules laid down in the Treaty. When the Community does take action, this by no means ends these powers though they no longer apply to the particular subject governed by the Community legislation.

4.05 Both the Community and the Member States are responsible, "competent" or empowered to take action on environmental issues. In view of the unlimited scope of the term "environment" in Title XVI and Article 130r(1) this holds true of *all* environmental issues. The Treaty assigns no particular area of environmental legislation exclusively to the Community or exclusively to Member States. As can be seen from Article 130t, this applies likewise to subjects already covered by Community legislation. Consequently, the interrelationship between the Community's and the Member States' competencies is flexible, dynamic and complementary.

Article 130t refers solely to protective measures. This possibility raises doubts whether measures could be taken under Article 130t to attain the other objectives stated in Article 130r(1), *i.e.* to preserve and improve the quality of the environment or to ensure rational utilisation of natural resources. However, "protective measure" must be interpreted as including *all* measures from Article 130s to attain the objectives set by Article 130r since, as explained earlier, there is no hard-and-fast dividing line between the various objectives set by Article 130r(1), all of which overlap. **4.06**

Article 130t applies only if the Community has adopted rules on the basis of Article 130s. Article 130t says nothing about the form which the Community rules must take. It is therefore immaterial whether they are set out in a directive, a regulation or a decision to accede to an international convention, whether they were adopted unanimously or by majority vote or whether they apply to exports from the Community or are enshrined in a directive applicable solely within the Community. **4.07**

The measures must be adopted "pursuant to Article 130s". Article 130t does not, therefore, apply if the Community adopts environmental legislation based on, say, Articles 43 or 100a. The thinking behind this is that in cases such as these the rules are concerned more with agricultural policy or the internal market and their prime aim is to attain the objectives of those sections of the Treaty. The fact that they are also of benefit to the environment in no way changes this. **4.08**

In the case of Article 100a this is the logical conclusion to draw from Article 100a(4), which allows the Member States to continue to apply their national provisions to protect the environment even after the Council has adopted a decision by qualified majority. This clause would be completely superfluous if Member States could invoke Article 130t to protect the environment after decisions had been taken on the basis of Article 100a. What is more, it would be incomprehensible why Article 100a(4) refers to decisions taken by qualified majority but Article 130t contains no such restriction. Finally, the objective of completing the internal market will never be attained if Member States remain free in 1995, 1998, or 2010, to take more stringent protective measures and can thus use environmental protection to prevent the free movement of goods.

Only "more stringent" protective measures are permitted under Article 130t. Consequently, the Member States may not adopt different measures from the Community. On the contrary, the tougher protective measures must aim in the same direction and come closer than the Community rules to attaining the objectives of Article 130r(1). It is important that the rules adopted by the **4.09** individual Member State are of the same type as the Community rules to give the Community and the other Member States a chance of aligning on the more stringent State and re-establishing uniform legislation throughout the Community. For example, if the Community decides, on the basis of Article 130s, to halve production and consumption of chlorofluorocarbons, any Member State may still impose an outright ban on production and consumption of CFCs.

However, it may not ban, on the basis of Article 130t, the use of aerosol cans containing CFC gas as a way of protecting the ozone layer. This is not a more stringent measure, but an aliud, another measure: the legality of such a measure is determined according to general Treaty provisions, in particular Articles 30 and 36 as well as Article 100a.

If the Community introduces a system of strict liability for environmental damage, but limits the amount of damages, each Member State may impose strict liability, the amount of which is unlimited. However, it may not provide for unlimited liability for negligence only—with a reversal of the burden of proof as regards negligence—since this is another system. A Member State could, however, prohibit industrial activities in such a case, arguing that experience had shown that these activities gave too often cause for environmental liability.

4.10 The protective measures must be compatible with the Treaty. Consequently, they must not conflict with any provision of the Treaty. In particular, they must not constitute a means of arbitrary discrimination or a disguised restriction on trade between Member States (Articles 30–36). Protectionism is still protectionism even if the aim is to protect the environment. Though Euratom and the Coal and Steel Treaty (ECSC) are not expressly mentioned in Article 130t, it is obvious that national measures must not either conflict with any of those provisions.

4.11 Any protective measures taken by the Member States must be compatible not only with the Treaty but also with the secondary Community legislation.[1] For example, if the Community adopts rules based on Article 130s, allowing the Member States to ban the use of regular leaded petrol but at the same time stipulating that, in order to protect carmakers, importers, dealers and vehicle users, any such ban must be published and communicated to the Commission six months in advance, no Member State may invoke Article 130t to evade this time limit or to ban unleaded regular petrol without prior notification. Since

---

[1] This opinion is contested in legal literature. See, for example, E. Grabitz, *EWG-Vertrag* (looseleaf) (München, 1987) Art. 130t(7): T. Schroer, *Die Kompetenzverteilung zwischen der Europaischen Wirtschaftsgemeinschaft und ihren Mitgliedstaaten auf dem Gebiet des Umweltschutzes* (Frankfurt-Berlin, 1992) p. 224.

Directive 87/416 allowing the Member States to ban leaded regular petrol[2] entered into force on July 21, 1987, the ban could not come into effect in Germany until January 21, 1988 at the earliest, not on January 1, 1988 as originally planned by the German authorities.

If a Community Directive on Article 130s sets limit-values for discharges of lead into waterbodies, any Member State is free to ban lead discharges into waterbodies altogether. However, the Member State may not ban the use of lead in paints since the Directive expressly permits the use of lead in paints, subject to certain limits.[3]

Jans has raised the question, whether measures under Article 130t are also admissable where Community secondary legislation has provided for a total harmonisation of a subject-matter. He concludes that Article 130t is not applicable in such a case and argues in particular that a total harmonisation measure under Article 130s could not be achieved any more since, via Article 130t, Member States were not bound to it.[4]

A practical example is Regulation 880/92 on the creation of a Community eco-labelling system.[5] Even if this Regulation had not contained the possibility for Member States to maintain existing eco-labelling systems, such a possibility would flow out of Article 130t. Therefore, Germany may maintain its Blue-Angel-System at national level, provided it is not seen as an aliud legislation; on this question doubts arise since the German system chose for a different symbol and the Community will never be able to "catch up". Indeed, since Regulation 880/92 is based on Article 130s, a total harmonisation of eco-labelling schemes is not reached at Community level.

Another practical example is Regulation 259/93 on the transport of waste, **4.12** which is based on Article 130s and introduced a "green list" of waste, which may be transported under less strict conditions than normally applicable.[6] The question is, whether Member States are allowed, under Article 130t, to reduce this green list or not to apply it at all, for instance, with the argument that also less dangerous waste should not be transported.

There is little doubt that the Regulation tried to introduce a total harmonisation of rules on the transport of waste. Nevertheless, the fact that the Regulation was based on Article 130s opens the possibility to apply Article 130t, even where the total harmonisation cannot be achieved. Indeed, Articles 130r to 130t do not aim at harmonising national legislation (the word "harmonisation" only appears once, in the newly inserted Article 130r(2)(2)) but aims at environmental protection. Had the Council wished to reach, as

---

[2] Dir. 87/416: [1987] O.J. L225/1.
[3] Dir. 88/379: [1988] O.J. L187/14.
[4] J. Jans, *Europees Milieurecht in Nederland* (Groningen, 1991) pp. 26 *et seq.*
[5] Reg. 880/82: [1992] O.J. L99/1.
[6] Reg. 259/93: [1993] O.J. L30/1.

regards the green list of waste or other aspects of waste transports, a total harmonisation or of rules at Community level, it should have based the Regulation of Article 100a. You cannot have your cake and eat it. The price of recurring to Article 130s is the farewell to total harmonisation. It is for this reason that product-related provisions have to be, in my opinion, normally based on Article 100a, since otherwise the internal market will never be capable of being achieved. And it is for this reason that it is difficult to see at present how an internal market can function where waste legislation, because of Article 130t, is and will continue to considerably diverge from one Member State to another.

4.13   Another opinion goes into an opposite direction and tries to require that measures adopted under Article 130t have only to be compatible with the Treaty but not with secondary Community law.[7] The argument is that otherwise the field of application of Article 130t would be too small, since there are such numerous secondary law provisions. This opinion is based on the assumption that there is a legal principle according to which environmental provisions of the Treaty must be optimised and that they prevail over other provisions of the Treaty.[8] It is thus not surprising to see this opinion principally defended in German environmental literature. In my judgment, this opinion places too much emphasis on the environmental provisions of the Treaty and not enough on the fact that the Community has to try to achieve the different objectives listed in Article 2 and other provisions, not only the best protection of the environment. The Court has ruled in a number of cases that, for instance, Articles 30–36 are no longer examined where the Community legislator has adopted provisions of secondary law. It would be, therefore, somehow absurd to believe that the consensus which was reached in Council in favour of a provision, based on Article 43, 84, 99, 100a or others could be put in question by virtue of Article 130t. After all, none of the different measures to complete the internal market or to put into practice the common agricultural policy appears in the Treaty. They are all secondary Community legislation measures and would, therefore, be called into question—i.e. be at the disposal of the national legislator—by the approach rejected here. Had the authors of the Treaty wished to give such a meaning to Article 130t, they should have made it of general application and not just allow it to be applied where measures are based on Article 130s. Therefore, in the above-mentioned example of eco-labelling schemes, Germany could not introduce, at national level, a provision under which products that are marketed with an eco-label other than the German Blue Angel were not allowed to be marketed in Germany. Such a provision would be in opposition to Regulation 880/92,

---

[7] See references in note 1 above.
[8] See, for a discussion of this principle para. above 2.35.

though it might even be justified under Articles 30–36 by the need not to confuse consumers.

Another example is Directive 89/369 which fixed air emission standards for new installations on the incineration of domestic waste.[9] The Directive is based on Article 130s. Member States are thus entitled to fix more stringent emission standards under Article 130t. However, they are not entitled to ignore Directives 80/779 on limit-values for SO_2, 82/884 on a limit-value for lead[10] or even 85/337 on environmental impact assessments.[11] Thus, where the authorisation for a new incineration installation would lead to an exceeding of the limit values for SO_2, or lead such an installation may not be authorised; where the conditions of Directive 85/337 are fulfilled, a domestic waste installation may only be authorised after an environmental impact assessment has been made.

4.14

Directive 91/689 fixed rules on dangerous waste.[12] The Directive is based on Article 130s. Member States may thus take more stringent protective measures. But they would not be entitled to get rid of the obligation under Article 8 of Directive 87/217 according to which asbestos waste must be disposed of in a way that no asbestos parts could enter the environment.[13]

It follows from this that Member States which follow the provisions of a measure adopted under Article 130s must respect the provisions of all other Community legislation. It makes no sense to allow a Member State to get rid of such an obligation just by introducing more stringent provisions under Article 130t.

4.15

Requesting that measures under Article 130t only need to respect the Treaty but not secondary legislation tries thus to reintroduce a general rule through the backdoor, while Article 130t is expressly limited to a specific situation, *i.e.* to measures adopted under Article 130s.

As stated above, this is exactly what the opinion of optimising the environmental protection aims at: whatever provision is adopted under Community law, Member States are allowed to introduce more stringent protective measures for the environment. This principle is not to be found in the Treaty.

Measures adopted under Article 130t must be notified to the Commission. There is no time-limit for such a notification and the measures must not be notified to the Commission in draft form. For practical reasons, the notification will in particular gain importance for new national measures and

4.16

---

[9] Dir. 86/369: [1989] O.J. L163/32.
[10] Dir. 80/779: [1980] O.J. L229/30; Dir. 82/882: [1982] O.J. L378/15.
[11] Dir. 85/337: [1985] O.J. L175/40.
[12] Dir. 91/689: [1991] O.J. L377/40.
[13] Dir. 87/217: [1987] O.J. L85/40.

for measures which are maintained after the adoption of new Community legislation under Article 130s. It follows from general principles of the Treaty and in particular from Article 5, that Member States are under obligation to inform the Commission as early as reasonably possible of their national measures—and of their intention to maintain them.

In contrast to Article 100a(4) there is no procedure for examination of the national measures as to their compatibility with Community law. Where the Commission is of the opinion that a national measure is not a more stringent protective measure, but something different—an "aliud"—or where it believes that the measure is not compatible with primary or secondary Community legislation, it has, in the last instance, to recur to procedures under Article 169 of the Treaty. The same possibility is open to any other Member State under Article 170 of the E.C. Treaty.

Article 100a(4)

4.17   Article 100a(4) reads as follows:

> "If, after the adoption of a harmonisation measure by the Council, acting by a qualified majority, a Member State deems it necessary to apply national provisions on grounds of major needs referred to in Article 36, or relating to protection of the environment or the working environment, it shall notify the Commission of these provisions.
> The Commission shall confirm the provisions involved after having verified that they are not a means of arbitrary discrimination or a disguised restriction on trade between Member States . . . "

The provision was introduced in the Treaty in 1987, as part of Article 100a which introduced majority decisions for the achievement of the internal market by the end of 1992. It was drafted at the last minute of the Intergovernmental discussions, and not amended by the Maastricht Treaty; its content and its legal consequences are very controversial in legal literature. This is in marked contrast to its use in practice. Indeed, the Commission received, until the end of 1993, only three notifications from Member States under Article 100a.

4.18   During the discussions on the introduction of emission standards for cars, the Danish Government informed the Commission at the end of the eighties that it intended to adopt national more stringent rules, but withdrew this notification when the Community reached agreement on car emission standards.

Germany notified the Commission in 1987 of its intention to prohibit the wood preserver, pentachlorophenol. The Commission informed Germany that it would submit proposals for a Community-wide measure. The proposal was made in 1988. In 1989 Germany adopted a regulation which provided for a total ban of production and marketing of PCP. In 1991 the Community adopted Directive 91/173 which restricted the use of PCP, but did not go as far as the German regulation. Germany notified the Commission of its intention to maintain its national ban. The Commission confirmed the German measure.[14] France considered the Commission decision illegal and seized the Court of Justice. On May 17, 1994 the Court voided the Commission's decision on the grounds of insufficient reasoning [Article 190, E.C. Treaty].

Denmark and the Netherlands have also introduced notifications as regards PCP, on which the Commission had not yet decided.

In 1989, the Council adopted Directive 89/428 on the reduction of waste from the titanium dioxide industry; the Directive was based on Article 130s.[15] On the request of the Commission, the Court of Justice declared that Article 100a would have been the correct legal basis.[16] Thus, the Council adopted Directive 92/112,[17] with practically the same content as Directive 89/428. However, the Council declared the standards in the Directive to be minimum standards, thus allowing Member States to adopt more stringent measures at national level.

The legal controversy on the interpretation of Article 100a(4) concerns the following aspects: **4.19**

(a) Is the provision also applicable where the Council takes unanimous decisions?

(b) Are also those Member States entitled to recur to this provision which have not voted against a Community measure?

(c) Is it possible, under this provision, to introduce new legislation at national level which did not yet exist at the moment of the adoption of the Community measure?

The opinion of legal writers is influenced on how they balance Community integration, the achievement of the internal market and environmental considerations. Those who answer the three questions above positively see in Article 100a(4) mainly a provision which allows optimising environmental protection. They argue as regards the first question that the wording does not indicate its application to unanimous decisions. Article 100a(4) is an exception and must therefore be interpreted restrictively. A Member State which agrees

---

[14] Dir. 91/173: [1991] O.J. L85/24; Commission (decision to confirm the German measure): [1992] O.J. C334/8.
[15] Dir. 89/429: [1989] O.J. L203/50.
[16] Case C-300/89, *Commission* v. *Council*: [1991] I E.C.R. 2867 (titanium dioxide).
[17] Dir. 92/112: [1992] O.J. L409/11.

to an E.C. measure, must, under an integration philosophy, not be allowed at a later stage to opt out of the consensus reached.

4.20   As to the second question, the writers who allow all Member States to recur to the provisions of Article 100a(4) argue that a Member State may have a clear interest of see a specific measure applied Community-wide, even if that Member State would think that the measure still does not go far enough. They also argue that a constraint to vote against a measure would easily lead to negative majorities, since even those Member States who generally approve of the measure would be obliged to vote against it in order to keep the option of Article 100a(4) open. As to the third question, the writers who also favour the application of Article 100a(4) to new measures, argue that the wording is not clear. Allowing new legislation to be adopted under this clause would increase environmental protection, at least in parts of the Community, it would enable the Community to profit from legal innovation in Member States and would allow environmentally progressive Member States to set up new protective measures thus generally increasing and optimising environmental protection. Also, an interpretation that only existing rules came under Article 100a(4) would favour those Member States which already have strict environmental standards.

4.21   The opponents see Article 100a(4) rather as an exceptional provision in the system for the achievement of the internal market, which must be interpreted narrowly. They answer all three questions in the negative.

As regards question (a), they invoke the wording of the provision, which only should apply in exceptional circumstances. Numerous, if not most measures under Article 100a are adopted unanimously and there is no reason at all to apply the exceptional provisions to such cases. On question (b), again the wording of the provision is taken as an argument. As to question (c), the wording of the Article 100a(4) is different from Articles 130t and 118a(3), where Member States have expressly been entitled to "maintain or introduce" national legislation. "Apply" in Article 100a(4) must thus have a more limited meaning, *i.e.* that a Member State is not compelled, by majority decisions, against its will, to lower its existing standards.

4.22   In my opinion, Article 100a(4) is a provision of rules on the internal market. Its aim is to contribute to achieving the completion of this internal market. Thus, the provision is not applicable where unanimous decisions are taken— though I admit that this result is influenced by the answer to the third question. As regards question two, it must be remembered that the wording of paragraph 4 does not mention specific Member States. Neither is there any provision which establishes with the necessary legal certainty—the formal indication in the Council minutes, publication in the Official Journal, etc.—

which Member State has voted against a specific proposal. Therefore, any Member State may, in the case of majority decisions, invoke Article 100a(4).

Finally, Member States are only allowed to continue to apply existing national **4.23** measures, but may not introduce new legislation. The following arguments are offered to support this opinion:

(1) If Article 100a(4) would also allow the introduction of new legislation, this would mean that the internal market could never really be completed, since Member States could, in 1995, 1998 or even later, opt out of the common rules and go their own way. Had the authors of the Treaty wished to introduce such far-reaching reservation of the achievement of the internal market, a clearer expression of this will would have been necessary.

(2) The Maastricht Treaty which revised the drafting of numerous Treaty provisions and in particular of the provisions of Articles 130r to 130t, has not changed the drafting of Article 100a(4); specifically, it has not adapted that provision to the wording of Article 130t ("maintain or introduce").

(3) Article 100a(4) does not apply to environmental legislation alone. It also refers to rules on health, safety, public security, industrial property and the protection of industrial and commercial property. Thus, all legislation on food, pharmaceuticals, chemicals, cars, workers' protection, etc. would come under this provision—which would mean that Article 100a(4) is a general opt-out clause of the internal market. Neither the Single European Act nor the Maastricht Treaty allow the slightest interpretation of this kind. Articles 7a—Article 8a old version—is clear and unambiguous and it is not possible to reinterpret the whole system of internal-market-completion via a single provision that was, according to its wording and its position within the system of Article 100a, conceived and drafted as an exceptional provision, which therefore needs to be interpreted narrowly.

(4) The introduction of specific, accelerated control rules in Article 100a(4) sub-paragraph 2 and 3, which deviate from the general rules of Articles 169 *et seq.*, make sense were, at the moment of the adoption of Community measures, pre-existing national legislation is in question. Indeed, in such cases it is important to quickly obtain legal certainty of which rules apply within the internal market. However, there is no need for such accelerated rules where new legislation would be introduced afterwards; such legislation must be notified in draft form to the Commission anyway and allows thus a control of its compatibility with the Treaty provisions. It is only logical that neither Article 130t nor Article 118a(3) provide for specific, accelerated control procedures in the case of national legislation.

109

It remains to be seen how the European Court will decide on this controversy, once a case is submitted.

The safeguard clause of Articles 130r(2)(2) and 100a(5)

4.24 The Maastricht Treaty inserted the new sub-paragraph of Article 130r(2)(2), which allows Member States to take, under certain conditions, provisional safeguard measures. The safeguard clause applies to decisions taken under Article 130s(1) and 130s(2). It allows Member States to provisionally use restrictive measures in respect of situations which have already been regulated by the Community legislator. The clause obviously followed the drafting of Article 100a(5), though its wording is slightly different.

4.25 The safeguard clauses of Articles 130r(2)(2) and 100a(5) both apply in those cases, where secondary E.C. legislation expressly contains a provision which enables Member States to take safeguard measures. As such this rule is not innovative. Indeed, a long time before Article 100a(5) was introduced in the Treaty, in 1987, E.C. Directives contained safeguard clauses which allowed Member States to provisionally deviate from E.C. standards.[18] Member States have made use of such clauses, sometimes, it is true, for protectionist reasons.[19] Therefore, the essential part in the provisions of Articles 130r(2)(2) and 100a(5) is less the possibility for the E.C. legislator to provide for a safeguard clause, but rather the provision that any national safeguard measure will be the subject of an E.C. control or inspection procedure. This clarifies that national measures under the safeguard clause may only be provisional, limited in time and subject of a decision by the E.C. as to its compatibility with E.C. law.

The question, whether Article 130r(2)(2) also applies to measures which are based on Articles 43, 84 or other provisions of the Treaty, is of academic value only. Indeed, nothing would prevent the E.C. legislator from including into a

---

[18] See, for instance the safeguard clause in Directive 67/548 in its present form (Dir. 92/32: [1992] O.J. L154/1): 1. Where a Member State has detailed evidence that a substance, although satisfying the requirements of this Directive, constitutes a hazard for man or the environment by reasons of its classification, packaging or labelling, it may provisionally prohibit the sale of that substance or subject it to special conditions in its territory. It shall immediately inform the Commission and the other Member States of such action and give reasons for its decision.
2. The Commission shall consult the Member States concerned within six weeks, then give its view without delay and take the appropriate measures.
3. If the Commission considers that technical adaptations to this Directive are necessary, such adaptations shall be adopted, either by the Commission or by the Council in accordance with the procedure laid down in Article 21; in such case, the Member State which has adopted the safeguard measures may maintain them until the adaptations enter into force.
[19] See, for instance Commission Decision 90/420: [1990] O.J. L222/49, informing Denmark that a specific substance is not carcinogenic.

measure adopted under Article 43 a safeguard clause for Member States, though there is no express provision for a safeguard clause in Article 43.[20]

Since Article 130t allows Member States generally to take more stringent protective measures, the field of application of the safeguard clause is likely to be rather limited. An example could be Regulation 259/93 on the transport of waste, which provides that "green" waste may be transported within the Community under relatively easy conditions.[21] Provided the Regulation contained a safeguard clause—which it does not—a Member State could invoke that clause and provisionally restrict the circulation of green waste, for instance because it is thought to present too high a risk to groundwater. Other examples could be taken from other waste Directives, which the Council bases on Article 130s,[22] on the Regulation of export and import of chemicals,[23] the Regulation on the ozone-depleting substances[24], etc. Generally, the safeguard clause has a potential field of application where Community measures that are product-related are based on Article 130s. Since the national measures are of provisional nature, they will mainly be used to take care of a specific, adhoc problem and thus be of administrative character, regulatory or legislative measures mainly coming under Article 130t.

4.26

Articles 30-36

Articles 130r-130t regulate the preconditions, content and consequences in the event that the Community adopts a measure to protect the environment. Articles 30-36, on the other hand, regulate the question of the relationship of the Community law to national law in the absence of Community measures to protect the environment.

4.27

Article 36 provides that Articles 30 to 34 "shall not prelude prohibitions or restrictions, justified on grounds of . . . the protection of health and life of humans, animals or plants . . . ". Such prohibitions or restrictions are, however, not permitted to be used as a means of arbitrary discrimination or a disguised restriction on trade between Member States. Thus, Article 36 does allow certain trade restrictions, though it enumerates the justifications for any such restriction.

---

[20] See, also, Dir. 91/414 on the licensing of plant protection products: [1991] O.J. L 230/1. This Directive is based on Article 43 and yet contains a safeguard clause in Article 11.

[21] Reg. 259/93 (note 6 above).

[22] See, in particular Dir. 91/156 on waste: [1991] O.J. L78/32 and Dir. 91/689 on hazardous waste (note 12 above).

[23] Reg. 2455/92: [1992] O.J. L251/13.

[24] Reg. 594/91: [1991] O.J. L67/1.

While actions in favour of the environment may contribute towards protecting human health, it is obvious that numerous measures which aim at the protection of the environment cannot be considered as protecting the health and life of humans, animals or plants; such measures include environmental taxes, environmental labelling, waste prevention measures, measures to assess the environmental impact and measures on environmental liability. Furthermore, even measures to reduce discharges of pollutants into water, air or soil, measures to reduce the noise level of cars or to provide for the designation of habitats, would only with very artistic interpretation methods be capable of being subsumed under Article 36. This again would contradict the interpretation rule used by the European Court on Article 36 that an exceptional provision must be interpreted narrowly.

4.28 Thus, while some environmental measures might be considered to aim at the protection of health or life of humans, animals or plants, the majority of environmental measures will not be capable of being subsumed under Article 36. The criteria whether a measure aims at the protection of health or life or whether this is not the case, seems to be the "direct effect" of a measure: where a measure directly affects the protection of humans or fauna/flora, it may be justified under Article 36; where this is not the case, the measure is an environmental measure. For instance, the restriction on the use of CFC's in products aims at the protection of the ozone layer. While damage of the ozone layer may increase diseases of humans, such as skin cancer, the measure remains an environmental measure, since the health risk of humans is an indirect one.[25]

Such measures include the hunting or capturing methods of plants and animals. Where these methods are either not humane or non-selective or both, Member States may, in the absence of E.C. measures, take action.

The E.C. itself has adopted a number of such measures, in particular:

— the prohibition of importing skins from seal pups, because of the methods of killing of the pups;[26]
— the import ban on ivory in order to protect the African elephant;[27]
— the prohibition of furs from animals caught by leg-hold traps or even from countries where leg-hold traps are in use;[28]
— the prohibition of use of drift-nets of more than 2.5 km length.[29]

[25] See, however, the Commission's proposal for a Regulation on trade in endangered species: [1992] O.J. C26/1.
[26] Dir. 83/129: [1983] O.J. L91/30.
[27] Commission Reg. 2496/89: [1989] O.J. L240/5.
[28] Reg. 3254/91: [1991] O.J. L308/1.
[29] Reg. 345/92: [1992] O.J. L42/15.

Except the second example, there is no question of protecting endangered species. The ban was rather pronounced to prohibit certain capturing methods.

Since the E.C. does not have greater or more environmental competence than—in the absence of E.C. measures—the individual Member States, such measures may also be taken by individual Member States.

Of particular importance is the question whether a Member State is allowed to   **4.29**
resort to Article 36 in order to protect the life of plants or animals in another Member State. To quote an example, Germany prohibits the marketing of corallium rubrum, a coral which lives in the Mediterranean, in particular in Italy, and whose existence is threatened, though no international convention has laid down its threatened status. The coral is used in Italy to produce jewellery.

Article 36 does not restrict the protection of health and life of humans, animals and plants to those living in the Member State which takes the restrictive measure. The requirement of nature protection and, more generally, of the protection of the environment is not geographically limited under the E.C. Treaty. Allowing the protection of the ozone layer or of the global climate by unilateral action of Member States, but not allowing such action in the case of nature protection seems contradictory. I am thus of the opinion that a Member State may protect the fauna and flora in another Member State where there is a threat to life of plants or animals. It is obvious, though, that a particularly careful examination as to whether such restrictions are scientifically justified and whether the measure does not constitute a disguised restriction on trade remains necessary. The examples given in paragraph 4.2.8 above show that European practice follows the same lines.

The European Court interprets Article 36 in a restrictive way and considers   **4.30**
the enumeration of reasons which could justify a trade restriction as exhaustive and as not being capable of being enlarged. However, in its landmark decision *"Cassis de Dijon"*, the Court interpreted Article 30 of the Treaty in a way that reached practically the same result as an enlargement of the grounds of Article 36.[30] Indeed, the Court declared that in the absence of Community legislation, a national restriction to the free circulation of goods from other Member States had to be accepted to the extent that it was justified by mandatory requirements; the Court mentioned as such mandatory requirements the necessity of fiscal controls, fair trading practices and consumer protection and indicated that there might be other mandatory requirements.

---

[30] Case 120/78, *Rewe-Zentral A.G.* v. *Bundesmonopolverwaltung*: [1979] E.C.R. 649, [1979] 3 C.M.L.R. 494 (*Cassis de Dijon*).

The Court added further that the measures taken in order to satisfy such a mandatory requirement had to be non-discriminatory and proportional. Furthermore, it is implicit in the Court's jurisdiction that the measure must aim at the protection of the environment and may not, in reality, pursue other objectives, such as protectionist objectives.

The discussion on the proportionality principle in Article 30 may be summarised by stating that a measure is proportional when it aims to pursue a legitimate political objective, when the measure is appropriate to approach this objective, when it is necessary to reach or approach the objective and when there is no measure which is less restrictive for the free circulation of goods. Despite numerous Court decisions on Article 30, many details of the proportionality principle remain open, particularly as regards environmental questions, since few environmental cases have ever been decided upon by the Court as regards Article 30.

4.31 In 1988, the Court recognised that the protection of the environment was a mandatory requirement which could justify restrictions to the free circulation of goods. In this case—Case 302/86, "Danish bottles"[31] the Commission attacked a Danish regulation which introduced a deposit-and-return system for drink containers. The Commission considered the system to be incompatible with Article 30. It was followed in its assessment by the Advocate General, but not by the Court.

The Court held, rather, that Denmark was entitled to introduce such a system since that system aimed at the protection of the environment, an objective of general Community interest. Denmark, so said the Court, was entitled to set up an efficient system of waste prevention and such an efficient system required the introduction of a deposit-and-return system, even though the practical complications might make it more difficult for non-Danish producers and traders to comply with the system.

4.32 Denmark had even gone one step further. In order to reach a particularly high number of returns it had prohibited the use of metal cans. And it had requested that all other drink containers had to be authorised, trying by this measure to standardise bottled and other containers, and thus reach a higher return percentage. Under certain conditions, foreign traders who marketed less than 3000 hl drinks per year in Denmark, were not obliged to use authorised (standardised) containers. As regards the ban of metal cans, the Commission accepted that this measure was taken in order to protect the (Danish) environment. Thus this ban was not attacked in Court. The attempts of the United Kingdom, as a third party intervenor, to obtain a judgment of

---

[31] Case 302/86, *Commission* v. *Denmark*: [1988] E.C.R. 4607, [1989] 1 C.M.L.R. 619 (Danish Bottles).

the Court on the ban of metal cans, failed; the Court did not address this ban.[32]

As regards the requirement of licensing containers, the Court admitted that the Danish measure was capable of achieving a higher number of returns than a simple deposit-and-return system.[33] Despite that—and in my opinion in some contradiction to its own statements on the deposit-and-return system— the Court found the licensing requirement excessive and therefore contrary to Article 30.[34] It did not accept that only traders with less than 3000 hl turnover in drinks were exempted from asking for a licence.

The Court indicated that Denmark was entitled to fix the degree of protection of the environment which it wanted. And if the degree which Denmark had opted for required, in order to be attained, the introduction of a deposit-and-return system, such a restriction to the free circulation of goods had to be accepted under Article 30. However, when Denmark wanted to introduce an even better system of environmental protection, the measures which were introduced to attain this better protection were considered excessive since they were not really necessary.

In the only environment case where a national court submitted a case to the European Court under Article 177, that national court did not ask whether the national measure was compatible with Article 30 but only asked for its compatibility with secondary environmental legislation,[35] so the Court of Justice did not decide on Article 30.   **4.33**

The ambiguity of the Court's decision in 302/86 led to numerous different interpretations. One of the most intricate questions is whether the Member States may, in the absence of Community legislation, themselves fix the degree of protection of the environment which they wish to achieve on their territory; if one reads the part of the judgment on the 3000 hl limitation, one must come to the conclusion that Member States may only introduce a "reasonable" degree of protection of the environment—whatever it is. Many authors have argued, that Article 30 and the free circulation of goods is of paramount importance to the E.C. Treaty, though there is no explicit decision of the Court with such a statement. This could lead to the conclusion that environmental considerations, as other considerations, should only be allowed

---

[32] The United Kingdom attempts can be seen in the Court's decision (note 31 above), section "Facts and procedure". See, also, P. Kromarek: "Environmental protection and the free movement of goods: the *Danish Bottle* case." [1990] *Journal of Environmental Law* 89.

[33] Court of Justice (note 31 above), para. 20, "It is undoubtedly true that the existing system for returning approved containers ensures a maximum rate of re-use and therefore a very considerable degree of protection of the environment".

[34] Court of Justice (note 31 above), para. 21: "Nevertheless, the system for returning non-approved containers is capable of protecting the environment". Thus, protection is allowed, but not maximum protection.

[35] Case 380/87, *Enichem Base Spa* v. *Cinisello-Balsamo*: [1989] E.C.R. 2491, [1991] 1 C.M.L.R. 313.

to restrict the free circulation of goods to the extent that this is "reasonable", in other words that in the case of conflict, free-trade considerations prevail over environmental considerations.

4.34   In my understanding, the Maastricht Treaty on European Union points to another interpretation. The environment is expressly mentioned in the Treaty and no indication seems to exist that it is less important than other objectives. On the contrary. The rule of Article 130r(2) phrase 2 is unique in the whole Treaty; environmental protection requirements are a component of other Community policies. Nowhere in the Treaty is the same said of free circulation of goods. Furthermore, Commission proposals in the area of the internal market must be based on a high level of protection (Article 100a(3)), the only provision in the Treaty which contains quality requirements for the Commission's proposals. Article 100a(4) and Article 130t allow Member States, once a Community environmental measure has been taken, to apply or to introduce[36] more protective measures at national level.

All these provisions clearly show the importance which the Treaty attaches to the protection of the environment. In view of this importance, I come to the conclusion that in the absence of Community rules, it is the Member States which decide the degree of protection they want to have for the environment, at least as regards their own territory. Thus, where, for instance, a Member State decides that there should be no metal cans in its environment, the inherent restriction to trade which such a ban of metal cans contains will have to be accepted by the Commission; and it could not be argued that such a ban is "unreasonable" or excessive.

The system of the E.C. Treaty itself seems to confirm this interpretation. Indeed, if one were thinking of a Community measure under Article 100a which is adopted by majority decision and declares all beverage containers, including metal containers, admissible a Member State would then, under Article 100a(4), be entitled to continue to have metal cans prohibited on its territory without any reasonableness-criterium applying. It seems contradictory then to apply criteria such as "reasonableness" when a national measure is examined under Article 30, *i.e.* before a Community measure is adopted.

4.35   The interpretation to be given to the Treaty system is rather, that it is the Member State which is entitled to determine the environmental measure in order to reach the level of protection which the same Member State has fixed. Where such measures are not an arbitrary discrimination or a disguised restriction on trade between Member States they cannot be questioned under Article 30. This interpretation thus takes the criteria established under Article

---

[36] It follows from what was said above in paras. 4.22 *et seq.*, that, as regards Article 100a, the introduction of new measures is not permitted.

100a(4)—"arbitrary discrimination" and "disguised restriction on trade"—as the means to determine the demarcation line in Article 30 between national measures and Community requirements. Indeed it does not seem possible to imagine a national measure which could be justified under Article 30 criteria but not (once a harmonisation measure under Article 100a(4) was adopted by a majority decision) be acceptable under Article 100a(4). Likewise, a measure which is unacceptable under Article 30 criteria cannot, it is submitted, be acceptable under Article 100a(4) criteria.

Article 100a(4) does not merely allow a "reasonable" degree of environmental measures by a Member State to continue to exist, despite a Community harmonisation measure adopted by majority decisions. Therefore, it seems impossible to declare, as to the European Court did in Case 302/86 (though admittedly in a case to which the Single Act provisions of the Treaty did not yet apply) that measures which go beyond the "reasonable" degree are contrary to Article 30. If one thought this argument through further, one would have to come to the conclusion that total bans of substances or products are almost always incompatible with Article 30, since an authorisation system, together with appropriate labelling and severe controls of use, elimination, etc. would reach a similar result, though perhaps not quite as effective as a total ban.[37]

A good illustration is a case concerning pentachlorophenol (PCP), a chemical substance which is used principally as a wood preservative and is considered dangerous to man and the environment. In 1987, Germany notified the Commission of its intention to severely restrict the use of PCP. The Commission asked Germany under Directive 83/189 to withhold its project since it intended to elaborate Community legislation. In 1989, Germany adopted its regulation which contained a total ban of PCP.[38] Directive 91/173 adopted in 1991, did not contain a total ban of PCP, but only severe restrictions on use.[39] Germany then notified the Commission under Article 100a of its intention to maintain its regulation. In 1992, the Commission confirmed this according to Article 100a(4).[40]

4.36

While the Commission decision is to be fully approved, it would be impossible to imagine that before the adoption of Directive 91/173 the German

---

[37] The Court has never explicitly objected against such a general interdiction. On the contrary, in case 125/88, Nijman: [1989] E.C.R. 3533, the Court expressly decided that Dutch bans of certain pesticides were compatible with Article 30.

[38] Reg. of December 12, 1989: Bundesgesetzblatt 1989, Vol. I, of December 22, 1989.

[39] Dir. 91/173: [1991] O.J. L85/24.

[40] Commission (note 14 above); France filed an application to the Court in this matter, not against the German measure, but against the Commission, for having incorrectly interpreted Article 100a(4), Case C-41/93. In a judgment of May 17, 1994, the Court decided that the Commission had not sufficiently stated the reasons of its decision [Art. 190 E.C. Treaty].

regulation was incompatible with Article 30, since it was disproportionate. Though the level of protection ensured by the Community Directive is effective, the German Regulation is even more effective; and one cannot, under Article 100a(4) and under Article 30, deny the right to a Member State to determine what kind of environmental protection it considers to be effective.

4.37 The Court is of the opinion that the criteria laid down in the last sentence of Article 36,—"arbitrary discrimination" and "disguised restriction on trade"—are an expression of the principle of proportionality. Thus, it is likely that it will give the same interpretation to the requirements of arbitrary discrimination and disguised restriction on trade in Article 100a(4). Following this line of argument, the national measures for protecting the environment would, in the absence of harmonisation measures, be allowed where they are necessary to attain the legitimate aim of protecting the environment. It seems obvious that the question of what is a legitimate degree of (environment) protection and what is necessary to attain this degree creates uncertainty and ambiguity in the interpretation of Article 30. Indeed, who shall decide whether a 100 per cent. use of returnable bottles is necessary to reach an appropriate environmental protection in Denmark or whether 80 per cent. would be enough. It is submitted that it is Denmark which has to fix the degree of environmental protection and that it is not possible to use criteria as "disguised restriction on trade" and declare such decisions to protect the environment to be disproportionate.

Such a conclusion is also in conformity with the principle of preventive and precautionary action which is one of the leading principles of environmental policy, not only at Community level, but independently of the acting body.

4.38 Some practical examples may help to illustrate these principles in the environmental sector:

Smog-Regulations. The Regulations, adopted in the 1980s by the German Lander, provide that private cars which are equipped with catalytic converters were allowed to continue circulating even in the event of a smog alarm, while other vehicles without this technology were not. The Commission took the view that this measure discriminated car producers from other Member States, since the Community provisions had taken the emissions from vehicles, whether or not equipped with catalytic converters, to be equivalent. According to the Commission, foreign vehicle manufacturers were more severely affected by the German measures than domestic producers.

When the Commission changed its policy in Spring 1989 and worked for Community emission standards which would require catalytic converter equipment, it filed the case.

There is no E.C. legislation on smog. Thus, Member States were free to decide on measures to take in the case of Smog, as long as these measures did not discriminate and were objectively capable of helping to fight air pollution. Since cars with catalytic converters emit less pollutants than cars without such converters, it was up to Germany to decide whether it wanted to make this difference a criterion for differentiation.

Phosphates in detergents. By regulation of April 20, 1988, Italy has limited **4.39** the phosphate content in detergents, in order to fight eutrophication of waters. Since there is a technology which produces detergents with little or no phosphate and since domestic products and imported products are equally affected by the regulations, there is no infringement of Article 30.

Prohibition of metal cans for beer. In 1988, Ireland planned to prohibit the **4.40** use of metal cans for beer. Environmental considerations might plead for prohibition of metal cans. However, it is obvious that the environment is in the same way affected, whether the metal can stems from soft drinks or from beer. Therefore, environmental considerations alone could not justify the envisaged measure; as a consequence other aspects of that case, such as competition, import of foreign beer as a possible reason for the measure, became prominent. When the Commission asked for evidence of which reasons other than environmental reasons, could justify the measure, Ireland abandoned its projects.

Prohibition of plastic bags. Several municipalities in Italy prohibited the **4.41** marketing of non-biodegradable plastic bags, based on Italian decrees of December 21, 1984, July 27, 1987, August 31, 1987 and September 9, 1988. In 1989, the European Court ruled that secondary Community legislation was not opposed to this ban. The Court left the question of compliance with Article 30 undecided—Community legislation does not exist. Since plastic bags may cause considerable environmental problems, an infringement of Article 30 does not seem to exist.

Lead capsules of alcoholic beverages. Legislation in the Federal Republic of **4.42** Germany to prohibit or to limit the use of lead capsules for wine and spirits could affect the marketing of those beverages from other Member States. However, lead capsules can easily be replaced by capsules of other substances. And the toxicity of lead is all too well known. A national measure which aims at reducing the quantities of lead in domestic waste and which affects all producers and traders in the same way is therefore compatible with Article 30.

The Community legislator has, in the meantime, adopted rules for a Community-wide ban.[41]

4.44 *Deposit for plastic bottles.* By regulation of December 1988, Germany introduced a mandatory deposit system for plastic bottles for beverages. It was the declared objective of the measure to limit the increase in the use of plastic bottles and in particular to stop the further increase in market shares of large plastic bottles. This measure had particular effects on the import of beverages from other member countries, since plastic is lighter in weight than glass and can thus be transported more easily.

The prevention of plastic waste is a legitimate objective of environmental policy. As the German measure affects all plastic bottles for beverages and equally efficient measures which affect imports less, are not available, the introduction of a mandatory deposit system is legitimate under Article 30.

4.45 In July 1993, Belgium adopted legislation on an environmental tax on a number of products, in particular packages for drinks, throw-away cameras and razors, batteries, pesticides and paper. Products, which were submitted to that tax had to carry a distinctive sign, showing that they were eco-taxed, and also the amount of tax.

The problem is, whether Article 30 applies at all in this case. The Belgian measure is clearly a national tax which comes under Article 95 rather than Article 30 of the Treaty.[42] Directive 92/12 expressly provides for rules on the fiscal marking of products.[43] The mere existence of Article 95 indicates that fiscal measures are not, generally, to be considered as measures that come under Article 30; this is confirmed by secondary legislation, which clearly distinguishes between the labelling of a product and its fiscal marking. There is thus no possibility to assess the compatibility of the Belgian eco-tax under Article 30. Belgium may, therefore, introduce such a tax, provided it does not discriminate between Belgian and other products.

4.46 *Taxes for plastic bags.* Section 1 and 9 of the Italian Act 397 of September 9, 1988 on industrial waste, together with Act 475 of November 9, 1988 imposed a production tax of 100 lire on producers of non-biodegradable plastic bags, which the trader hands over to consumers; an equal tax is raised from importers of such bags. The Act expressly mentions environmental reasons for this tax. Furthermore, all plastic bags which are handed over to the consumers, shall have to have a minimum size and shall have an indication

---

[41] See, for instance Reg. 3280/92: [1992] O.J. L327/3.
[42] Case 74/76, *Janelli et Volpi*: [1977] E.C.R. 557, [1977] 2 C.M.L.R. 688; Case 78-83/90, *Compagnie Commerciale de l'Ouest and others* v. *Receveur principal des douanes de la Pallice Port*: [1992] I E.C.R. 1847; Case C-17/91, *Lornoy*, judgment of December 16, 1992, not yet reported; Case C-266/91, *Celulosa Beira*, judgment of August 2, 1993 not yet reported.
[43] Dir. 92/12, [1992] O.J. L76/1.

informing the user of the raw material used and asking him not to throw away the plastic bag. The notion "non-biodegradable" shall be defined by regulation.

The taxes are not raised for plastic bags that are bio-degradable or that are not handed over to the consumer. Thus, they clearly aim at protecting the environment, since the taxes do not affect the production, import and use of all plastic sacks, but only of those whose elimination as waste leads to considerable changes in the environment.

The same Italian Act provides from July 1, 1989 on—with transition periods till end 1990—the use of specific materials for the production of plastic sacks; it is the purpose of this rule to obtain a biodegradability of at least 90 per cent.

The general character of those measures which apply to Italian and foreign producers and traders in the same way, cannot be put into question by Community law because there are no Community rules for plastic sacks.

Eco-taxes. Eco-taxes (on CFC's, packaging containers or others) are not to **4.47** be examined under Article 30, but rather under Article 95. National tax on a product is not a product-related measure which comes under Articles 30 to 36 and which is to be harmonised under Article 100a, but there are specific rules: in the absence of E.C. legislation, Article 95 applies and the harmonisation of national measures is to take place according to Article 99. Article 95 provides for prohibition of discrimination. The proportionality principle is not mentioned. This is a consequence of the fact that (environmental) taxes do not have the improvement of the environment as their only objective. They also have other objectives, such as to ensure income to the administration or to finance staff, equipment or research. The cumulative effect of the different objectives can only be reached by fixing a specific tax rate, whatever the concrete amount of that rate is. Tax rates, therefore, cannot be disproportionate.

The European Court has only in one case considered that Article 30 could be of application, *i.e.* in cases where no national production exists and the tax would effectively bar the import of products from another Member State.[44] This theoretical consideration by the Court is to be completed, as far as an environmental tax is concerned, with the observation that even in such cases a national tax may be compatible with Article 30, namely, in those cases where a Member State has environmental grounds to raise such a tax. Where, for instance, a Member State would not like to have metal cans in its environment, it would be entitled, instead of prohibiting their use, to charge a high, dissuasive tax for them.

---

[44] Court of Justice, Case C-47/88, *Commission v. Denmark*: [1990] I. E.C.R. 4509.

4.48 *Product use.* Greece prohibited, by way of legislation, the import of diesel cars for private use, arguing that air pollution in Athens and in Thessaloniki required such a measure. Later, Greece amended its legislation. It now authorises the sale of diesel cars in Greece, but prohibits, again for reasons of air pollution, their use in the Athens and Thessaloniki regions. Ireland prohibited, by regulation, the sale of bituminous coal in the Dublin area in order to fight air pollution.

A total ban of imports (sales) for private diesel cars in order to combat air pollution in two regions is obviously disproportionate. There is no reason for such a far-reaching ban. This is different from the regional ban for bituminous coal in Dublin which the Commission had actually accepted and which enabled Ireland to finally comply with the requirements of Directive 80/779 on limit-values for sulphur dioxide and black smoke in the Dublin area. The Irish measure is neither discriminating nor disproportionate, since most of the air pollution in Dublin came from private households which used bituminous coal.

Whether the prohibition to use diesel cars in the two Greek regions is an appropriate means to fight air pollution, seems very doubtful. It would have to be shown that the air pollution in the two regions is primarily due to the use of diesel cars, but not due to the use of petrol-driven cars, nor due to industrial or other economical activity nor to household heating. In view of the substances contained in diesel, compared to petrol, this can be excluded. I am therefore of the opinion that the Greek measure is discriminating and objectively not capable of reaching its aim, *i.e.* the reduction of air pollution in the two Greek regions.

No rule prevents, of course, local authorities from banning traffic from cities in order to fight air pollution or noise, or to prevent traffic congestion and other nuisances as long as such measures apply to cars without discrimination. The Commission also accepted that lorry traffic through a village was prohibited and that exceptions for local trucks were made.[45] Such local exceptions still apply to local trucks, independently from the type of the truck. There is thus no discriminatory element in such a measure.

4.49 *Ban of ammunition and CFCs.* In 1991, the Netherlands, following in that similar measures taken by Denmark prohibited, the sale of lead-containing ammunition for hunting purposes in order to reduce the quantity of lead in the natural environment.

There are no E.C. rules on the lead content of ammunition. The eating of lead-containing ammunition by ducks and other animals (birds) creates environmental problems. Even if lead-free ammunition is not quite as apt for hunting purposes, it is up to the Dutch authorities to decide whether they

---

[45] Commission Written Question 1715/90: [1991] O.J. C130/5.

want to have lead-containing ammunition used for hunting purposes in the Netherlands or not. The measure cannot be considered to be disproportionate.

In 1990, Luxembourg prohibited the use of CFC's and HCFC's in the equipment of air conditioning for buildings. E.C. legislation on CFC's does not cover products, so that Article 30 is the appropriate legal yardstick for assessment. Since ammoniac is capable of being used instead of CFC's or HCFC's, there exists neither an element of discrimination nor of disproportionality visible in the legislation adopted by Luxembourg.

Aluminium, PVC and tropical timber. A number of German Länder have **4.50** taken measures to stop State aids to the construction of houses, where construction material is used that consists of aluminium, tropical timber or PVC. Since I am of the opinion that financial measures, fiscal incentives and taxes have to be assessed under Articles 92 and 95, Article 30 does not apply to these German measures, even if they had as a consequence that the use of this construction material would diminish.

However, if one were slightly changing the case and considered measures which provide for the restriction or the prohibition of use of aluminium, tropical timber or PVC, the provisions on the free circulation of goods would become relevant. Directive 89/106[46] provides for the free circulation of construction material. It fixes the general conditions for health, safety and environmental protection to which construction material must correspond. These requirements aim at the protection of man and the environment during and after the construction period and try to ensure that buildings do not, during their construction period and use, constitute a risk to man (including workers) and the environment. Environmental considerations which deal with the production of raw materials or with the disposal of construction material after the end of the lifetime of the building, are not the subject of the Directive. In the absence of secondary E.C. legislation, the compatibility of such restrictions/bans has to be assessed according to Articles 30–36.

As regards tropical timber, it seems obvious that the environmental concern is **4.51** less the environmental protection in the specific tropical country otherwise such restrictions would also have to apply to timber from the Alps, the Pyrenees, from Portuguese oaks, United States or Canadian forests or other regions. The restriction rather aims at the prevention of climate change, which is seen to be influenced by the progressive disappearance of tropical forests. However, it is not proven that the disappearance of tropical rain forest could not be rebalanced, as far as climate is concerned, by the tree-planting in European countries. It is not either evident, that the restriction/ban is the less

---

[46] Dir. 89/106: [1989] O.J. L40/12.

restrictive means to protect the environment. Indeed the marking of such tropical timber with a quality label in order to show that it was produced under "sustained conditions" could be such a less restrictive means. In view of this, the restriction/ban of tropical timber seem disproportionate. This result is, of course, very arguable. By acceding the United Nation Convention on Climate Change in December 1993, the Council has, for the very first time, legislated in the area of a "global common"; the legal evolution of international environmental law is difficult to assess, as environment will have to be weighed against interests such as national sovereignty, free trade and the right of States to dispose of their resources. The European Union tries to pursue, at international level, the line that restrictions to free trade are only allowed, in particular under GATT rules, where there is an international agreement to protect a species or a "global common". My own opinion goes somehow further: whether this be the case or not, no international agreement or scientific consensus exists as to the protection of tropical forests.

In 1993, the Netherlands set up a national Covenant on Tropical Hardwoods, which provides that after 1995 only timber from sustainably managed forests is used for trade or processing. The Covenant, a voluntary agreement, was signed by the Government, the timber trade and timber processing industry, trade unions and environmental organisations. It is intended to introduce an approval mark in the Netherlands in order to distinguish sustainably produced timber from other timber. The Covenant is a voluntary agreement; however, since it is backed by the Dutch Government, which even played a very active part in its setting up, it is to be considered as a national measure and as such is to be measured under Articles 30–36. According to the line of principle adopted here, I am of the opinion that a Member State may take measures to protect the environment outside its own jurisdiction, as long as the measure is neither discriminating nor disproportionate. As regards discrimination, the problem of the Covenant is that timber import from other hardwood producing countries, such as Canada and Russia (Siberia) are not covered by the Covenant. Since there is no commitment to enlarge this Covenant to other competing countries, I would consider the Covenant to be in contradiction with Article 30.

4.52   Aluminium restrictions aim at the (polluting) production methods for aluminium. Thus, admitting such a restriction would mean that any Member State would be allowed to restrict the import of any product with the argument that the production methods in another Member State or in a third country do not comply with its own national production methods or with methods which the prohibiting Member State considers sufficiently "clean" for the environment. Recurring to production methods and their environmental impact in order to block the import or use of products, would affect the core of Article 30. In the absence of E.C. rules on production methods, national production methods must thus be accepted and considered to be equivalent. This excludes the possibility of restricting imports from other Member States on grounds of production methods. Such restrictions are objectively not capable of effectively protecting the environment in another Member State. The same reasoning would apply to protection methods in third countries. And for the same reason a Member State is not entitled to restrict imports from another Member State with the argument that E.C. environmental law had not been respected during the production process, for instance on accident prevention, air emissions or water discharges.

The borderline between allowed and disallowed measures is rather difficult to trace. I would consider that a Member State may legitimately ban the imports of products containing CFCs or HCFC's, but which have been produced by production methods where CFC's/HCFC's were used.[47] In this last case, the "product element"—free circulation of goods—prevails over the "production" element.

As stated above, these observations do not apply where the measures aims directly protecting persons, animals or plants, the interests mentioned in Article 36. In these cases, life is in question which has still, even in the area of environmental protection, a higher need of being protected than other environmental issues. The higher value of the protection of life has found its expression in the mentioning of persons, animals and plants in Article 36. Thus, national measures which try to protect life, including by regulating inhumane capturing or killing methods of animals or, indeed inhuman working conditions such as children's work, may in my opinion be allowed under Articles 30–36.

PVC-bans PVC is a plastic product which is, as such, not dangerous. It is **4.53** mainly used as a construction material, packaging, as car parts, in toys and office equipment. However, when incinerated, it is thought to contribute to the generation of dioxins and furans. Its recycling is particularly difficult.

Under Article 30 the relevant question is therefore, whether Member States may, in view of complications with waste disposal, restrict the use of certain products. No jurisdiction exists. The Commission had accepted, in the mid-1980s that Denmark banned the use of metal cans for drinks because of environmental disposal problems.[48] If this line of thinking is accepted also the use of PVC will be capable of being legitimately restricted because of disposal problems. It might be added that the Netherlands and Denmark have introduced by way of voluntary agreements between public authorities, trade and industry, measures to gradually phase out the use of PVC without any intervention from the side of the Commission.

---

[47] In 1993, Denmark published draft legislation which intends to prohibit the import of products which were produced in a process where CFC's or HCFC's were used.
[48] See above, para. 4.32.

4.54 ***Throw-away plates.*** Several German local authorities have prohibited or restricted the use of one-way plates and cutlery at fares, exhibitions and public festivities. As far as taxing the use of such products is concerned, Article 95 is of application; since no discrimination between national and other products is made, no problem exists under E.C. law for such taxes. For other restrictions on bans, Article 30 applies: according to what was said earlier, as long as there is no discrimination between products because of Member States, the use of products may be restricted or prohibited because of disposal problems; such problems include quantitative aspects of waste generation.

Marks. In Germany, a private association has set up a system to identify reptile skins from animals which were either bred in farms or caught in compliance with Regulation 3626/82.[49] Commerce in Germany refuses to take skins that are not marked with the association's label.

Private labels or identification marks do not come under Article 30, though they might raise problems under Article 85. However, where public authorities take part in the labelling scheme, recognise it or promote it, Article 30 may become relevant. In such a case, the scheme would have to based on objective criteria which allow every producer or trader who complies with the conditions for attribution of the label, to accede to the scheme. As regards the question of proportionality, the scheme seems appropriate to allow combatting illegal trade in skins from reptiles which are endangered species. The scheme thus seems acceptable under Articles 30–36.

4.55 ***Dioxin levels.*** Germany intends to limit the levels of dioxins and furans in substances, preparations and products. Where such limits are exceeded, the product is to be withdrawn from the market.

There are no Community limits fixed for dioxins and furans. Thus, Germany has to decide whether it wants to fix such limit-values for dioxins and furans or, indeed, for other additives or undesirable substances. At present, there are numerous such rules at national level, particularly in the food sector.

4.56 ***Thermometers.*** Denmark plans to prohibit the marketing of thermometers containing mercury. E.C. legislation on thermometers has not, until now, concerned the mercury content. However, in 1993, the Commission made a proposal for a directive to the Council, suggesting that thermometers containing mercury should not be marketed within the E.C. as from 2004 onwards.

---

[49] Reg. 3626/82: [1982] O.J. L384/1. A number of reptiles are endangered species and listed in that Regulation.

This proposal shows, that the Commission recognises the environmental risk of mercury-containing thermometers. In the absence of E.C. rules, Denmark may well pronounce such a ban. This also follows from the idea underlying Article 100a(4): supposing the E.C. adopted a ban by the year 2004, then Denmark could, under Article 100a(4) maintain its legislation that provides for an earlier ban. If such a national ban were allowed even in cases where E.C. legislation is adopted, then it can hardly be illegal where no such E.C. rules yet exist. The Danish measure is therefore permitted under Article 30.

PVC in capsules. The Netherlands have drafted legislation which provides that PVC in wine capsules shall be forbidden from 1996 onwards. There is no E.C. legislation on the use of PVC in bottle capsules. Thus, it is up to each Member State to decide what measures it wants to adopt in order to protect the environment. It is true that wine is not produced in the Netherlands, thus the measure exclusively affects imports. However, the measure is part of an overall national programme to reduce the use of PVC. It is therefore to be treated in the same way as other national bans or restrictions of use.   **4.57**

In further development of the *Dassonville* and *Cassis de Dijon* decisions of the Court,[50] the following general rule can be established for Member States' environmental measures: in the absence of Community provisions, a national measure to protect the environment is permissible, to the extent that it is objectively capable of reaching the aim that it is not discriminatory and that the desired objective cannot be attained by less restrictive means.   **4.58**

---

[50] The Court of Justice, Case 8/74, *Procureur du Roi v. Dassonville*: [1974] E.C.R. 837, [1974] 2 C.M.L.R. 436: (measures of equivalent effect are) "all trading rules enacted by Member States which are capable of hindering, directly or indirectly, actually of potentially, intra-Community trade". Case 120/78, *Rewe-Zentral*: [1979] E.C.R. 649, [1979] 3 C.M.L.R. 494: "Obstacles to movement in the Community resulting from disparities between the national laws relating to the marketing of the products in question must be accepted in so far as those provisions may be recognised as being necessary in order to satisfy mandatory requirements relating in particular to the effectiveness of judicial supervision, the protection of public health, the fairness of commercial transactions and the defence of the consumer."

FIVE

Financing and Implementing Community Legislation

Financing legislation

The provision of Article 130s(4) was introduced in 1987 by the Single   **5.01**
European Act which stated, however, that Member States were to finance and
implement "the other measures". The Maastricht Treaty replaced these
words by "the environment policy".

Article 130s(4) stipulates as a principle that the Union's environment policy
is financed by Member States. Thus, it is for the Member States to provide for
the necessary budgetary means and the other measures in order to comply
with the requirements which flow out of the measures adopted at European
level. The Court of Justice has made it absolutely clear that no Member State
may invoke financial difficulties in order not to fulfil its obligations.[1] Also,
Member States are obliged to take all necessary steps to contribute to the
achievement of the environmental objectives of Article 130r(1). This obligation exists independently from a specific measure which was adopted by the
Union and is, as such, an emanation of the general obligation of Member
States "to ensure fulfilment of the obligations arising out of the Treaty"
(Article 5). Of course, such an obligation exists all the more, where a specific
environmental measure was adopted in pursuance of the Union's
environmental policy. Member States are therefore obliged to take the
necessary financial and legal measures in order to implement the Community
requirements.

---

[1] See, Case C-42/89, *Commission* v. *Belgium*: [1990] I E.C.R. 2821, [1992] 1 C.M.L.R. 22, para.
24: "It should be borne in mind that according to the case-law of the Court, a Member State
may not plead practical or administrative difficulties in order to justify non-compliance with
the obligations and time limits laid down in Community Directives. The same holds true for
financial difficulties which it is for the Member States to overcome by adopting appropriate
measures".

5.02 As a general rule, the Member States will finance the measures decided at Community level, for example, the protection of habitats, the cleaning up of surface or groundwater, the elimination of air pollution, disused waste tips, etc. How Member States finance such measures, whether it be by taxes or charges, by charging private persons or otherwise, is left to their discretion.

The Court of Justice's statement that the protection of the environment is in the general Community interest, has led one Member State to request that environmental measures which were decided by the Community should, in principle, also be financed by the Community. Article 130s(4) makes such a solution impossible. It is probably also for this reason that the Community environmental fund, LIFE, which was set up in 1991, only co-finances demonstration and pilot projects.[2]

Measures of a Community nature may be financed by the European Community. It is not quite clear what such measures are. Since the early 1980s, the Community has co-financed, measures of nature conservation in Member States, in particular the protection of biotopes and habitats.[3] The LIFE fund expressly provides for such funding. In knowledge of this funding the Intergovernmental Conference for the Maastricht Treaty adopted the following declaration:

> "The Conference considers that, in view of the increasing importance of nature conservation at national, Community and international level, the Community should, in exercising its powers under the provisions of Part Three, Title XVI, take accounts of the specific requirements of this area".[4]

5.03 Thus, nature conservation measures are, in principle, measures of a European Union nature. For the rest, it is submitted that it requires an express European decision to finance or co-finance, by Community money, measures of environmental nature. A general Community fund as a way of effectively combating environmental pollution would hardly be compatible with this clause. This does not mean, however, that it would not be legal to target payments from E.C. sources such as the Structural Funds or the Cohesion Fund on environmental protection schemes, such as projects to improve environmental infrastructure—water treatment works, waste disposal facilities, etc. Overall, any such spending, which the Courts of Auditors estimated run up to one billion ECU per year,[5] remains marginal compared with the funding by the individual Member States of environmental measures. However, since Community funding is, under paragraph 4 of Article 130s, the

---

[2] Reg. 1973/92: [1992] O.J. L206/1.
[3] Reg. 1872/84: [1984] O.J. L176/1.
[4] [1992] O.J. C191/99.
[5] Court of Auditors, Special Report 3/92: [1992] O.J. C245/1, points 1.1 to 1.6.

exception, any decision which may be taken by the Council or the Commission within their respective spheres of responsibility must take the form of a legal instrument under Article 189 of the Treaty; a pure internal decision such as in the case of ENVIREG would not be compatible with the requirement of Article 130s(4). Examples of past formal decisions of this kind are the decisions on LIFE, MEDSPA,[6] ACE/ACNAT[7] or NORSPA.[8]

Implementation: general questions

Under Article 130s(4) it is, in principle, the Member States which have to implement Community environmental policy and the different individual measures which form part of that policy. Member States have thus, first of all to transpose and incorporate the Community environmental legislation into their national legal system and then to ensure that the environmental provisions are effectively applied in practice. However, their obligations do not end here. They have also to create the necessary local, regional and national administrative, technical and scientific infrastructure to be able to effectively preserve, protect and improve the quality of the environment; to create bodies that are capable of systematically analysing and monitoring emissions, discharges and other environmental impairment; to create, improve and maintain environmental awareness with the public; to make the polluter pay and to prevent environmental damage. The implementation of Community environmental policy by Member States therefore requires an active, dynamic national environmental policy which contributes to the achievement of the objectives of Article 130r(1).   **5.04**

As regards the legal aspects of implementation of the Community's environmental protection measures, the Member States are required: **5.05**

— to transpose the binding Community provisions into their national legislation;
— to ensure that the national legislation covers the whole of the national territory and completely and correctly transposes the Community legislation;
— to ensure that these transposed rules are effectively applied in practice.

Member States are free to choose whether they act by parliamentary legislation or governmental regulation, by central government action or by

---

[6] Reg. 563/91: [1991] O.J. L63/1.
[7] See, Reg. 1872/84 (note 3 above); 2247/87: [1987] O.J. L207/8; 3907/91: [1991] O.J. L370/1.
[8] Reg. 3908/91: [1991] O.J. L370/28.

regional or local rules. In this context, it must be remembered that regional authorities have large responsibilities for environmental issues in Spain, Italy, Germany, Belgium and to some extent the United Kingdom, Denmark and the Netherlands. Administrative provisions, such as circulars, directions, *Verwaltungsvorschriften*, etc., which, by their nature can be changed at the discretion of the administration, are generally not considered to be an effective means of transposing Community laws requirements into national law.[9]

5.06 Community environmental legislation has some unique features which seriously affects its full application in practice. Since it is legislation that tries to protect a general interest of the Community, it markedly differs from agricultural, transport or industry legislation which affects first of all specific, vested interests. Where vested interests are in question, law-making and law enforcement takes place, in Western Europe, in a constant public—or not so public!—discussion with the representatives of vested interests; this discussion continues inside administration, parliaments and decision-making bodies. The general interest "environment" has no vested interest defenders. Environmental organisations in Western Europe are structurally and financially too weak to effectively defend environmental general interests over a long period of time. While there is consensus that the environment needs adequate protection, the implementation of concrete, legally binding measures proves difficult, where other diverging vested interests exist. The environment, being without voice, almost necessarily loses in every specific conflict of interests.

5.07 Vested interest groups are also used to ensure transmission of knowledge on—transport, competition, agriculture, etc.,—legislation and in this way contribute to either ensuring compliance with the legal rule or bringing about concerted action against that rule, often even preventing its generation. Almost no such groups exist with regard to the environment and since local, regional and national administrations in the 12 Member States are not all to the same degree convinced that Community environmental standards are to be enforced, very considerable implementation gaps exist.

The Community does not, in principle, have to implement environmental policy. However, under Article 155 of the Treaty, the Commission has the task of ensuring that "the provisions of the Treaty and the measures taken by the institutions pursuant thereto are applied". The Treaty provides no means to enable the Commission to assume this function. And while inspection bodies and other sophisticated control mechanisms were created at Community level in order to ensure effective supervision in the area of competition,[10]

---

[9] See, Case C-131/88, *Commission* v. *Germany*: [1991] I E.C.R 825.
[10] See, Reg. 17 of February 6, 1962: [1962] O.J. point 13.

fishery,[11] veterinary questions, customs and regional policy, no such instruments were set up for the environment. Questions of a green police or a Community inspectorate for the environment were discussed but, so far, without concrete results. Article 20 of Regulation 1210/90 on the European Environmental Agency[12] provides that the Regulation shall, after two years, be revised with a view to examining to what extent the Agency is to participate in monitoring compliance with Community environmental provisions; since the Regulation only entered into effect at the end of 1993, this provision has not yet become operational.

Under the Fifth Environmental Action Programme, the creation of an implementation network is announced, whose primary task is the "exchange of information and experiences and the development of common approaches at practical level, under the supervision of the Commission".[13] At present (end of 1993) an informal network exists as an intergovernmental co-operation network, without direct relation to the implementation of Community legislation.

Numerous directives contain obligations for Member States to report on implementation measures. However, these reports were largely not sent at all, were incomplete, inconsistent or otherwise defective. In 1992, a new system was set up which provides for national reporting on the basis of questionnaires; the system will become operational from 1997 onwards.[14]   **5.08**

State of the Environment Reports have not been published systematically, and when published did not deliver a very precise picture of the state and the evolution of the environment within the E.C.[15]

Environmental directives have been adopted at the Community level since 1975. Control of implementation during the first years following that date focused on the question of whether any national legislation was adopted in order to transpose the directive into national law.

In 1983 some barrels containing highly toxic waste from the Seveso (Italy) accident in 1978, suddenly disappeared while being transported. The incident caused enormous public concern in almost all EEC Member States. The European Parliament, for the first time in its history, instituted an enquiry Committee which was to examine the implementation of EEC environmental

---

[11] See, Reg. 2847/93: [1993] O.J. L261/1.
[12] Reg. 1210/90: [1990] O.J. L120/1.
[13] Fifth Environmental Action Programme: [1993] O.J. C138/1, Chap. 9.
[14] Dir. 91/692: [1991] O.J. L377/48.
[15] The following reports on the state of the environment have been published, to date:
   1: State of the Environment, First Report (Bruxelles-Luxembourg, 1977);
   2: State of the Environment, Second Report (Bruxelles-Luxembourg, 1979);
   3: The State of the Environment in the EEC (Luxembourg, 1986);
   4: The State of the Environment in the European Community, COM(92) 23 fin. Vol III of April 3, 1991.

legislation and in particular Council Directive 78/319 on toxic and dangerous waste.[16] The final report of the Committee and Parliament's resolution on the question were highly critical of the Commission and the Member States and called for effective measures in order to improve the implementation of environmental legislation by Member States and control by the Commission.[17] This led the Commission to increase its activities in monitoring the implementation of EEC environmental law by Member States.

5.09   When a directive is adopted, the Commission sends a formal letter to each Member State, referring to the directive, the deadlines laid down in it and the need to adapt national law to the requirements of Community law. Some three months before the deadline for incorporating the directive into national law, the Commission again sends a formal letter to those Member States which have not notified the Commission of such incorporation. In this letter the Commission once again explains the legal position and points out the Member States' obligations to comply with the provisions of the directive.

Such letters are sent in connection with each directive adopted. The convening of meetings of experts or representatives of the Member States before or after a directive has come into force is less systematic. While meetings take place regularly in connection with such fields as chemicals, atmospheric pollution and flora and fauna, and the opportunity at least exists for discussing jointly within the Waste Management Committee[18] the implementation of the Directives on waste in the Member States, meetings related to water and noise pollution tend to be few and far between.

Alongside meetings with representatives of the Member States, the Commission carries out its own investigations into the execution and application of Community environmental regulations and assesses its findings. In this context there are numerous formal or informal, written or personal contacts between Commission departments and the national authorities responsible for putting the Directives into effect.

Occasionally the Commission conducts informal appraisals of draft legislation submitted by the Member States before definitive adoption. Although the Commission can give no definite opinion on implementing measures at the draft stage, it attempts to help the Member States at their request.

Finally, in 1990 the Commission started to organise bilateral "package" meetings with the national authorities to discuss the facts of the case or legal aspects of alleged infringements, complaints or measures to implement the Directives on the environment with all the central, regional or local authorities

---

[16] Dir. 78/319: [1978] O.J. L84/43.
[17] European Parliament Resolution of April 11, 1984: [1984] O.J. C127/67.
[18] Commission Decision 76/431: [1976] O.J. L115/73.

concerned. The Commission announced that it would try to have one package meeting per Member State and per year.[19]

Monitoring implementation by the Commission

In the absence of other instruments at its disposal, the Commission tried **5.10** mainly to fulfil its obligation under Article 155 of the Treaty by developing action under Article 169 of the Treaty.

Article 169 reads as follows:

> "If the Commission considers that a Member State has failed to fulfil an obligation under this Treaty, it shall deliver a reasoned opinion on the matter after giving the State concerned the opportunity to submit its observations.
>
> If the State concerned does not comply with the opinion within the period laid down by the Commission, the latter may bring the matter before the Court of Justice."

Thus, there is a three-stage procedure under that Article:

(1) formal notice to the Member State concerned;
(2) reasoned opinion;
(3) referral to the Court of Justice.

The letter of formal notice from the Commission does not follow a specific pattern, though it has by now acquired a more or less standard content. This is, in part, due to the view held by the Court of Justice that the Commission's letter has already been defined the object at issue in any subsequent court proceedings.[20] The Commission is thus unable to include any additional points of complaint in its reasoned opinion or when bringing the matter before the Court of Justice, even if the Commission has itself discovered the infringement by the Member State.

The rules allow the Member State in question two months in which to reply to the Commission's letter of formal notice. However, since on average, the Commission discusses and decides on an Article 169 procedure only once every six months, the time available to Member States to reply is almost always much longer.

---

[19] Commission Monitoring application of Community law, Eighth Report: [1991] O.J. C338/1, p. 206.
[20] Court of Justice, Case C-337/89, *Commission v. United Kingdom*: [1992] I E.C.R. 6103.

5.11   The Commission's reasoned opinion closes the administrative part of the procedure. The facts of the case have been clarified and the Member State informed of the Commission's definitive stand on the legal issue involved. The opinion gives a detailed account of how Community law has been infringed. Should proceedings subsequently be initiated with the Court of Justice, the facts no longer need to be clarified; the dispute can be confined to legal issues.

The judgment by the Court of Justice pursuant to Article 169 establishes an infringement of Community law provisions, unless the Commission's complaint is dismissed. The Court, in a judgment, can only state a breach of Community environmental law; Member States have then to take the necessary steps to comply with the judgment. Only where a Member State does not comply with a judgment may the Court, in a second judgment, impose a lump sum or a penalty payment on that Member State. This sanction, which was inserted into Article 171 by the Maastricht Treaty, has not yet been applied in an environmental case, which becomes understandable if one realises that it takes at present some six years between the opening of a procedure under Article 169 and the (first) decision of the Court.

5.12   Until now, little has been done to tackle the problem of sanctions, provided for by national legislation implementing the Community rules. Recently, the Court of Justice ruled that Member States are under an obligation to impose sanctions for non-compliance with their national provisions implementing a Community Directive.[21] Each Member State is free to choose whichever sanctions it considers appropriate as long as they provide an adequate, effective deterrent in proportion to the offence and are of equivalent force to the sanctions imposed in similar cases by the national legislation.

Financial situations came to Community environmental policy almost through the back-door. Following the amendment of the EEC Treaty in 1987 and the implementation of its Article 130d, the Council, in 1988, adopted Regulation 2052/88 on the reform of the Community Structural Funds[22] or, in more simplistic terms, on the main instruments of financial intervention of the EEC in matters of agricultural, regional or social policy. Article 7 of this Regulations states:

> "Measures financed by the Structural Funds or receiving assistance from the European Investment Bank or from another existing financial instrument shall be in keeping with the provisions of the Treaties, with the instruments adopted pursuant thereto and with Community policies, including those concerning . . . environmental protection."

---

[21] Case 68/88, *Commission* v. *Greece*: [1989] E.C.R. 2965, [1991] 1 C.M.L.R. 31.
[22] Reg. 2052/88: [1988] O.J. L185/13.

Thus, according to this provision, measures may not be financed with resources from the Structural Funds if they fail to comply with all the provision of secondary environmental legislation and, in addition, the objectives of Community environment policy, as set out in Article 130r(1) of the Treaty.[23]

Subsequently, on several occasions the Commission suspended payments in the framework of regional policy which were destined to co-finance projects that did not altogether comply with environmental legislation. The main areas covered were the construction of motorways or other infrastructure projects without a proper environmental impact assessment according to Directive 85/337. As evaluated from the echo in the national media, this blocking of funds had a far greater impact on national or regional decision-making procedures than any procedure under Article 169 could have hoped to achieve. What is more, the systematic approach by the European Investment Bank and by the Commission, to ask whenever a project is submitted for financial assistance whether environmental legislation is complied with, has a marked, though admittedly slowly increasing, preventive effect on local, regional or national administrations, particularly in the transport, infrastructure, or economic development sectors.

The threat of financial sanctions is, of course, limited. Until now, there does not seem to have been one single decision to definitely refuse payment due to disregard of environmental legislation. And in the area of large or important infrastructure projects the political pressure exercised becomes overwhelming—casting some doubt on whether the threat of refusal to give financial assistance really is an effective tool in monitoring implementation. In the end, much probably depends on the determination to give full effect to Article 7 of Regulation 2052/88.

All three stages of Article 169 require an explicit, formal decision by the Commission itself based on a proposal from the departments concerned. In view of the rather formalised procedures, it always takes a considerable amount of time from the start of the Article 169 procedure to the eventual Court judgment. One way to speed up the procedure is to start "urgency procedures", in other words to shorten the gap between the formal decision and its implementation and the time which the Member States are allowed to send in their replies. However, for lack of staff and objective criteria for selecting the right dossiers, such urgency procedures are rather exceptional.   **5.13**

The Commission is not empowered to take interim measures against individual Member States. It is only when a case has been brought before the Court that it can request the Court to impose a provisional injunction if it fears

---

[23] Reg. 792/93: [1993] O.J. L79/74 on a (temporary) Cohesion Fund provides for a similar provision.

that irreversible damage could be caused pending the final ruling [Article 786 E.C. Treaty].

Three aspects of implementation of Community environmental laws are monitored. The Commission checks whether:

(1) the Member States have adopted and submitted their national measures to implement the Directives;
(2) these national measures fully and correctly discharge the obligations imposed by Community law;
(3) these national implementing provisions are applied correctly in practice.

5.14 All Community Directives contain a provision to the effect that Member States must adapt their national legislation to the provisions of the Directive within a specific time-period and give notification of these implementing measures to the Commission. When this specified period has expired without the Commission having received notification of the required implementing measures, the Commission decides without further ado, to initiate a procedure under Article 169. This is justified by the fact that the Member States have twice been formally reminded of their obligations during the period of grace, that these obligations are clearly and unequivocally set out in the Directive, and that past experience has shown that incorporation into national law of environmental Directives within the fixed time-period is the exception rather than the rule.

These non-notification procedures reflect a certain slowness on the part of the Member States to implement new Directives rather than any deliberate attempt to evade their obligations to the Community. The Member States often step into line shortly after the Directive enters into force. As a result, the Court rarely has to give a ruling.[24] Thus, an infringement procedure on the grounds of failure to give notification of national implementing measures should be seen primarily as a means of pressuring the Member States into incorporating Community environmental provisions into their national law within the specified period of time.

The letters of formal notice sent to the Member States regarding failure to notify are of a purely formal nature. If notification is subsequently received from a Member State, the Article 169 procedure has to be closed. If necessary, a new procedure on the grounds of incomplete implementation may be initiated, which is a most intricate process.

The Commission is not informed of the national measures taken to implement international conventions on the environment, even in those cases where the Community is a contracting party in its own right. Consequently,

---

[24] Up to the end of 1993, the Court had issued some 25 judgments because of failure to communicate national implementation measures.

the Commission does not monitor implementation of such conventions within the Community. However, if the Community adopts specific legal provisions governing fields covered by an international convention, the Member States are, of course, required to inform the Commission of the national measures adopted to implement these Community instruments. Consequently, these are monitored as provided by Article 155 of the Treaty.

The second stage of monitoring by the Commission is to check whether the **5.15** national rules fully and correctly implement Community law on the environment. It is not simply a question of making sure that each Article of the Directive is echoed by the national legislation submitted. In practice, the entire national legislative, administrative and regulatory framework, with all its peculiarities and unique operating procedures, has to be examined to make sure that all the objectives of the Community regulations are attained. This examination is sometimes further complicated by the interdependence of national and regional legislation.

Special problems arise if the Community Directive is incorporated not by central government but, for example, by regional authorities, Länder, autonomous provinces, etc. Each Member State is free to devolve powers in its country as it sees fit, for example to delegate the responsibility for adopting the measures to implement the Directive to regional or local authorities. The Commission must make sure that the Directive is applied throughout each Member State's entire territory.

The Commission has repeatedly taken action in cases where a Community Directive on the environment has been incorporated into national legislation by an administrative circular. Circulars are widely used in environmental law and practice. The form of these circulars varies considerably from one Member State to another. So, too, do their scope, legal status and, hence, compatibility with Community law. Following the line consistently taken by the Court of Justice, the Commission is of the opinion that Directives conferring rights or imposing obligations on private individuals cannot be properly implemented by internal circulars which can be amended at any such time as the national administration sees fit. The same applied to unpublished circulars or to published circulars which can subsequently be amended by unpublished circulars. In all such cases, the public has no way of knowing which is the exact law applicable. As the Court of Justice stated, in such cases legal certainty commands that rules with a mandatory character are issued:

> "It should be pointed out that the fact that a practice is consistent with the protection afforded under a directive does not justify failure to implement that directive in the national legal order by means of provisions which are capable of creating a situation which is sufficiently precise, clear and open to permit individuals to be aware of and enforce their rights. As the Court held in its judgment in Case C-339/87, *Commission* v. *Netherlands*: [1990] I E.C.R. 851,

paragraph 25, in order to secure full implementation of directives in law and not only in fact, Member States must establish a specific legal framework in the area in question."[25]

It may be deduced from this case law that, generally speaking, administrative measures are not sufficient to incorporate environmental Directives in national law and that regulations or even laws are needed for this purpose, as soon as these Community instruments pronounce prohibitions, fix concentrations or otherwise refer to rights or obligations of individuals.

Furthermore, these legal measures must be published in an official gazette or some other suitable form, so as to inform all persons subject to the law about measures to protect the environment and enable them to ensure they are complied with.

Another important problem is that of limit-values. Sometimes, it is argued that there is no need to explicitly include the limit-values set at the Community level for the concentration of certain pollutants in the air or water in the national legislation, but that all Member States have to do is to ensure that the values are observed in practice. The Commission has always firmly asserted that the Community limit-values must be enshrined in generally applicable legislation or regulations. It must be possible to find the limit-value set by the Community in the national rules. The Court of Justice stated in this regard:[26]

> "Thus, it is clear that legal certainty also requires the specific transposal of individual limit-values, maximum permissible concentrations and emission values into national legislation. A general reference to Community legislation is not permitted."

A Directive is also deemed to be incompletely incorporated if, for example, national law allows administrative authorities to make exceptions to the provisions of the national law in question, while the Directive does not provide for such exceptions. The same applies if the definitions of the Directive are not incorporated in their entirely into national law—which would alter the scope of the Directive.

5.16 National legislation implementing a Community Directive on the environment cannot provide automatic protection for the environment. It must be applied in practice. In other words, plans or programmes must be adopted and implemented, limit-values must be enforced, official licences must be adapted, etc. Even national legislation copying a Directive word for word will remain meaningless unless it is applied.

---

[25] Case C-131/88, (note 8 above), para. 8.
[26] Case C-361/88, *Commission* v. *Germany*: [1991] I E.C.R. 2567, [1993] 2 C.M.L.R. 821.

Every Community Directive on the environment includes a clause requiring the Member States to inform the Commission of the national rules adopted to implement the Directive and to send the text to the Commission. Consequently, incorporation of the Directives into national legislation and the compatibility of this national legislation with the Commission provisions can be monitored by examining the texts adopted. However, the Community Directives do not normally contain a clause requiring the Member States to inform the Commission of the effective implementation of the Community rules on the environment.

It is true that many of the Directives on the environment require the Member State to submit regular reports on the measures taken to implement the Directives of specific aspects of the Community rules. However, as mentioned above, not all Member States systematically submit these reports to the Commission.

Also, the national reports on the implementing measures usually give no detailed evidence of effective implementation of the rules on the environment. Instead, they primarily provide a brief summary of the technical and administrative measures already in place or adopted.

The reports from the Member States therefore, are rarely a source of information on effective implementation of Community environmental rules.

The Commission has conducted some studies of its own on effective implementation of the Directives on the environment in the Member States, although inevitably only in a limited number. An added problem which necessarily limits the values of such studies is that it has proved extremely difficult to gain access to the data held by the national, regional or local authorities on, for example, the frequency and results of the inspections, the firms inspected, the conditions laid down in the licences granted or the pollution levels recorded.

Consequently, the Commission's main sources of information are the complaints. The complaints system introduced by the Commission in the late 1960s, originally to smooth the way for the completion of the internal market, has mushroomed spectacularly in recent years where the environment is concerned. This trend has been boosted by the growing number of written and oral questions or petitions reporting inadequate implementation of the rules on the environment. The Commission has decided to treat these in the same way as complaints. The fact that individuals are able to register a complaint with the Commission, can promote the creation of a Community-wide awareness of the environment, strengthen the accessibility of the institutions of the European Communities for the man-in-the-street, and bring home to the individual the fact that he bears part of the responsibility for his environment and can contribute to its protection and preservation. This is of particular importance in regions where pollution was long considered as an Act of God. Administrations and polluters were not used to seeing their

5.17

141

environmental behaviour challenged by an outside body. Environmental complaints, about 500 per year at present, come from individuals, environmental as well as from professional organisations, national, regional or European deputies, local administrations, political parties, embassies, occasionally even from environmental ministers. Not seldom is the formal notification of the existence of the complaint to a Member State sufficient to prompt that Member State to ask questions, check its internal monitoring system, inspect or control, or otherwise re-examine its own rules.

Every letter complaining that Community environmental law, or Community laws relating to other fields, is being infringed is entered in a special register of complaints maintained by the Commission. The Commission has even published a form which is designed to facilitate on introductions of complaints.[27]

The Commission requests the factual and legal information from the Member State needed to assess the complaint. It obtains its own expert's opinions and where necessary requests that documents be submitted to it. As yet there have been no formal hearings of witnesses of the parties involved; as part of the process of investigating a complaint such action would seldom have any practical relevance.

5.18 Disadvantages of the complaint system are that the Commission has to concentrate its efforts on the cases brought to its attention by the plaintiffs. These are not necessarily either the most serious or the most urgent cases. Above all, a complaint is a sign that the citizens are willing to seek a solution to the problem facing them. If the public resigns itself to a deteriorating environment, there is virtually nothing the Commission can do. Also, effective implementation of the rules on the environment depends on application at the local, regional or national level, and this is more effective in some places than in others—a situation that runs counter to the principle that Community rules must be applied identically throughout the Community.

Another major obstacle to monitoring the practical implementation of the Community Directives is that the Directives, which are addressed to the Member States and not to private citizens or undertakings, are often imprecisely worded. For example, several stipulate that companies emitting pollutants must use "the best available technology not entailing excessive cost".[28] Since the Community has given no clear, precise definition of the implications of this concept for individual industries, it is interpreted differently from one Member State to another, from one industry to another and, probably, even from one company to another. Article 13 of Directive 84/ 360 requires the Member States to "implement policies and strategies . . . for

---

[27] [1989] O.J. C26/1.
[28] See, for instance Dir. 84/360: [1984] O.J. L188/20, Art. 4; Dir. 89/369: [1989] O.J. L163/32, Art. 3.

the gradual adaptation of existing plants . . . to the best available technology . . . not entailing excessive costs." The loose wording of this clause makes it virtually impossible to monitor whether a given Member State has fulfilled its obligations under Article 13 of this Directive at any given installation.

Article 3 of Directive 85/210 on the lead content of petrol[29] requires the Member States "to take the necessary measures to ensure the availability and balanced distribution within their territory of unleaded petrol from October 1, 1989". The Commission has initiated several Article 169 procedures to ensure the effective implementation of this clause. Nevertheless, the difficulties hampering rigorous application of Article 3 are only too obvious.[30]

Directive 75/442 on waste and 78/319 on dangerous waste[31] stipulate that waste should be disposed of "without endangering human health and without harming the environment", and in particular, "without risk to water, air, soil, plants or animals". It is submitted, that this clause would be precise enough to oblige clean-up measures for leaking landfill sites, but obviously gives broad scope for interpretation.

Article 6 of Directive 76/160 on bathing water quality,[32] in conjunction with Annex V to the Directive, calls for the monitoring of the salmonella content in bathing water, "should inspection . . . reveal that there is a discharge or a probable discharge of substances likely to lower the quality of the bathing water". Monitoring can therefore be avoided simply by not carrying out the inspections, which are left to the discretion of the Member States.

On rare occasions the Commission departments visit a place in order to find out more about the facts of a particular complaint. These visits take place at the initiative of the Commission, which informs the Member State and the complainants of its intention, in order to ensure that all facts can be clarified on the site. Though the repercussions of such visits are sometimes considerable, they cannot be called inspections, since no investigation is carried out. It would seem more appropriate to call them fact-finding missions, since their main purpose is to clarify all the facts of a case in order to allow a proper legal assessment of whether there is a breach of Community law.

The correspondence between the Commission and Member States on compliance is not made public. The letters of formal notice and reasoned opinion are not published either. Occasionally the Commission publishes a press release on such cases as it considers important. The impact of these press releases is very great, particularly in the United Kingdom with its outstanding, highly sensitive journalism. The decision to refer a case to the Court of Justice follow the same rules.

---

[29] Dir. 85/210: [1985] O.J. L96/25.
[30] See, also, for figures, Chap. 1, note 72, p. 12.
[31] Dir. 75/442: [1975] O.J. L194/39; Dir. 78/319 (note 16 above).
[32] Dir. 76/160: [1976] O.J. L31/1.

5.19 Beginning in 1990, the Commission published separate reports on the monitoring of the application of environmental legislation in Member States.[33] Despite a very considerable echo within the European Parliament and the European Council, it abandoned this practice in 1993 and now publishes findings on the application of environmental legislation within its general reports on the monitoring of application of Community legislation.[34]

Implementation of Community environmental measures occurs exceptionally at Community level, where Regulations need to be monitored. Examples are Regulation 880/92 on the eco-labelling,[35] Regulation 1836/93 on an eco-audit,[36] or the arrangements for administering the quotas imposed on use and production of CFCs.[37] Sometimes also Directives provide for a constant concentration at Community level, such as the prior notification procedure of bringing chemicals or genetically modified organisms on the market,[38] or the exchange of experience on accident prevention of industrial installations.[39] Generally, however, the administration of implementation by bodies at Community level would increase the powers of Community institutions and is thus resisted by Member States.

---

[33] Commission Document P-5 of February 8, 1990; Commission Monitoring application of Community law, 8th Report: [1991] O.J. C338/1 p. 204.
[34] Commission Monitoring application of Community law, 10th Report: [1993] O.J. C233/1; 11th Report [1994] O.J. C154/7.
[35] Reg. 880/92: [1992] O.J. L99/1.
[36] Reg. 1836/93: [1993] O.J. L168/1.
[37] See, Reg. 594/91: [1991] O.J. L67/1.
[38] Dir. 90/220: [1990] O.J. L117/15.
[39] Dir. 82/501: [1982] O.J. L230/1.

SIX

Assessment

The Treaty framework for law and policy

There is no European Community environment different from the environ-   **6.01**
ment of Member States. For this reason, Community environmental law and
policy cannot be evaluated completely independently from national environmental law. For the environment it is irrelevant whether it is protected
through local, regional, national, European or international rules: what
matters is the result, the effective preservation, and the protection of the
environment. Evaluating Community environmental law is, therefore, more a
question of addressing whether the methods, tools and instruments exist and
have been made operational to enable the law to contribute its part to the
protection of the environments inside the Community and at international
level.

The Treaty provisions give broad competence to the Community. The
environmental objectives in Article 130r(1) which complete the general
Community tasks of Article 2 and 3a, are sufficiently large to allow the
Community to tackle any environmental question of some significance.

The obligation to attain a high level of environmental protection (Article
130r(2)(2), see also Article 100a(3)), which the Treaty only provides as regards
other sectors for public health and consumer protection, contains a quality
requirement and obliges the institutions of the Community to take the
protection of the environment seriously. The principle of majority decisions,
introduced by the Maastricht Treaty and further strengthened by the formal
adoption of action programmes by way of a majority co-decision procedure, is
likely to speed up decision-making and to ensure that individual Member
States can no longer block Community decisions. At the same time, the Treaty
does not prevent Member States from progressing at national level with the
adoption of environmental standards in areas not yet covered by the
Community legislation or going beyond Community standards (Article 130t).
The integration clause (Article 130r(2)(2)) ensures that environmental
requirements are integrated into other policies of the Community. Finally, a

145

participation in international environmental negotiations is ensured (Article 130r).

6.02 The Treaty does not provide for environmental enforcement bodies, nor for individual rights with regard to the environment—right of information, right of participation in decision-making, rights of access to justice—nor for sanctions. To these specific aspects are joined the general omissions of the European Union Treaty: the democratic deficit, the subordinate role of the European Parliament and the absence of transparency in the work of the institutions. The Treaty also enshrines a number of notions which are anything but clear, such as "sustainable", "precautionary principle", "the polluter should pay", "benefits and costs of lack of action", "measures of general nature", "management of water resources" and others. In a Union with, at present, 12 Member States with different legal cultures, the risk is high that diverging interpretations are given to such notions, according to the specific interests of the different Member State. The tendency of using diffuse notions has long been observed in national and international environmental law and policy, and might be unavoidable in such a young sphere as is environmental law. It is doubtful, though whether the use of a notion such as, for instance, "sustainable", will really contribute to better environmental protection.

6.03 Overall, it might be said that the "constitutional" framework of environmental law and policy at Community level is satisfactory. In view of the fact that the Community is not a nation-State and that the political making of an integrated European Union is anything but easy, major revisions of the Treaty do not seem necessary at present in order to ensure the elaboration and application of standards which give appropriate protection to the environment.

Programmes and secondary legislation

6.04 The absence of specific environmental provisions in the Treaty prior to 1987 was the main reason why Community environmental policy was conceived around multiannual action programmes which fixed objectives, principles and priorities. The basic conception of these programmes was that of a preventive policy with the objective of preventing the creation of problems rather than combating their consequences. Economic decisions were to take environmental considerations into account and the fixation of stringent standards was considered necessary in order to prevent pollution and suggest a more prudent use of resources. The first action programmes also aimed at creating public awareness of environmental problems and fixed a general framework for environmental measures.

146

A considerable amount of measures which were announced in the action **6.05** programmes were not proposed or adopted; other measures which were taken at Community level had not been previously announced.[1] There is a lack of assessment of the achievements and failures of the respective action programmes made at the end of each programme. Since the Member States have not prepared reports on the environmental policy on a regular basis[2] and since the ones they prepared contained neither precise information nor comparable data on Community environmental action, the success of the Community activity remained uncertain, as well as the analysis of the reasons for successful and less successful actions. Each programme announced continuous and progressive environmental protection.

As regards its general evaluation, the following observations can be made:

Water legislation

Community water legislation lacks consistency. Some Directives concern **6.06** discharges, others deal only with quality objectives. Dangerous substances shall be reduced through either emission standards or quality objectives. Some try to reduce polluting discharges, others aim at protecting the receiving waters.

The main sources of pollution have so far not all been covered. Emission standards were set differently for seventeen dangerous substances, according to different industrial sectors.[3] Municipal waste water—but not industrial waste water—is to be treated before discharge, by the year 2005 at the latest.[4] In place of emission standards quality objectives may be set, which were to be fixed, by Member States, also on all other dangerous substances.[5] At Community level, quality objectives were fixed for surface waters, drinking

---

[1] Examples for measures which were announced under the Fourth Environmental Programme, but not proposed by the Commission: mandatory information on draft legislation [Fourth Action Programme, no. 2.1.7]; sea pollution measures [point 4.2.6]; noise measures [point 4.5.3.]; for further examples see Chap. 2, note 51.

Examples for measures which were adopted between 1987 and 1994 by the Council, without having been announced in the Fourth Environmental Programme: Reg. 1210/90 on the Environmental Agency: [1990] O.J. L120/1; Reg. 880/92 on an eco-label: [1992] O.J. L99/1; Reg. 1836/93 on an eco-audit system: [1993] O.J. L168/1.

[2] So far, the Commission has published the following reports: "State of the Environment. First Report" (Bruxelles-Luxembourg, 1977), "State of the Environment Second Report" (Bruxelles-Luxembourg, 1979); "The State of the Environment in the EEC" (Luxembourg, 1986); "The State of the Environment in the European Community", COM(92) 23 fin., Vol. III, of April 3, 1992.

[3] See, Directives mentioned in Chap. 1, para. 1.14 to 1.16.

[4] Dir. 76/464: [1976] O.J. L129/23, Art. 7.

[5] Dir. 91/271: [1991] O.J. L135/40.

water, fish, shellfish and bathing water.[6] A general directive on the ecological quality of water has been suggested, which will again leave it to Member States to fix quality standards.[7]

6.07   The trend in Community water legislation—as with air pollution legislation— is moving towards regionalisation of standards for water, a trend which is also influenced by the subsidiarity discussions and the requirement of unanimous decisions for the management of water resources. Legally, this trend finds its expression, for instance, in the regional differentiation for urban waste water—normal situation, sensitive zones, less sensitive zones—and in the use of the legal requirement to use the best available technologies not exceeding excessive costs, a notion which allows for different regional if not local decisions. Such differentiations are also likely to lead to differences in the competitive situation, especially of industrial discharges, and to differences in effective implementation of the standards. Indeed, the approach allows national, regional or local authorities to work towards a high level of water protection within the Union, if they so wish. However, where there is less will to reach this objective, European Union legal rules will hardly be capable of ensuring that this objective is reached.

Air pollution

6.08   Air pollution is also far from being homogeneous. Air emission standards and quality objectives were set and product-related standards and general requirements were fixed, according to the different circumstances.
      Air emission standards exist for CO, HC and NOx and particles from cars,[8] SO_2, NOx and black smoke from large combustion plants,[9] smoke, some heavy metals, SO_2, HC_1 and HF from incineration installations for household wastes,[10] asbestos emissions from installations producing or processing asbestos,[11] smoke, SO_2 and HC_1 from the titanium dioxide industry[12] and

---

[6] Dir. 75/440 (surface water); [1975] O.J. L194/2; 80/778 (drinking water): [1980] O.J. L229/11; 78/659 (fishwater): [1978] O.J. L222/1; 79/923 (shellfish water): [1979] O.J. L281/47; 76/160 (bathing water): [1979] O.J. L31/1.
[7] Commission Legislative Programme 1993: [1993] O.J. C125/1, point 241.
[8] Dir. 70/220 (car emissions): [1970] O.J. L76/1 and subsequent amendments; 73/206 (diesel car emissions): [1973] O.J. L190/1 and subsequent amendments.
[9] Dir. 88/609, [1988] O.J. L336/1.
[10] Dir. 89/369 (new installations): [1989] O.J. L163/32; 89/429 (existing installations): [1989] O.J. L203/50.
[11] Dir. 87/217: [1987] O.J. L45/40.
[12] Dir. 92/112: [1992] O.J. L409/11.

aluminium, nickel, chromium, copper, vanadium, lead, chlorine, fluorine, sulphur dioxide from the incineration of used oils.[13]

Air quality objectives have been fixed for SO_2 and black smoke, lead and NO_x.[14] Product standards were developed for the lead and benzol content of petrol as well as for sulphur in diesel petrol.[15] PCBs and PCTs were considerably restricted in use,[16] volatile, monomer, vinyl chloride was prohibited as a propellant[17] and CFCs and similar, ozone-depleting substances were restricted in use or even completely prohibited.[18]

For the rest, air pollution legislation refers to the necessity of authorising new installations on the basis of "best available technologies not entailing excessive costs"[19] and to the progressive adaptation of existing installations, either by reducing the total quantities of emissions or by refitting them.[20] The trend, as in water legislation, is towards drafting general clauses, which leave ample room for regional differentiation in standards, rather than to integrate uniform standards. Aspects of competitivity and of controlling air pollution rank secondary in such a scenario. **6.09**

Product-related measures to combat air pollution are gradually strengthened in time, such as lead-related measures in petrol which passed from 0.64/0.40g per litre in 1978 to lead-free petrol in 1985;[21] sulphur in gas oil which passed from 0.6/0.8g per cubic metre between 1975 to 0.2g in 1987;[22] reductions and bans of CFCs which were phased out between 1980 and 1995, other ozone-depleting substances being significantly restricted in use;[23] car emission standards which were very seriously reduced between 1970 and 1992,[24] etc. New air quality standards are not planned under the Fifth Action Programme.

Whether air pollution will be capable of being stabilised (a political commitment to stabilise carbon dioxide emission exists[25]) is speculation, since increases in car use and traffic as well as increased energy use will increase pressure on the air. The present data does not allow an accurate assessment to

---

[13] Dir. 75/439: [1975] O.J. L194/23 and subsequent amendments.
[14] Dir. 80/779 (SO_2 and suspended particulates): [1985] O.J. L87/1.
  82/884 (lead): [1982] O.J. L378/15; 85/203 (NOx): [1985] O.J. L87/1.
[15] Dir. 85/210 (lead in petrol): [1985] O.J. L96/25; 93/12 (gas oil and diesel fuels): [1993] O.J. L74/81.
[16] Dir. 85/467: [1985] O.J. L269/56.
[17] Dir. 76/769: [1976] O.J. L262/201.
[18] Reg. 594/91: [1991] O.J. L67/1, which replaced earlier regulations.
[19] Dir. 84/360: [1983] O.J. L188/20.
[20] Dir. 84/360 (note 19), Art. 13; 89/429 (note 10); 88/609 (note 9).
[21] Dir. 85/210 (note 15), which replaced Dir. 78/611: [1978] O.J. L197/19.
[22] Dir. 75/716 (note 15); 87/219: [1987] O.J. L91/19.
[23] See, Reg. 594/91 (note 18).
[24] Dir. 70/220 and 72/306 (note 8), with subsequent amendments.
[25] See, [1990] 10 E.C. Bull. 91, point 1.3.77.

be made on the impact of air pollution on urban agglomerations, water pollution, acidification or forest decline.

Chemicals

6.10   Legislation on chemicals has produced total harmonisation rules: all products marked in the Community must conform to the harmonised provisions. The basic rules are in place: new substances and genetically modified organisms are to be tested before marketing.[26] Dangerous chemicals are labelled and packed accordingly and, where necessary, restricted in use.[27] These principles now need to be applied in reality to the some 100,000 chemical substances on the Community market, out of which 2,500 are regulated, as well as to the some seven million chemical preparations. Uniform methodologies for risk assessment,[28] risk management and risk reduction will be developed under that scheme.

Industrial chemical installations are faced with Community measures on risk prevention mainly.[29] A number of horizontal rules such as those on eco-auditing,[30] impact assessment[31] or access to environmental information[32] also apply to chemical installations. Once the proposed legislation on integrated pollution control has been adopted,[33] the legislative framework will be, more or less, in place.

Noise

6.11   The product-related noise legislation aims at the free circulation of products rather than at protection against noise. No legislative instruments have been developed at Community level to reduce ambient noise levels in sensitive areas or elsewhere, of course with the obvious exception of noise levels at the workplace.

---

[26] Dir. 92/32 (dangerous substances): [1992] O.J. L154/30; 90/220 (genetically modified organisms): [1990] O.J. L117/15.

[27] Dir. 92/32 (note 26); 76/769 (restrictions of use): [1976] O.J. L262/201.

[28] Reg. 793/93: [1993] O.J. L83/1.

[29] Dir. 82/501: [1982] O.J. L230/1.

[30] Reg. 1836/93: [1993] O.J. L168/1.

[31] Dir. 85/337: [1985] O.J. L175/40.

[32] Dir. 90/313: [1990] O.J. L158/56.

[33] Proposal for a Directive: [1993] O.J. C311/6.

Nature

Legislation on important habit conservation has just been put in place, in an   **6.12**
attempt to preserve natural islands for fauna and flora.[34] Scenic landscapes,
biotopes and other parts of the natural environment are entirely left to
Member States' protection measures. The control of abuse and trade of wild
species, in particular of endangered species, is by and large legally possible,[35]
but suffers from the well-known problem of ineffective monitoring. Land-use
management remains in the hands of Member States and sustainable policies
for tourism, transport, energy, extractive industries and forestry are neither
politically conceived nor legally shaped at Community level.

Wastes

The Community has not been able to set up a network of disposal installations   **6.13**
and it is unclear when this network will be fully available.[36] Also it is not clear
at all, what relation exists between national disposal, self-sufficiency and
Community self-sufficiency.[37] There is no obligation for Member States to
dispose of waste within their territory and criteria for planning, authorising
and controlling of installations are very general.

Horizontal measures

Horizontal environmental measures very markedly try to increase transpar-   **6.14**
ency and awareness, information of individuals and the public in general, and
to cover procedural aspects. Their relatively recent adoption hardly allows an
assessment of their legal and ecological efficiency. Similar observations are
applicable on measures in other policy areas, such as agriculture, energy,
regional policy, competition, transport or development policy.

Only a minority of Member States have a consistent, coherent, medium-to-   **6.15**
long-term environment policy. By contrast, in approximately half the
Member States legislative initiatives to protect the environment concern

---

[34] Dir. 92/43 (habitats): [1992] O.J. L206/7; see, also, Dir. 79/409 (birds): [1979] O.J. L103/1.
[35] Reg. 3626/82: [1982] O.J. L384/1.
[36] Dir. 91/156: [1990] O.J. L42/1, Art. 6: "Member States shall take appropriate measures . . . to
     establish an integrated and adequate network of disposal installations . . . "
[37] Dir. 91/156 (note 36), Art. 6: "The network" (see note 36 above) must enable the Community
     as a whole to become self-sufficient in waste disposal and the Member States to move towards
     that aim individually . . . ".

almost exclusively, the implementation of measures adopted, or in the process of adoption, by the Community.[38]

For this reason, it is not surprising that some of the Community instruments have a significant impact on the direction of national policies; examples include the Directives on drinking water quality,[39] groundwater protection,[40] urban waste water[41] and on nitrate levels in water,[42] those on limit-values for certain pollutants in the atmosphere,[43] vehicle emissions,[44] large combustion installations[45] and incineration standards;[46] Directives on hazardous wastes and their transport, including the export of wastes to third countries;[47] the Directives on major accident hazards in the chemical industry[48] and the notification of new chemicals,[49] the Directive on the protection of species of wild birds,[50] on habitats,[51] access to information,[52] environment impact assessment[53] and the Regulation on eco-audit.[54]

6.16   Most of the Directives adopted before 1987 already contained the provision now anchored in Article 130t, that Member States could maintain or introduce more stringent protective measures. This is an expression of the general principle that Member States' social achievements, particularly in the field of health, safety environmental protection and social policy, cannot simply be sacrificed on the altar of harmonisation and market unity. The general objective of the Union Treaty to provide for a high level of environmental protection, which is laid down in Article 130r(2), 100a(3) and (4), tries to make it superfluous to make use of the possibilities of Articles 130t and 100a[4].

6.17   If one looks at European Union secondary environmental legislation generally, one is marked by the fact that most of the measures adopted are not self-executing. The legal notions are general, definitions often imprecise and general obligations prevail. Methods of measurement and analysis, the

---

[38] With all the risk of simplification, Greece, Italy, Spain, Portugal, Ireland and Belgium may be named.
[39] Dir. 80/778 (note 6).
[40] Dir. 80/68: [1980] O.J. L20/43.
[41] Dir. 91/271 (note 4).
[42] Dir. 91/676: [1991] O.J. L375/1.
[43] Dir. 80/779: 82/884 and 85/203 (note 14).
[44] Dir. 70/220 and 73/206 (note 8).
[45] Dir. 88/609 (note 9).
[46] Dir. 89/369 and 89/429 (note 10).
[47] Dir. 91/689: [1991] O.J. L377/20.
[48] Reg. 259/93: [1993] O.J. L30/1.
[49] Dir. 82/501 (note 29).
[50] Dir. 79/409 (note 34).
[51] Dir. 92/43 (note 34).
[52] Dir. 90/313 (note 32).
[53] Dir. 85/337 (note 31).
[54] Reg. 1836/93 (note 30).

frequency of sampling and other procedural rules for ensuring compliance have often remained general. This type of law-making, which might at least to some extent have been promoted by environmentally progressive Member States such as Denmark, the Netherlands or Germany, needs an active administrative infrastructure in Member States, which continuously fills in the legislative gaps, completes omissions, monitors full compliance and enforcement and endeavours to live up to the words and the spirits of Community legislation. In Member States where environmental protection policy has a low priority and/or where such an active administration lack Community legislation, even if it is transposed word by word into national law, it must contribute little to improve the quality of the environment. Since there cannot be, in these lines, a discussion on the necessity for a change in national environmental policy, law and administrative infrastructure, only the European Community level can be considered.

Community secondary legislation should be drafted in a more systematic way and more clearly be based on long-term, medium-term and short-term objectives, as the case might be. The emotionalised discussion on subsidiarity has increased the likelihood that also in future, Community legal measures will consist of umbrella rules, use general terms and definitions and will leave national implementation and enforcement measures, largely to the Member State's own discretion.

This situation, however, increases the need to follow more closely the practical application of rules within the Member States in order to ensure an equivalent interpretation. If one looks, for instance, closely at such a notion as "best available technology" one is obliged to state that despite its existence in Community legislation for more than 15 years, its interpretation still varies considerably between Denmark and Portugal, Germany and Greece, or the Netherlands and Spain. Unless more integration is ensured in future, this state of affairs will continue for a long time. Neither the environment nor Community integration profits from this situation. **6.18**

Implementation and enforcement

The Commission's attempt to systematically monitor the implementation of European environmental law by Member States had a number of rather important consequences. Despite the somewhat limited publicity which surrounds the procedures, public opinion has become aware of the possibility of taking action against environmental degradation, contamination or pollution. While in some Member States pollution was, and partly still is, considered to be some "act of God", the possibility of sending complaints to **6.19** the European Commission and having a local environmental problem examined, has promoted awareness and increased sensitivity. The Commission is seen rather as a central body, capable of even taking a stand against national administrations—a possibility which the public does not seem to have in all Member States. The turning of "soft law" into hard law and the application of European Community Directives as rules of binding law rather than as some form of recommendation has probably surprised many local, regional and national administrations. This process of integrating European Community environmental law into national environmental law is far from being completed. Furthermore, many administrations were not accustomed to seeing their practice being questioned by an outside body and having to justify why this or that authorisation was given, or this or that habitat destroyed. This challenging of administrative sovereignty was, at the same time, a monitoring of the European environment despite national sovereignty. Generally, it can be said that Member States accepted the Community monitoring process, since it also brought advantages: for instance, central environmental administration was made aware of imperfect implementation at the local level, or it was able to successfully argue an environmental case against other, more powerful departments of the same administration, using the Commission's letter as support for its own arguments.

6.20   Other aspects were also important, for instance, changes of national legislation in order to adapt it to European environmental requirements; or the preventive effect which a threat to expose the Member State to a sort of public blame from Brussels inevitably had. Since environmental protection profits most from public awareness and public participation, the media echo brought about by decisions from the Commission may have contributed to avoiding some deterioration of the environment.

The monitoring process went so far as to influence the form of environmental law-making. The most obvious evidence for this is the gradual reduction in the use of circulars. The fact that more and more regulatory instruments are used demonstrates a growing maturity of European Community environmental law. Other notable changes concern the content of legislation and its application in practice which became more similar from one Member State to the other than would have been the case without the European Community monitoring procedure. Also, the evidence that quality objectives can hardly be monitored and are, in fact, almost never monitored in Member States will undoubtedly have some impact on legislators. Lastly, more attention is being given at the drafting stage of Community legislation as to how it would be implemented in practice.

The specific nature of Community environmental law also creates a number of problems for monitoring its implementation. Procedures take a very long time and all too often the damage to the environment is irreparable by the time the Community steps in. No direct contact with polluters or local authorities exists.

A further major hindrance to promoting efficiency is that of administrative secrecy. The whole procedure under Article 169 is largely non-public or even secret.[55] Since the Commission does not have inspectors of its own, it must rely largely on the complainants' arguments and the administration's reaction. It is often doubtful whether these two sources of information are sufficient to assess a situation properly. Mobile measuring stations and inspectors would probably be very useful in two-thirds of all complaints. Their absence is felt very heavily.

To these problems must be added that of the absence of sanctions. It is well known that a number of Member States quite openly do not respect Community law requirements, or disregard some Directives for years without being sanctioned. Public blame is almost the only sanction, and even that needs reception by the media in order to condemn the action. Access to national courts in environmental matters is very difficult in practice because of the limited right to bring an action and the high costs involved.

The punctual action undertaken by the Commission can be and is successful in some cases, leading to changes in legislation or to changes in practice. However, this action is unable to remedy any weakness in the environmental infrastructure of a Member State. Where an administratif sees environmental impact assessments, protection of habitats, reduction of emissions to air, soil or waste as a nuisance, which is still sometimes the case, the Commission's intervention under Article 169 is likewise seen as a nuisance rather than as an opportunity to properly protect the environment—and to properly respect legal obligations under the E.C. Treaty. And, while Community intervention might be supportive to the environmental administration or at a local or regional level in the discussion with other administrations, it cannot permanently establish a balance in the influence of these different administrations.   **6.21**

The implementation procedure does not contribute greatly to the establishment and implementation of clean-up plans and programmes either. Where a national administration is not able or not willing to honour the corresponding commitments under E.C. environmental legislation, it is normally extremely difficult to change such an attitude.

Major advantages which the Community's implementation actions in the environmental sector have brought about and are essentially the following: **6.22**

---

[55] See, Commission 10th Report on the monitoring of application of Community law: [1993] O.J. C233/8; it should be noted that Article 169 does not provide for procedures to be non-public. The Dutch Government also gives access to the letters of formal notice, which the Commission issues.

— There is a "central" body which looks into national environmental legislation and—at least as important—into environmental practice in order to level its compliance with European environmental rules. Neither national parliaments nor national administrations therefore necessarily have the last word on environmental issues;

— Controversies are decided by the Court of Justice, which is highly respected and has sufficient authority for its judgment to be accepted;

— Individuals may raise the question of the compliance of any measure with European environmental rules and have a guarantee from the Commission that their case will be examined. Thus, they no longer regard environmental pollution as an "act of God", but become aware of the possibility of protecting "their" environment;

— The European Parliament's activities, the Commission's own initiatives, as well as actions from non-governmental organisations contribute to bringing cases of non-compliance to the attention of the public. This feature, which is linked to the functions of public opinion within the Member States, is the environment's greatest potential ally;

— Administration in Member States is gradually accepting that its environmental actions can be questioned by the administration. Thus, not only does environmental law-making go beyond the nation-State, but its implementation control as well.

6.23 Major deficiencies in the procedure are the absence of neutral measuring and of inspection possibilities on the one hand and of sanctions on the other. Both deficiencies would not be too important if, at the level of all Member States total monitoring and inspection facilities existed and appropriate sanctions were practised—which is the case only in a minority of Member States.

General evaluation

6.24 Any review of Community environment policy has to bear in mind that it is not a question of protecting the environment in one or the other part of the Community, e.g. France, Germany, the North Sea or the Mediterranean. The objective of Community environment policy is to maintain, protect and improve the environment in the whole Community—the "European eco-system". In addition, Community environment policy has a general integrative role and ought also to contribute towards protecting the environment outside the Community to the extent that the Community acquires such responsibilities. Consequently, any criticism which measures Community environment policy against the environment policy of an individual Member State is based on incorrect assessment criteria.

Community environment policy developed and flourished and the absence of explicit powers in the original E.C. Treaty; these powers were only granted when the Treaty was amended in 1987. It says a great deal for the tactical and strategic skills of the Community administrations and the environment authorities in the Member States that the design and implementation of a Community environment policy was possible. A comparison of starting positions and results between environment policy and other areas—consumer policy, social policy, energy policy or transport policy—provides an eloquent illustration of this.

The following positive effects of Community environment policy are apparent: **6.25**

(1) Community environment policy helps to ensure that environmental thinking and policies in the Member States are based on identical principles and developed along similar lines; in this way it prevents Member States drifting apart on environmental matters.

(2) Community environment policy provides the most suitable physical and political framework for certain measures. This is true, for instance, of measures regulating specific products or production processes in order to combat environmental pollution, the tackling of transboundary environmental pollution, the co-ordination of national and international research and collection, evaluation and dissemination of data on the environment.

(3) The Community participates as an entity in international negotiations on environmental issues and *vis-à-vis* international organisations, it co-ordinates its views with those of the Member States and in this way is able to bring its economic and political weight into play in formulation and implementation of international agreements.

(4) With regard to half, perhaps the majority, of the Member States, Community solutions provide a stimulus for legislative measures, changes in administrative structure and practices and changes in conduct of economic operators; thus Community arrangements often also function as the transmission belt for transfer of environment policy know-how.

(5) Community environment provisions help to avoid or eliminate distortions of competition, therefore have an integrative effect and so implement the objectives of the Treaty on European Union.

The problems of Community environment legal policy are to be found, among others, in the following circumstances: **6.26**

(1) Community measures in concert with national measures have not so far succeeded in permanently halting and gradually reducing the progressive pollution of the environment: "a new report on the State of the Environment . . . shows a slow but relentless deterioration of the

157

general state of the environment of the Community, notwithstanding the measures taken over the past two decades particularly as regards . . . climate change, acidification and air pollution of water resources, deterioration of the urban environment, deterioration of coastal zones, and waste".[56] This statement is probably the most severe criticism of Community and national environmental policy and law which can be issued. It is confirmed by statements, reports and data, wherever these are trying to assess the European eco-system.

6.27   (2) Many of the existing instruments are not satisfactorily coping with current levels of environmental degradation. Legislation is sometimes drafted in an inconsistent, even contradictory way. A loose drafting of texts and the use of notions which hide subsistent differences among Member States, an increasing number of exemptions and derogations, the reference to national administrative decisions, etc., lead to legal texts which are interpreted differently from one Member State to another. Since national administrations and political bodies often have a different perception of the need to protect the environment, these divergencies are increasing. Directives thus quite often give an added value to the environmental protection where a national administration is willing to provide for such an added protection. Where, however, national, regional or local administration is less convinced of the need to protect the environment, the loose and general drafting of the Community legislation considerably reduces this added value.

6.28   (3) Community environmental policy in the past did not manage to keep public opinion as its ally. The common view that the more the environment is discussed in public the better, is especially true for the Community environment. The Commission has not always managed to ensure transparency and openness of discussions on the environment in the Community.

(4) There is a considerable gap between the different Community Directives and Regulations and their application in practice.

The mere existence of Community provisions on environmental protection does not in itself improve environmental quality. Carriers and their passengers may ensure compliance with the provisions of transport law, competitors compliance with competition law and farmers compliance with agricultural legislation, but environment law has to be applied on the spot in order to be effective. There are considerable differences from one Member State to another in the practical application of Community law.

---

[56] Fifth Environmental Action Programme: [1993] O.J. C138/11 point (i).

Rehbinder-Stewart have already warned of the possible political consequences of a consistent policy of implementation, namely that decision-making process for Community instruments will be slowed down for fear of strict implementation or that the content could be diluted.[57] There are signs that this is so. In the past, Member States quite often treated directives as recommendations. Courts and authorities knowingly or unknowingly, frequently ignored Community environment law. The fact that environmental protection provisions of Community law may be directly applicable in national law does not generally appear to be known.

(5) The very considerable differences in the importance attached to environment policy in the Member States, combined with the lack of a Community "environment" infrastructure (European environment association have relatively little influence, there is no European Union press, radio or television service, and no European documentation and information), the absence of democratic controls and the fact that decisions in the Council and Commission are taken out of sight of the public, have resulted in decisions at European level that are not always a model of progressive environment policy.

    6.29

The integration of environmental requirements in other policies remains an ongoing problem at Community as well as Member State level.

(6) Member States with their well-defined environment policy tend to seek solutions to problems at national level while not always contributing their know-how to the Community environment structures. The necessity for common solutions in some cases—product standards, ozone problems, marine pollution—may be a certain qualifier. Essentially, however, Community environment policy seems to be comprehended as an environmental foreign policy rather than a domestic policy.

(7) Environment problems in the Mediterranean area—soil erosion, forest fires, water management from the point of view of the Mediterranean countries, and in addition waste disposal, clean-up, biotope protection, protection of fauna and flora from a Community point of view in Eastern Europe—and global issues are shifting the focus for the Community as a whole, leading to new priorities and an inevitable slowing down of the decision-making process. Furthermore, the emotionalised subsidiarity discussion seems to lead to more umbrella legislation, which is not really helpful to the Community environment.

---

[57] E. Rehbinder, R. Stewart, *Environmental Protection Policy* (Berlin-New York, 1985) 316 *et seq.*

6.30 On the whole, there cannot really be any doubt that Community environment policy has been a success to the extent that it has led to measures to protect the environment in all sectors throughout the Community. The quantitative and qualitative legislation gap between Member States would doubtless be even greater in the absence of a Community environment policy. And the Community legal measures increasingly set the pace of environmental legislation for Member States as well as for other countries.

Bibliography

ASSER INSTITUUT (ed.), *Europees Milieurecht: praktische problemen bij de totstandkoming en nitvoering* (s'Gravenhage, 1989).

AUBIN, A., *La Communauté européenne face à la pollution atmosphérique* (Rennes, 1993).

AUTRAND, A., "Fiscalité et environnement" *Revue du Marché Commun et de l'Union Européenne* (1992), p. 894.

BALDOCK, D., "The status of special protection areas for the protection of wild birds" (1992) *Journal of Environmental Law*, p. 139.

BALDOCK D., BENNETT, G., *Agriculture and the polluter pays principle: a study of six E.C. countries* (London, 1991).

BARENTS, R., 'Milieu en interne Markt' *Tijdschrift voor europees en economisch recht* (1993), p. 5.

BECKER, U., *Der Gestaltungsspielraum der E.G.-Mitgliedstaaten im Spannungsfeld zwischen Umweltschutz und freiem Warenverkehr* (Baden-Baden, 1991).

BEHRENS, P., KOCH, H.J. (ed.), *Umweltschutz in der Europäischen Gemeinschaft: Spannungsfelder zwischen nationalem und europäischen Gemeinschaftsrecht* (Baden-Baden, 1991).

BENNETT, G. (ed.), *Air pollution control in the European Community* (London, 1991).

BENNETT, G., *The internal market and environmental policy in the Federal Republic of Germany and the Netherlands* (Arnheim, 1989).

BOCKEN, H., RYCKBOST, D. (ed.), *L'élaboration et l'application des directives européennes en matière d'environnement* (Gent, 1990).

BRADLEY, K., "The European Court and the legal basis of Community legislation" (1988) 13 E.L. Rev. 379.

BREIER, S., "Die Bedeutung der umweltrechtlichen Querschnittsklausel des Art. 130r Abs. 2 Satz 2 EWG-Vertrag für die Verwirklichung des Europäischen Binnenmarktes" (1992) *Natur und Recht*, p. 174.

BREIER, S., "Das Schicksal der Titandioxid-Richtlinie" (1993) *Europäische Zeitschrift für Wirtschaftsrecht*, p. 315.

BREUER, R., "EG-Richtlinien und deutsches Wasserrecht" (1990) *Wirtschaft und Verwaltung*, p. 79.

BREUER, R., "Umweltrechtliche und wirtschaftslenkende Abgaben im europäischen Binnenmarkt" (1992) *Deutsches Verwaltungsblatt*, p. 485.

BREUER, R., *Entwicklungen des europäisches Umweltrechts – Ziele, Wege und Irrwege* (Berlin-New York, 1993).
BRINKHORST, L.J., *Subsidiariteit en milieu in de Europese Gemeenschap. Doos van Pandora of Panacee?* (Leiden, 1992).
BRINKHORST, L.J., "Subsidiarity and E.C. environment policy" (1993) *European Environment Law Review*, p. 8.

CALLIESS, C., WEGENER, B. (eds.), *Europäisches Unweltrecht als Chance: die Umweltpolitik der E.G. und die Einflussmöglichkeiten der Umweltverbände* (Taunusstein, 1992).
CAMPINS, ERITJA, M., *La gestión de los residuos peligrosos en la Comunidad Europea* (Barcelona, 1994).
CAPRIA, A., *Direttive ambientali CEE. Stato di Attuazione in Italia* (2nd ed. Milano, 1992).
Centrale Raad voor de Milieuhygiene, *Europa 1992: naar een ecologische gemeenschap?* (s'Gravenhage, 1989).
CORCELLE, G., "Agriculture et environnement: une liaison tourmentée, mais tellement naturelle" (1991) *Revue du Marché Commun*, p. 180.

DAVIES, P., GOH, J., "E.C. law on aircraft noise: recent developments" (1993) *European Environmental Law Review*, p. 229.
DEMARET, P., "Environmental policy and Commercial policy: The emergence of trade-related measures (TREMs) in the external relations of the European Community" in *The European Community's Commercial Policy after 1992: the legal dimension*, M. Maresceau ed. (Deventer, 1993), p. 315.
DEMMKE, C., *Umsetzung und Vollzug von E.G.-Umweltpolitik in den nationalen Verwaltungen der E.G.-Mitgliedstaaten. Die Implementation der Trinkwasser-reichtlinie* (Diss. Speyer) (Baden-Baden, 1994).
DEMMKE, C., "Umweltpolitik im Europa der Verwaltungen" (1994) *Die Verwaltung*, p. 49.
DE SADELEER, N., "La circulation des déchets et le marché unique européen" (1994) *Revue du Marché Unique Européen*, p. 71.
DE VILLENEUVE, C., "Les mouvements transfrontiers des déchets dangereux (Convention de Bâle et droit communautaire)" (1990) *Revue du Marché Commun*, p. 658.
DIEZ DE VELLASCO VALLEJO, M., *Aspectos jurídicos de la protección del medio ambiente en la Comunidad Europea y en especial la contribución de su Tribunal de Justicia* (Granada, 1991).

EPINEY, A., "Einbeziehung gemeinschaftlicher Umweltschutzprinzipien in die Bestimmung mitgliedstaatlichen Handlungsspielraums" (1993) *Deutsches Verwaltungsblatt*, p. 93.
EPINEY, A., FURRER, A., "Umweltschutz nach Maastricht. Ein Europa der drei Geschwindigkeiten?" (1993) *Europarecht*, p. 369.

ERICHSEN, H.U., "Das Recht auf freien Zugang zu Informationen über die Umwelt. Gemeinschaftsrechtliche Vorgaben und nationales Recht" (1992) *Neue Zeitschrift für Verwaltungsrecht*, p. 409.

EVERLING, U., "Umsetzung von Umweltrichtlinien durch normkonkretisierende Verwaltungsanweisungen" (1992) *Recht der Internationalen Wirtschaft*, p. 392.

EVERLING, U., "Durchführung und Umsetzung des Europäischen Gemeinschaftsrechts im Bereich des Umweltschutzes unter Berücksichtigung der Rechtsprechung des EUGH", 16.wiss. Fachtagung der Gesellschaft für Umweltrecht, Dokumentation (Berlin, 1993), p. 65.

FECLAY, M.S., GILHALY, P.M., "Green law-making: a primer on the European Community's environmental legislative process" (1991) *Vanderbilt Journal of Transnational Law*, p. 653.

FEHR, H., VAN DER STELT-SCHEELE, D., "The E.C. Environmental policy in relation to the E.C. structural funds: a critical analysis of its application" (1992) *European Environmental Law Review*, pp. 121 and 143.

FLUCK, J., "Zum Abfallbegriff im europäischen, im geltenden und im werdenden deutschen Abfallrecht" (1993) *Deutsches Verwaltungsblatt*, p. 590.

FORSTER, M., "Enforcing the drinking water directive" (1991) *Land Management and Environmental Law Report*, p. 56.

FREES, C.P., "Maßnahmen und rechtliche Möglichkeiten der E.G. zur Bekämpfung und Verhütung von Öltankerunfällen vor ohren Küsten" (1992) *Natur und Recht*, p. 16.

FÜHR, M., "Umweltmanagement und Umweltbetriebsprüfung – neue E.G.-Verordnung zum Öko-Audit verabschiedet" (1993) *Neue Zeitschrift für Verwaltungsrecht*, p. 858.

FÜHR, M., ROLLER, G. (eds.), *Participation and litigation rights of environmental associations in Europe: current legal situation and practical experience* (Frankfurt/M, 1991).

GEBERS, B., ROBESIN, M. (eds.), *Licensing procedures for industrial plants and the influence of E.C. directives* (Frankfurt/M, 1993).

GEDDES, A., "Locus standi and EEC environmental measures" (1992) *Journal of Environmental Law*, p. 29.

GERADIN, D., "Free Trade in an Integrated Market; a survey of the case law of the United States Supreme Court and the European Court of Justice' (1993) *Florida Journal of Transnational Law and Policy*, p. 141.

GLIM, M., *European Enviromental Legislation, what does it really mean?* (Delft, 1990).

GORNIG, G., "Vom Ökodumping zum Ökoprotektionismus. Umweltzeichen im Lichte von EWG-Vertrag und GATT" (1992) *Europäische Zeitschrift für Wirtschaftsrecht*, p. 753.

HAIGH, N., *Manual of Environmental Policy: the E.C. and Britain* (London, 1993) (looseleaf).

HAILBRONNER, K., *Umweltrecht und Umweltpolitik in der Europäischen Gemeinschaft* (Linz, 1991).

HANCHER, L., SEVENSTER, H., Note on European Court of Justice, Case C-2/90, Commission v. Belgium, judgment of 9 July 1992. 30 C.M.L. Rev. 351.

HANNEQUART, J.P., *Le droit européen des déchets* (Bruxelles, 1993).

HANNEQUART, J.P., Le règlement européen sur les mouvements de déchets (1993) *Aménagement-Environnement*, p. 67.

HENKE, J., *EUGH und Umweltschutz. Die Auswirkungen der Rechtsprechung des Gerichtshofs der Europäischen Gemeinschaften auf das Umweltschutzrecht in Europa* (Diss. Bayreuth) (München-Firenze, 1992).

HESSION, M., MACRORY, R., "Maastricht and the Environmental policy of the Community: legal issues of a new Environment policy' in *Legal issues of the Maastricht Treaty* (D. O'Keeffe, P. Twomey, eds. London-New York, 1994), p. 151.

HILF, M., "Umweltabgaben als Gegenstand von Gemeinschaftsrecht und Politik" (1992) *Neue Zeitschrift fü Verwaltungsrecht*, p. 105.

HOWARTH, W., SOMSEN, H., "The E.C. nitrates directive" (1991) *Water Law*, p. 149.

JADOT, B., DE SADELEER, N. (ed.), *Le label écologique et le droit* (Bruxelles, 1992).

JAHNS-BÖHM, J., "Güterkraftverkehrspolitik und Umweltschutz im EWG-Vertrag" (1991) *Europäische Zeitschrift für Wirtschaftsrecht*, p. 523.

JANS, J.H., MORTELMANS, K.J.M., SEVENSTER, H.G., *Zo sterk als de zwakste schakel: Nederlands produktgericht milieubeleid in Europees en internationaal-rechtelijk verband* (Amsterdam, 1993).

JANS, J.H., *Europees Milieurecht in Nederland* (2nd ed. Groningen, 1994).

JANS, J.H., "Het EEG-Verdrag en nationale financiele milieubeleidsinstrumenten" in *Financiele instrumenten in het milieurecht* (R.J.J. van Acht, R. Uylenburg ed., Zwolle, 1993), p. 65.

JARASS, H., "Binnenmarktrichtlinien und Umweltschutzrichtlinien" (1991) *Europäische Zeitschrift für Wirtschaftsrecht*, p. 530.

JUIN, D., *L'application de la législation communautaire de l'environnement en France* (with A. Comolet, V. Fernandez, F. Gras), (Paris, 1992), Vol. 1 and 2.

KAHL, W., *Umweltprinzip und Gemeinschaftsrecht* (Diss, Augsburg) (Heidelberg, 1993).

KAMMINGA, M.T., KLATTE, E.R., "Twintig jaar EG milieubeleid en het integratiebeginsel" (1994) *Milieu en Recht*, p. 2.

KISS, A., SHELTON, D. (ed), *Manual of European Environmental Law* (Cambridge, 1993).

KOPPEN, I., "The role of the European Court of Justice in the development of the European Community environmental policy", EUI Working Paper 92/18 (Firenze, 1993).

KRÄMER, L., "The implementation of environmental laws by the European Economic Communities" *German Yearbook of International Law* (1991) p. 9,

KRÄMER, L., *Focus on European Environmental Law* (Sweet & Maxwell, London, 1992).

KRÄMER, L., *European Environmental Law Casebook* (Sweet & Maxwell, London, 1993).

KRÄMER, L., "Environmental protection and Article 30 EEC Treaty" 30 C.M.L. Rev. 111.

KROMAREK, P., "La Cour de Justice des Communautés européennes et l'environnement" *Jurisclasseur-Environnement* (Paris, 1992) Fascicule 1120.

LECLERC, S., *Politique agricole commune et environnement* (Rennes, 1993).

LIEFFERINK, J.D., LOWE, P.D., MOL, A.P.J. (eds.), *European integration and environmental policy* (London, 1993).

MACRORY, R., "The enforcement of Community environmental laws: some critical remarks" 29 C.M.L. Rev. 347.

MAHMOUDI, S., "EG-medlemskap och strängere nationella miljöutgärder" (1993) *Svensk Juristtidning* p. 419.

NIJMAN, M., "Le développement du principe de subsidiarité avec une étude de cas sur la politique de l'environnement dans la Communauté européenne et le principe de subsidiarité" (Diss. Amsterdam, 1991).

PAGH, P., *E.F.-miljoeret* (Copenhagen, 1990).

PAGH, P., "Farlige stoffer og EF-retten" (1991) *Ugeskrift for Retsvaesen*, B 353.

PAGH, P., "Unionstraktaten og milioeet" (1992) *Juristen*, p. 225.

PAGH, P., "Luftforureningsbekaempelsen i retlig belysning" (1992) *Ugeskrift for Retsvaesen*, B 361.

PAGH, P., "Miljoegarantien efter PCP-dommen" (1994) *Ugeskrift for Retsvaesen*, B 276.

PALME, C., *Nationale Umweltpolitik in der E.G. Zur Rolle des Art. 100a IV im Rahmen einer europäischen Umweltgemeinschaft* (Diss. Tübingen) (Berlin, 1992).

PEETERS, M., "Towards a European system of tradable pollution permits" (1993) *Tilburg Foreign Law Review*, p. 117.

PERNICE, I., "Umweltschutz und Energiepolitik" (1993) *Recht der Energiewirtschaft*, p. 45.

PILLITU, *Profili costituzionali della tutela ambientale nell'ordinamento communitario europeo* (Perugia, 1992).

REHBINDER, E., STEWART, R., *Environmental Protection Policy* (Berlin-New York, 1985).

RENAUDIÈRE, P., "Le droit communautaire de l'environnement après Maastricht" (1992) *Aménagement-Environnement*, p. 70.

RENGELING, H.W. (ed.), *Umweltschutz und andere Politiken der Europäischen Gemeinschaft* (Köln-Berlin-Bonn-München, 1993).

ROMI, R., *L'Europe et la protection juridique de l'environnement* (Paris, 1990).

RYLAND, D., "The European Environment Agency" (1994) *European Environmental Law Review*, p. 138.

SCHERER, J., "Umweltrecht: Handelshemmnis im EG-Binnenmarkt?" (1992) *Umweltrecht in der Praxis*, Heft 1, p. 76.

SCHERER, J., "Umwelt-Audits: Instrument zur Durchsetzung des Umweltrechts im europäischen Binnenmarkt?" (1993) *Neue Zeitschrift für Verwaltungsrecht*, p. 11.

SCHMIDT, A., "Transboundary movements of waste under E.C. law: the emerging regulatory framework" (1992) *Journal of Environmental Law*, p. 61.

SCHMIDT-RÄNTSCH, A., "Besitz und Vermarktung von geschützen Tieren und Pflanzen nach der Vollendung des EG-Binnenmarktes" (1992) *Natur und Recht*, p. 49.

SCHRÖDER, M., "Aktuelle Konflikte zwischen europäischem und deutschem Abfallrecht" (1991) *Die Öffentliche Verwaltung*, p. 910.

SCHRÖDER, M., "Zusammenwirken von Gemeinschaftsrecht und nationalem Recht auf dem Gebiet der Umweltabgaben" in *Umweltschutz im Abgaben und Steuerrecht* (P Kirchhoff ed., Köln, 1993), p. 87.

SCHRÖER, T., "Die Kompetenzverteilung zwischen der europäischen Wirtschaftsgemeinschaft und ihren Mitgliedstaaten auf dem Gebiet des Umweltschutzes" (Diss. Frankfurt) (Berlin, 1992).

SEVENSTER, H.G., "Milieubeleid en Gemeenschapsrecht" (Proefschrift Leiden) (Deventer, 1992).

SIMON, D., RIGAUX, A., "Les contraintes de la transcription en droit français des directives communautaires: le secteur de l'environnement" (1991) *Revue juridique de l'environnement*, p. 269.

SOMSEN, H., "E.C. Water directives" (1990) *Water Law*, p. 93.

STEIGER, H. (ed.), *Umsetzung der Richtlinie 85/337 zur Umweltverträglichkeitsprüfung in den Mitgliedstaaten der E.G.* (Giessen, 1992).

STEINBERG, R., BRITZ, G., "Die Energiepolitik im Spannungsfeld nationaler und europäischer Regelungskompetenz" (1993) *Die Öffentliche Verwaltung*, p. 313.

VANDERMEERSCH, D., "Twintig jaar E.G.-milieurecht in retrospectief: van casuistiek naar modern beleid?" (1992) *Sociaal Economisch Wetgeving*, p. 532.

V. WILMOWSKY, P., "Grenzüberschreitende Abfallentsorgung: Ressourcen-konflikte im gemeinsamen Markt" (1991) *Neue Zeitschrift für Verwaltungsrecht*, p. 1.

V. WILMOWSKY, P., "Abfall und freier Warenverkehr: Bestandsaufnahme nach dem EUGH-Urteil zum wallonischen Einfuhrverbot" (1992) *Europarecht*, p. 414.

V. WILMOWSKY, P., ROLLER, G., *Civil Liability for Waste* (Frankfurt-Berlin-Bern-New York-Paris-Wien, 1992).

WÄGENBAUR, R., "Regulating the European Environment: the E.C. experience" *The University of Chicago Legal Forum* (Chicago, 1993), Vol. 1992.

WARD, A., "The right to an effective remedy in European Community law and environmental protection: a case study of United Kingdom judicial decision concerning the environmental impact assessment directive" (1993) *Journal of Environmental Law*, p. 221.

ZULEEG, M., "Umweltschutz in der Rechtsprechung des Europäischen Gerichtshofs" (1993) *Neue Juristiche Wochenschrift*, p. 31.

Index

Accidents,
  industrial plants and, 1.33, 2.20,
                                        3.36
  industrial policy and, 1.58
Administrative circulars,
  implementation of Community
      legislation by, 5.15
Agricultural,
  activities,
    labelling and, 1.47
    pollution by, 1.13, 1.17, 1.40
  policy, 1.52, 3.24–3.25
Air pollution, 1.20–1.24, 3.36 *see,*
  also, **Catalytic converters,**
  Emissions, Ozone
  coal from, 4.48
  diesel cars and, 4.48
  nuclear energy and, 1.56
  regional differences and, 2.41
  standards, 6.08–6.09
  transboundary, 1.24, 1.50
Alcoholic beverages,
  lead capsules of, 4.42
Aluminium, 4.50
Ammunition, 4.49
Animals, *see, also,* **Endangered**
  species, Flora and fauna
  conservation of, 1.50
  experiments, 1.36
  protection of, 1.34–1.37, 2.03,
                            4.28–4.29
Aquatic environment *see* **Marine**
  pollution, Water
Article 30, 4.27–4.58
Article 36, 4.27–4.58

Article 100a, 4.17–4.23
  free movement of goods
    under, 2.10–2.11
  internal market and, 2.15–2.16
  safeguard measures and, 2.05,
                           4.24–4.26
Article 130d,
  cohesion fund under, 2.05
Article 130r,
  benefits and charges under, 2.40
  derogation clause, under, 1.09
  co-operation with other countries
    under, 3.20–3.22
  environment policy
    under, 2.06–2.09,
          2.15–2.18, 2.37–2.41
  import ban on waste, under,
                    2.18
  integration principle, under,
          1.07, 2.26–2.27,
          6.01–6.02
  international measures, under,
                  6.01
  precautionary principle,
    under, 1.08, 2.19
  preventive principle
    under, 2.19–2.20, 6.04
  qualified majority voting
    under, 1.07
  safeguard measures
    and, 4.24–4.26
  subsidiarity and, 2.28–2.32
Article 130s,
  chlorofluorocarbons, and, 1.24

169

Article 130s,—*cont.*
Community action programmes
    and,   3.14–3.19
decision-making and,   2.41,
    3.01–3.39
energy tax and,   3.07
financing of environment policy
    under,   5.01–5.02
fiscal measures and,   3.07
implementation of environmental
    policy under,   5.04
majority voting under,   1.08,
    3.02–3.06
unanimous decisions,
    under,   1.09, 3.06–3.13
Article 130t,
environmental protection
    under,   1.24, 2.05, 2.08
free movement of goods
    and,   2.11
industrial policy under,   1.58
notification of national
    measures on environment
    under,   4.02–4.16
Asbestos,   1.32, 4.14
Assessment,
environment policy, of,   2.41,
    6.01–6.30

Bathing water,   1.11–1.12, 5.18
BATNEEC,
industrial plants and,   1.22
interpretation of,   6.18
notes for industrial sectors
    on,   1.22
water standards and,   6.07
Batteries,   1.40, 1.42, 3.30, 3.33
Beer cans,
prohibition of metal,   4.40
**Best available techniques not
    entailing excessive costs** *see*
    BATNEEC
Birds,
conservation of, wild,   1.34, 3.09

Blue flag scheme,   1.12

Cadmium,   3.19
quality objectives for,   1.15
restrictions on,   1.29, 1.32
Catalytic converters,   1.20, 3.30,
    4.38
financial incentives and,   1.58
CE marks *see* **Certification marks**
Certification marks,   1.59
CFCs *see* **Chlorofluorocarbons**
Chemicals,   1.27–1.33, 3.36
Commission Committee on,   2.38
export of,   1.31, 2.10
harmonization of rules on,   6.10
installations,   1.33, 1.58
import of,   1.31, 2.10
labelling of,   6.10
marketing of,   1.28
pollution by,   1.50
Chlorofluorocarbons,   1.24, 4.09,
    4.28 *see, also,* **Ozone**
bans on,   4.49, 4.52, 6.09
Classification,
chemicals, of,   1.27–1.28
dangerous substances, of   1.02,
    1.27–1.28
pesticides, of,   1.28–1.29
Clean-up,   2.09, 2.20
costs,   2.23–2.24
Climate change *see* **Greenhouse
    effect**
Coal,   4.48
Cohesion Fund,   1.53, 2.05, 3.05
polluter pays principle and,   2.24
Commercial agreements,   3.38
Commercial policy,   3.37–3.38
Commission,
complaints to,   5.17–5.18
Energy and Environment
    (1990),   1.56
*Industrial Competitiveness and
    Protection of the
    Environment (1992),*   1.58

Commission,—*cont.*
GreenBook
*Impact of Transport on the
Environment* (COM (92)
46), 1.55
*Liability for Environmental
Damage* (COM (93)
97), 1.49
*Remedying Environmental
Damage* (COM (93) 47)
monitoring of implementation
by, 5.10–5.19, 6.19– 6.23
notification of national measures
on environment to,
1.44–1.45, 4.02–4.16
opinions, of, 5.17
Political Union, on, 1.07
press releases of, 5.18
proposals of, 3.02–3.03
Scientific Committee on Toxicity
and Ecotoxicity of
Chemicals, 2.39
visits, 5.18
WhiteBook,
*Community Strategy on
Sustainable Mobility*
(COM (92) 494)
Committee of the Regions,
environment policy and, 3.04
Common Agricultural Policy *see*
Agricultural policy
Community action programmes,
1.02–1.04, 2.02
adoption by majority co-
decisions, 1.08
assessment of, 6.04–6.05
decisions on, 3.14–3.19
Fourth, 1.18
Fifth,
air pollution standards
in, 6.09
competition policy and, 1.54
implementation network
and, 5.07

**Community action
programmes,**—*cont.*
Fifth,—*cont.*
ozone-depleting substances
and, 1.59
regional policy and, 1.53
subsidiarity and, 3.16, 3.19
transport policy and, 1.55
voluntary agreements
under, 1.54
integration with
other Community policies
of, 1.51
natural resources, use of,
and, 2.12
traffic infrastructure, on, 1.55
water resources and, 3.10-3.11
Community law,
national law, relationship
with, 4.01–4.58
Competition,
environmental protection
and, 3.34–3.35,
4.31–4.37
packaging waste and, 1.40, 3.29
trade restrictions and, 4.09–4.10
Complaints, 5.17–5.18
Conservation, 1.34–1.37, 1.50,
2.09
financial assistance for, 3.05,
5.02–5.03
forests, of, 1.52, 3.25 *see, also,*
Timber
Co-operation,
other countries, with, 3.20–3.22
Costs,
environmental protection,
of, 2.40, 3.05
CO$_2$,
emissions from, 1.56
energy tax and, 3.12–3.13
Council,
decision-making procedures
of, 3.01–3.39

Council,—*cont.*
Declaration of the Environment
(1990),   2.02
environmental protection
and,   1.07

Damage *see* **Environmental damage**
Dangerous substances,   1.02, 1.27
see, also, **Chemicals,**
Chlorofluorocarbons,
Pentachlorophenol,
Pesticides, PVCs
groundwater pollution, by,   1.13
industrial policy and,   1.58
list of,   1.14–1.16
quality majority voting and, 1.28
water, pollution, of, by   1.14,
3.13
Decision-making procedure,   2.41,
3.01–3.39
see, also, **Majority voting, Majority
co-decisions, Unanimous
decisions**
Deposits,
bottles, on,   4.31–4.32, 4.44
Derogation clause,   1.09
Detergents,   3.18, 4.39
Developing countries,   2.08, 2.33
Development policy,   1.57
Dioxin levels,   4.55
Direct effect,   4.28
Discrimination,   4.35–4.58
Disposable plates,   4.54
**Dooge Report on European
Political Union,**   1.05
Drinking water,
abstraction of,   1.11
pollution of,   2.07
quality of,   1.13, 2.23
subsidiarity and,   2.32
Drinks containers, 3.29, 4.37, 4.40
deposits on,   4.40, 4.44
Dumping of waste at sea,   1.19,
1.40, 2.09

Eco-auditing,   3.36
chemical installations and,   1.33
industrial installations and, 1.47
Eco-labelling,   1.47, 4.11, 4.13
see, also, **Labelling**
Economic and Social Committee,
decision-making and,   3.06
environmental policy and,   3.04
Eco-taxes,   1.54, 4.45–4.47
Emissions, *see, also,* **Air pollution,
Petrol**
CO_2 of,   1.56
industrial plants from,   1.22
motor vehicles, from,   1.02,
1.20–1.21, 1.55
see, also, **Catalytic converters**
fiscal measures against,   3.07
standards,   3.28, 3.30, 4.18
regional differences in,   2.39
standards,   1.14, 2.21, 4.14
waste incinerators, from,   1.22
Endangered species,   1.37, 4.28,
4.54
Energy,
policy,   1.56, 2.12
supply,   3.12–3.13
tax,   1.56, 3.07
**Enforcement of environmental
law,**   6.19–6.23
Environment,
frontiers of,   2.04
notion of,   2.01–2.05
Environmental damage,
evidence of,   2.38
rectification of, 2.18, 2.21–2.23
**Environmental impact
assessment,**   1.43, 3.36
chemical installations of,   1.33
infrastructure projects of, 1.55,
2.20, 3.08, 5.12
limit-values and,   4.14
rectification of, at source, 2.21
regional policy and,   1.53

Environment measures,
 legal basis of, 3.23–3.39
Environmental policy, *see, also,*
  Member states
 assessment of, 2.41, 6.01–6.30
 financing of, 5.01–5.03
 implementation of, 5.04–5.19,
  6.19–6.23
 integration with other policies,
  of, 1.51–1.59
 objectives of, 2.06–2.09,
  2.15–2.16
 origins of, 1.01–1.09
 principles of, 2.19–2.41
Environmental protection,
 benefits of, 2.40
 level of, 2.14–2.18, 2.29–2.33,
  3.35
European Commission *see*
  Commission
European Council *see* **Council**
European Environment Agency,
 information collecting role of,
  2.38
 monitoring role of, 5.07
 reports of, 1.46
European Parliament *see*
  Parliament
European Political
  Union, 1.05–1.09
Evidence,
 environmental damage of, 2.38
Export,
 chemicals of, 1.31
 endangered species of, 1.37
 ozone-depleting substances
  of, 1.23
 waste, of, 1.57, 2.20
 see also **Transport**
Financial incentives,
 catalytic converters and, 1.58
Financing,
 environmental policy, 5.01–5.03
 suspension of, 5.12

Fiscal measures,
 sovereignty and, 3.07
Fish life,
 drift nets and, 3.25
 quality of water for, 1.11, 1.13
Flora and fauna, 1.34–1.37, 6.12
 see, also, **Animals, Birds**
 imports of, 1.57
 protection of, 3.05, 3.08–3.09,
  4.28–4.29
Forest conservation, 1.52, 3.25
see, also, **Timber**
Free movement of goods,
 dangerous chemicals and, 2.11
 environmental protection
  and, 3.27–3.28, 3.31,
   4.33–4.34
 noise and, 6.11
 protective measures and, 4.08
Free trade, 4.30, 4.51
Fuels, 1.21, 3.18
Funds *see, also,* **Cohesion Fund,**
  Structural Funds
 environmental protection
  and, 1.48, 5.02

GATT Rules, 4.51
General Consultative Forum, 1.49
General measures,
 environmental protection,
  on 1.43–1.50
Genetically modified organisms,
  1.32
Global warming *see* **Greenhouse**
  effect
Greenhouse effect, 1.56, 2.19,
  4.51
 energy tax and, 3.12–3.13
 evidence of, 2.38
Groundwater pollution, 1.11, 1.13,
  2.34

Habitats, 1.34–1.37, 1.50,
  3.08–3.09

Habitats,—*cont.*
conservation of, 3.36, 6.12
financial assistance for protection
of, 3.05
Hazardous waste, 1.38–1.42, 1.50
transboundary shipment of, 3.22
Health *see* **Human health**
Horizontal measures.
environment on, 6.14–6.18
Human health,
protection of, 2.09–2.11,
3.24–3.25, 4.27–4.29

Identification marks, 4.54
Implementation,
environmental policies,
of, 5.04–5.19, 6.19–6.23
Import,
bans, 2.18, 2.22
chemicals of, 1.31, 2.10
endangered species, 1.37
Industrial plants,
accidents, in, 1.33, 2.20, 3.36
eco-auditing and, 1.47
emissions from, 1.22
Industrial policy, 1.58–1.59
Information,
access to, environment
on, 1.44–1.45, 3.36
European Environmental Agency
and, 2.38
Infrastructure,
environmental impact
assessments and, 1.55,
3.08, 5.12
projects, 2.20, 3.08
Integration principle, 1.07,
2.25–2.27, 6.01– 6.02
**Intergovernmental Conference on
European Political Union,**
1.05–1.09
energy resources and, 2.12
Interim measures, 5.13

International
agreements, 2.13, 3.20–3.22,
3.38
free trade and, 4.51
transboundary air pollution, 1.24
Internal market, 4.17–4.23
environment protection
and, 3.27–3.37
protective measures and, 4.08
Injunctions, 5.13
Ivory,
ban on imports of, 2.08, 4.28

Labelling, 3.36, 4.54
see, also, **Eco-labelling**
chemicals, of, 1.27–1.28
dangerous substances, of, 1.02,
1.27–1.28
pesticides, of, 1.28
Land use, 3.08–3.09
Landfills, 1.40
waste management of, 3.08
Lead, 1.23, 4.11
ammunition, in, 4.49
capsules of alcoholic
beverages, 4.42
petrol, in 1.21, 4.11, 5.18, 6.09
Life,
protection of, 4.52
Local authorities,
implementation of directives,
by, 5.15

Majority co-decisions, 3.01, 6.01
Community action programmes,
adoption by, 1.08
water resources on, 1.16, 3.11
Majority voting, 1.08–1.09,
3.01–3.05, 6.01
commercial policy on, 3.37–3.38
dangerous substances on, 1.28
environmental matters
on, 1.06–1.09
qualified, 1.07, 3.02, 3.13

Majority voting,—*cont.*
  qualified,—*cont.*
    commercial policy on,
                      3.37–3.38
    research and development
      and,   3.39
Marine pollution,   1.19
  land-based sources, from,   1.50
  Mediterranean Sea of, 1.50, 6.29
Marks,
  identification,   4.54
Mediterranean Sea,
  pollution of,   1.50, 6.29
Member States, *see, also,*
  Implementation, National
  law
  economic growth and,   2.41
  environmental impact
    assessments and,   1.43
  environmental policies, of 1.03,
                  1.06, 2.12
  international agreements
    on environment
    and,   3.20–3.22
  level of standards in,   3.35
  monitoring bathing water
    standards by,   1.12
  reporting obligations
    of,   1.44–1.46
  see, also, **Commission,**
    Information
  subsidiarity principle
    and,   2.28–2.32
  transport policy, of   1.55
  waste management and, 1.41
Mercury,   4.56
Motor vehicles,
  emissions from, 1.02, 1.20–1.21,
                  1.55
    diesel cars and,   1.20, 4.48
    fiscal measures against, 3.07
    standards, 3.28, 3.30, 4.18
  transport policy and,   1.55

National law,
  relationship with Community
    law,   4.01–4.58
Natural resources,
  utilisation of,   2.12
Nature conservation, 1.34–1.37,
                   6.12
see, also, **Endangered species,**
  Flora and fauna
Nitrogen dioxide,   1.23
Noise,   1.25–1.26,
               3.36, 6.11
  aircraft,   1.25
  levels,   1.02, 1.55
  subsidiarity and,   2.30
Nuclear energy,   1.56
  sustainable development
    and,   2.34
Nuclear waste,
  transport of,   1.39

Opinions *see* **Commission**
Ozone,
  concentrations,   1.23
  depleting substances, 1.59, 3.32,
                 3.36
    ban of,   6.08
  export of,   1.24
  layer,   1.24, 1.50, 4.09
    CFCs and,   4.28

Packaging, *see, also,* **Drinks**
  containers
  chemicals of,   1.27–1.28
  dangerous substances, of, 1.02,
                1.27–1.28
  pesticides, of,   1.28
  waste of,   1.40, 3.29
Parliament,
  committee on environment,
    public health and consumer
    protection,   3.03
  decision-making and, 3.06, 3.14
  opinions of,   3.03

Pentachlorophenol, 3.30, 4.18
trade restrictions and, 4.36, 4.37
Pesticides, 1.13, 1.28, 1.52
marketing of, 3.25
Petrol, *see, also,* **Emissions**
lead, in, 1.21, 4.11, 5.18, 6.09
Phosphates, 4.39
Planning, 3.08–3.09
Plastic bags, 4.41, 4.46
Polluter pays principle, 2.23–2.24,
3.05
state aids and, 1.54, 2.24
Precautionary principle, 1.08, 2.19
Press releases,
Commission of, 5.18
Preventive principle, 2.19–2.20,
6.04
Product safety, 1.59
Product standards, 3.31–3.35
Proportionality principle, 4.30,
4.37
eco-taxes and, 4.47
endangered species and, 4.54
Protectionism, 4.10
Protective measures, 4.06–4.11,
4.44
Public health, 2.10
PVCs, 4.53, 4.57

Qualified majority voting *see*
Majority voting
Quality,
objectives, 2.22–2.23, 6.08–6.09
standards, 1.11, 1.14
Quantitative measures,
water supply and, 3.10–3.11

Railways, 1.55
Regional diversity,
environmental protection
and, 2.17, 2.39
water standards on, 6.07
Regional policy, 1.53, 2.39
see, also, **Subsidiarity**

Regional policy,—*cont.*
Committee of the Regions
and, 3.04
development and, 2.41
local environmental issues
and, 2.04
suspension of financing for, 5.12
Research and development, 3.39
Resolutions,
legally binding nature of, 3.18
Rivers,
protection of, 1.19, 1.50, 2.39

Safeguard measures, 2.05,
4.24–4.26
Sandoz accident, 1.33, 1.58
Scientific and technical data,
environmental protection
and, 2.38
Scientific Committee on the
Toxicity and Ecotoxicity of
Chemicals, 2.38
Secrecy, 6.20
Seveso accident, 1.58, 5.08
Shellfish waters, 1.11, 1.13
Smog, 4.38
Smoke, 1.23
Sovereignty, 6.20
fiscal measures and, 3.07
Standards, 1.59
air pollution, 6.08–6.09
emission, 1.14, 2.21, 4.14
noise, 1.26
product, 3.31–3.35
technical, 1.59
State aids,
discrimination and, 4.50
environmental policy and, 1.54
polluter pays principle
and, 1.54, 2.24
Structural funds, 1.53, 5.12
Subsidiarity,
Community action programmes
and, 3.17, 3.19

Subsidiarity,—*cont.*
environment policy, effect
on,   6.17, 6.29
local environmental issues
and,   2.04
member states and,   2.28–2.32
noise pollution and,   2.30
water standards and,   6.07
Sulphur dioxide,   1.23
Surface water,   1.13
Sustainable development,   1.43,
2.33–2.34

Tax,
eco,   1.54, 4.45–4.47
energy,   1.56, 3.07
Technical standards,   1.59
see, also **Standards**
Thermometers,   4.56
Third world countries *see*
Developing countries
Timber,   1.57, 4.50–4.52
see, also, **Forest conservation**
Titanium dioxide industry,
pollution by,   1.18–1.19
waste from,   1.40, 1.58, 3.30
competition and,   3.33–3.34
reduction in,   4.18
Trade restrictions,   4.09–4.10,
4.35–4.58
CFCs and,   4.09
Trans-European networks,   2.05,
3.08
Transport,
animals of,   1.36
policy,   1.55, 3.26
waste of,   1.39–1.42, 1.50, 2.20
green list of,   4.12
transboundary,   3.22
Treaty of Rome *see* **Individual**
Treaty articles
Tropical rain forests,   1.57,
4.50–4.52

Unanimous decisions,   3.01–3.05
Article 130s, under,   1.09,
3.06–3.14
energy supply and,   3.12–3.13
Trans-European network
and,   3.08
water resources and,   3.10–3.11
United Nations,
development policy of,   1.57

Vested interest groups,   5.06–5.07
Visits,
Commission by,   5.18
Voting *see* **Majority voting**

Waste,   1.38–1.42, 3.33, 5.18
disposal installations,   3.35, 4.14,
6.13
dumping at sea, of,   1.19, 1.40,
2.09
exports of,   1.57
imports of,   2.18, 2.22
incinerators, emissions
from,   1.22
landfills of,   1.40
management,   1.41, 5.18
unanimous decisions
and,   3.08
packaging of,   1.40, 2.39
tips,
groundwater pollution,
through,   1.13
transport of,   1.39, 1.41–1.42
water treatment,   1.17
Water,   1.11–1.19, 3.36
bathing,   1.11–1.12, 5.18
dangerous substances of,
pollution by,   1.14, 3.13
drinking,   1.11, 2.07
quality of,   1.13, 2.23
subsidiarity and,   2.32
fish,   1.11, 1.13
ground,   1.11, 1.13, 2.34
legislation on,   6.60–6.07

Water,—*cont.*

majority decisions on,   1.16

resources,   3.10–3.11

shellfish,   1.11, 1.13

supply,   3.10–3.11

surface,   1.13

Water,—*cont.*

waste,   6.06–6.07

World Commission on Environment and Development *Our Common Future,*   2.33